THE GRANDMOTHERS' MOVEMENT

Solidarity and Survival in the Time of AIDS

MAY CHAZAN

McGill-Queen's University Press
Montreal & Kingston | London | Ithaca

© McGill-Queen's University Press 2015

ISBN 978-0-7735-4485-7 (cloth)
ISBN 978-0-7735-4486-4 (paper)
ISBN 978-0-7735-8174-6 (ePDF)
ISBN 978-0-7735-8178-4 (ePUB)

Legal deposit first quarter 2015
Bibliothèque nationale du Québec

Printed in Canada on acid-free paper that is 100% ancient forest free (100% post-consumer recycled), processed chlorine free

This book has been published with the help of a grant from the Canadian Federation for the Humanities and Social Sciences, through the Awards to Scholarly Publications Program, using funds provided by the Social Sciences and Humanities Research Council of Canada.

McGill-Queen's University Press acknowledges the support of the Canada Council for the Arts for our publishing program. We also acknowledge the financial support of the Government of Canada through the Canada Book Fund for our publishing activities.

LIBRARY AND ARCHIVES CANADA CATALOGUING IN PUBLICATION

Chazan, May, 1974–, author
The grandmothers' movement : solidarity and survival in the time of AIDS / May Chazan.

Includes bibliographical references and index.
Issued in print and electronic formats.
ISBN 978-0-7735-4485-7 (bound). – ISBN 978-0-7735-4486-4 (pbk.). –
ISBN 978-0-7735-8174-6 (ePDF). – ISBN 978-0-7735-8178-4 (ePUB)

1. Grandmothers – South Africa.   2. Grandmothers – Canada.   3. Solidarity – South Africa.   4. Solidarity – Canada.   5. AIDS (Disease) – South Africa.   6. AIDS activists – Canada.   7. Social change – South Africa.   I. Title.

HQ759.9.C53 2015   306.874'5   C2014-907977-X
                                          C2014-907978-8

Set in 10/14 Calluna with Gotham
Book design & typesetting by Garet Markvoort, zijn digital

THE GRANDMOTHERS' MOVEMENT

CONTENTS

....

MAP, TABLE, AND FIGURES

ACKNOWLEDGMENTS

I would like to extend my sincerest thanks to all of the women and men in the Valley of 1000 Hills who courageously shared their stories with me: ngiyabonga, Inkosi inkubusise. I am profoundly grateful to Cwengigile Myeni for her insights, guidance, energy, passion, and optimism. I also appreciate the support and input offered by Julie Hornby, Princess Mkhize, and the staff at the Hillcrest AIDS Centre Trust. In Canada, I thank all those affiliated with the Grandmothers to Grandmothers Campaign who participated in my research and encouraged me in my journey, including Peggy Edwards, Pat Evans, Carolyn Nixon, Kathleen Wallace-Deering, Jenny Wilson, the Capital Grannies, and the One World Grannies, to name just a few. I thank all of the leaders from within the Grandmothers Campaign who followed their convictions and worked, often against the current, to create the Grandmothers Advocacy Network; they are a continual source of inspiration. My research benefitted greatly from a longstanding relationship with the Stephen Lewis Foundation, and I am grateful for that. I would also like to acknowledge Michelle Valberg, for allowing me to use her provocative photo on the book's cover, and Ben Hodson, for drawing the map of South Africa.

Over the course of my journey, I worked closely with a number of dedicated and skilled research assistants. I sincerely thank Phumzile Cele, Gugu Ndlovu, and Nonkululeko Nzama for helping me conduct, transcribe, and translate the interviews and focus groups in the Valley. Their patience, sensitivity, and commitment to the project were remarkable. I thank Stephanie Kittmer for her longstanding interest and significant contribution to the Canadian research. I am also very grateful to Melissa Baldwin and Ziysah von Bieberstein for their assistance in the preparation of this manuscript, and for their keen diligence, intellectual input, and general spunk.

This book has drawn from many collaborations and from the insights of many scholars before me. The research and writing of this book would not have been possible without the thoughtful critique, genuine enthusiasm, logistical support, and longtime friendships of Mike Brklacich, Belinda Dodson, Blair Rutherford, and Alan Whiteside. Belinda read an earlier version of this manuscript with an incredibly detailed but supportive eye. Blair's generosity of time and supportive words strengthened my analysis and shaped my approach to scholarship more broadly. I extend my gratitude to Alan for sharing his vast knowledge of HIV/AIDS and South Africa with me. And I would especially like to thank Mike for his incredible mentorship, open-mindedness, sensitivity, and unwavering belief in me and my work.

I owe an enormous debt to Mark Hunter for reading and re-reading my manuscript, and for his invaluably critical comments. I have learned much from him – from our conversations and from his pivotal book, *Love in the Time of AIDS*. I am also hugely indebted to Jenny Wilson, who had the unenviable task of editing this manuscript multiple times prior to its submission to McGill-Queen's University Press. Jenny helped me find my voice, choose my words, and stay true to my vision, and I thank her for her compassion, pragmatism, and commitment. In addition, I appreciate the encouragement and helpful feedback offered by Paula Meth.

Over the course of my research in South Africa, I received outstanding support from the Health Economics and HIV/AIDS Research Division (HEARD) at the University of KwaZulu-Natal (UKZN) in Durban. I must give special thanks to Nkosinathi Ngcobo, Tim Quinlan, S'bo Radebe, Nina Veenstra, and Samantha Willan, among others, for their contributions to my work. I also benefitted enormously from the funding and institutional support offered by the Canada Research Chairs Program, Carleton University, the P.E. Trudeau Foundation, the Social Sciences and Humanities Research Council of Canada (SSHRC), Trent University, and the University of Toronto. I am particularly thankful to Gillian Balfour, P.G. Forest, Marg Hobbs, Fran Klodawsky, Fiona Mackenzie, Alex Neve, Colleen O'Manique, Joan Sangster, and Josée St-Martin for their mentorship and encouragement.

At McGill-Queen's University Press, Jacqueline Mason supported my work early on and helped me navigate a process that was entirely new to me. I also extend my thanks to my entire editorial team at MQUP, especially Ryan Van Huijstee and Joan McGilvray, to Noeline Bridge for her help with the index, and to my two anonymous reviewers, whose thoughtful feedback greatly improved my manuscript.

After an incredibly rewarding and challenging journey spanning the past decade, I am grateful to so many other people that I could never name them all. For their friendship, logistical support, and generosity of spirit, however, I thank Jessica Brando, Richard Brooks, Dana Capell, Catherine Collingwood, William Cooke, Corina Crawley, Earth Mother Organics, Dan Flanders, Erica Gilmour, Jeremy Grest, Brandy Humes, Tasha Lackman, Laura Madokoro, Patrycja Maksalon, Andy Mason, Kristin Nelson, Gretha Quinlan, Becky Rosen, Judith Shier, Nicola Spunt, Emily Wilson, and my many kindred Trudeau Foundation scholars; in so many different ways you have been my fellow travellers.

Finally, my family has shown me endless love and commitment. While I could never match her for strength of will, work ethic, or determination, I owe much to my mother, Beverly Kraft, for what she has taught me through her own actions; I am also incredibly grateful for her editorial help and for reserving a spot for this on her bookshelf. Gayle Trupish regularly provided the highest level of grandmothering support; without her countless hours of work, I am quite certain this book could never have been written. Elyse Chazan managed to appear on the scene at many of my most critical moments; I cannot be sure how she knew, but I am very glad she did. I thank Marion Little, Ted Hodson, and Abi Hodson for their quiet support, their genuine caring, their lightness of spirit, and their laughter. Melissa Baldwin stepped into our home in 2012 with a truly exceptional generosity of time and love; I am deeply appreciative for our provocative conversations, her music, and the peace of mind she brings me. During the course of this journey, my two beautiful daughters, Zoe Hodson and Alexandra Hodson, were born, in 2007 and 2011 respectively. The process of becoming a mother changed me more profoundly than I ever could have expected and in ways that I do not fully comprehend; my ability to connect with the women in my research, the depth of my analysis, and my approach to writing were undoubtedly intertwined with this experience. I thank Zoe and Alex for reminding me about miracles, for making me act silly, and for forcing me to learn the art of time management. Lastly, Ben

Hodson embarked on this journey with me and stood with me unconditionally throughout. He shared in my worlds in South Africa, at times with a baby on his back, making many personal and professional sacrifices to do so. His humour, faith, understanding, and partnership mean so much that "thank you" does not begin to capture my gratitude.

Royalties from the sale of this book will be donated to the Hillcrest AIDS Centre Trust.

ACRONYMS

....

ABSA	Amalgamated Banks of South Africa
AIDS	acquired immunodeficiency syndrome
ANC	African National Congress
ARV	anti-retroviral therapy
CAMR	Canadian Access to Medicines Regime
CBC	Canadian Broadcasting Corporation
CD4	cluster of differentiation 4 (T-cell count)
CIDA	Canadian International Development Agency
COSATU	Congress of South African Trade Unions
DAFTA	Durban Association for the Aged
FBO	faith-based organization
GAA	Global Action on Aging
GRAN	Grandmothers Advocacy Network
HACT	Hillcrest AIDS Centre Trust
HAI	HelpAge International
HEARD	Health Economics and HIV/AIDS Research Division
HIV	human immunodeficiency virus
IFP	Inkatha Freedom Party
IMF	International Monetary Fund
KZN	KwaZulu-Natal
NAC	National Advocacy Committee
NGO	non-governmental organization
PEPFAR	President's Emergency Plan for AIDS Relief
RA	research assistant
SLF	Stephen Lewis Foundation
SSHRC	Social Sciences and Humanities Research Council
SWAPOL	Swaziland Women for Positive Living
TB	tuberculosis

UDF	United Democratic Front
UKZN	University of KwaZulu-Natal
UN	United Nations
UNAIDS	Joint United Nations Programme on HIV/AIDS

THE GRANDMOTHERS' MOVEMENT

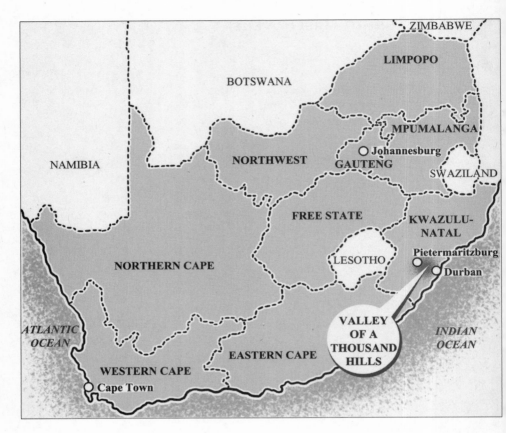

Map of South Africa

"Tell me, May," S'fiso[1] asked me one day in late 2008, with a teasing grin on his face, "will I make it into your book?"

I must have looked confused. Not only was I far from being ready to write about my experiences or findings, but I did not see why I would include S'fiso in a work about grandmothers ("gogos" in isiZulu). He and I were colleagues at the Health Economics and HIV/AIDS Research Division (HEARD) at the University of KwaZulu-Natal, a well-known South African institute in Durban, where I had been based intermittently since 2004. On my first trip to Durban, he had worked as my research assistant (RA), helping me navigate a situation that was entirely foreign to me: my first time on the African continent, speaking not a word of isiZulu, I was attempting to interview street traders on the sidewalks of Warwick Junction, Durban's bustling inner-city transport hub and informal trading area. S'fiso was intelligent, hard-working, and insightful, and through our work we had become close friends. I knew I owed much to him for his guidance and support; still, I could not envision why I would write about him alongside the gogos.

"I just thought I'd ask," he chuckled. Then, in a more serious tone, he added, "Will I at least be able to understand it?" He left my office before I had a chance to answer. It was the last time I saw him. A little over a year later, S'fiso was dead.

In the weeks following the news of his death, I felt trapped in an agonizing cycle of grief, rage, guilt, and helplessness. It was not the first time I had lost someone close to me in the six years I had been working in South Africa, but it was the time that hit me the hardest. S'fiso was the same age as me – thirty-five at the time – and, like me, he had a young child at home. He had grown up in Umlazi, a township outside Durban, where in recent years he, along with every one of his friends, had lost loved ones to gun violence, road accidents, alcohol and drug overdoses, and treatable illnesses. He had come of age, forging his most intimate relationships, as part of a peer group where he suspected at least half were HIV-positive, in a province where forty percent of adults were estimated to be infected, and at a time when treatment was accessible only to those with significant financial resources. The stigma facing those believed to have "this thing," as it was cryptically known, was enormous. By any measure, his chances of escaping unscathed, of living to see his child grow up, were low. He worked in HIV/AIDS research because he believed in what he was doing and wanted to see change. In a context where unemployment levels were soaring and the income gap was widening, he also took pride in his ability to provide for the many people close to him.

The questions he asked me in 2008 have stayed with me – so much so that I want to respond to them in this preamble, situating them among the philosophies, methodologies, ethics, and politics that have underpinned my research journey and my writing of this book.[2] What drew me, a young, "white," able-bodied Canadian woman, into a decade-long engagement with HIV/AIDS research in South Africa? How did I come to focus my work on grandmother caregivers, documenting their associations and transnational connections? What ideas, events, and relationships guided my research? What are my goals for this book, and why have I written it the way I have? It is these broader questions that are invoked for me when I reflect on my relationship – and especially on my final encounter – with S'fiso. I address these questions by recounting the story of my research in South Africa, from some of my earliest experiences through to the writing of this book.

EARLY ENCOUNTERS AND GUIDING PHILOSOPHIES

As a twenty-nine-year-old Canadian student working on my master's degree, I was initially drawn to Durban by some combination of serendipity and deeply held convictions. I was, most significantly, committed to an *engaged* research practice: in embarking on graduate studies, I hoped to contribute not only to producing sound, thought-provoking knowledge but also to improving the lives of those who participated in my research in any way that was feasible. I aligned myself with the longstanding intellectual project of democratizing knowledge production and thus sought to carry out research that was, to the greatest extent possible, community-sanctioned and community-driven. Maintaining a critical perspective on the power relations shaping the research, I wanted to involve participants in my research in some or all aspects of the process, from defining the questions to producing, interpreting, disseminating, and acting on the findings. I also questioned who would have access to the knowledge produced and how it might be used. I was guided, then, by what are often called anti-oppressive epistemologies and methodologies: I was committed to valuing the perspectives of those historically excluded from knowledge sanctioned by the academy and to remaining critical of, while working to shift, the power dynamics between myself, as researcher, and those whom I was researching.

In early 2004, when I initially proposed the research for my MA at Carleton University in Ottawa, my focus was on youth vulnerabilities to HIV/AIDS in Indigenous communities in Canada. My undergraduate training in the 1990s had been in health studies; I had followed the unfolding of the global HIV/AIDS epidemic for some time, concerned particularly with the ways in which its uneven impacts revealed patterns of social marginalization and interlocking systems of oppression, as starkly illustrated by the disproportionate levels of infection and illness observed within Indigenous communities. However, as an unknown and relatively inexperienced graduate student, establishing trust with Indigenous-run organizations proved difficult – for good reasons. I understood how research had been used as a colonial tool – generating homogenizing and objectifying knowledge about Indigenous peoples for use in their domination – and I aligned myself with efforts to break this cycle by valuing and privileging those knowledges historically devalued, or even exploited, in academic research. I decided that I would engage in this work only if I was invited to do so in partnership with an appropriate Indigenous-led organization. But, although the research I was proposing was considered by my advisors to be academically sound, and although I had secured funding for it, I was unable to establish the relationships that I felt were necessary to do the work in an ethical way. Faced with the choice of carrying out my research in a manner that was incompatible with my own politics or returning my research funding and re-conceptualizing my project, I chose the latter.

At this point, serendipity came into play. I took on a short contract with the Canadian-based North-South Institute, helping to organize an international workshop to review Canada's global HIV/AIDS policies. Through this, I met the program director of HEARD, a young woman with whom I had much in common. Over the course of the workshop, she asked if I would consider working with her team in Durban. She offered to host me as a visiting scholar and to help me identify a project that would dovetail with HEARD's larger research initiatives. Shortly thereafter, a funding opportunity presented itself. When I boarded the flight to South Africa a few months later, I had many lingering, critical questions about my role and positioning within this work, and I remained unsure about what the project we had jointly proposed – the work in Warwick Junction – would entail. I took some comfort, though, in the prospect of working with a local, like-minded research institute and contributing to a larger initiative, and I hoped there would be opportunities for the kind of engaged work I envisioned.

Within a week of my arrival in Durban, and after visiting the vibrant (albeit chaotic and insecure) area that was to be my research site, I was overwhelmed. On the advice of colleagues at HEARD, I hired S'fiso. He was keen to assist, and he seemed to have friends in every corner; he taught me how to manoeuvre safely through the area and made it possible for me to begin meeting street traders. For five months, he acted as my translator and guide, offering a depth of insight I could not have found anywhere else – not in my research interviews, and certainly not in all the books I had read. He also taught me to speak enough isiZulu to begin to forge my own relationships. Those relationships, especially with the gogos in the market, set me on the road to the research for this book.

While I had initially intended to focus on gendered vulnerabilities to HIV/AIDS among transient urban youth, I was quickly drawn to the older women's stories. I listened to women in their forties, fifties, and sixties recount, one after another, how they were supporting growing numbers of young children because other adult income-earners in their families were either unemployed, ill, or dead. Although they worked in the city, they regularly travelled between Warwick Junction and their rural homes, where their families resided. They saw themselves as the primary caregivers and felt displaced while away at work. They were not only the pillars of their families but, despite immense calls on their time and energy, the key organizers within their communities as well. While each woman in my research came from a different rural or peri-urban area outside Durban, each belonged to a similar community association designed to respond to their similar stresses, including the compounding pressures associated with HIV/AIDS. The pattern I observed was so pronounced that I grew determined to learn more about these seemingly widespread community groups. By early 2005, I had focused in on the effects of HIV/AIDS on this generation of South African women as a topic that I would continue to explore through a PhD, and I was increasingly interested in the roles these women played in community mobilization. At that time, "grandmothers" had yet to be fully incorporated into global AIDS discourses, and the issues faced by older women in South African communities were under-studied.

My early work in Durban, in 2004 and 2005, was not, in retrospect, as community-engaged as I had hoped it might be. While I facilitated a number of gatherings with traders' organizations and disseminated research findings widely in Warwick Junction, the traders with whom I worked never initiated the research; they also never contributed to its design or used the knowledge produced in their own advocacy efforts. Where I was able to make some contribution beyond the scholarly contribution of my research was in my work with HEARD. In 2005, HEARD was still a small and relatively new research institute and, as part of its broader effort to build local research capacity and grow its team, I was invited to take on a number of short contracts. Through this, I helped extend the work in Warwick Junction, so that the project spanned, intermittently, the next three years. I also set out to build relationships with a number of community-based organizations across the country, investigating in a preliminary way the roles of older women in community AIDS response. One such organization was the Hillcrest AIDS Centre Trust (HACT), a multi-dimensional project located forty kilometres inland from Durban in an area called the Valley of 1000 Hills; I later partnered with the HACT to carry out the research for this book. My primary role at HEARD, however, was to help recruit and train a team of fieldworkers and RAs – young people from the surrounding areas who were eager to obtain job skills and work experience – and it was through this work that I most significantly connected my research with advocacy.

S'fiso was my first RA, and our evolving relationship was illustrative of the many ways in which the distinctions between my roles as researcher, advocate, and friend became blurred. Indeed, I resisted the idea that, as a researcher, I should remain detached from, or minimize disturbance in, the lives of those whom I drew into the research; instead, I attempted to adopt an ethics of care, allowing my practice to be guided by caring for each person I involved in my work.[3] In 2005, S'fiso confided in me that the mother of his child had passed away. He did not reveal (and perhaps did not know) the cause of her death, but it was obvious that he was terrified that she might have had the dreaded virus. After that, each interview we carried out seemed to further trigger his fears. While having S'fiso share his own experiences with me at the end of each interview clearly deepened my understanding of the epidemic, I realized that asking him to continually engage in such emotionally laden interviews was taking a toll on him; I felt responsible for helping him access counselling and medical advice. I also advocated for him to secure more permanent work at HEARD and to purchase life insurance.

I was drawn to doing HIV/AIDS research in South Africa, then, by my academic interests and by my desire to make a contribution both within and outside academia. Through my work with HEARD, and especially in my relationships with RAs like S'fiso, some opportunities to do the latter emerged; these encounters, in turn, revealed to me the importance of remaining conscious of the emotional dimensions of this kind of practice while also reflecting critically on the various ways my roles and positions would blur. It was not until the following year, however, when I began the research for this book, that the opportunity arose to carry out a more community-engaged and community-driven research practice.

Relationships, Timing, and Community Engagement

In March 2006, serendipity once again steered the course of this project. The Stephen Lewis Foundation (SLF), a Toronto-based organization that supports and funds community-based AIDS projects across sub-Saharan Africa, launched its Grandmothers to Grandmothers Campaign, seeking to mobilize Canadian grandmothers in solidarity with gogos from the region. I took an immediate interest as I was hopeful that this campaign might bring recognition and support to older women who were struggling to care for their families in the context of AIDS. It also prompted me to turn my gaze closer to home: it spoke to the nagging questions I had about what roles Canadian women (myself included) could and should play in the struggles of women on the other side of the globe. I was drawn, furthermore, to think about how such a transnational network would play out in the lives of the South African gogos with whom I had been working. In the lead-up to the launch of the Grandmothers to Grandmothers Campaign, I spoke about my research at a small meeting at the SLF. Later that year, when the SLF organized its inaugural Grandmothers' Gathering in Toronto, bringing grandmothers from Canada and southern Africa together, I volunteered to assist with documenting the event.

At this gathering in Toronto, I reconnected with two nurses from the HACT whom I knew from my earlier work with HEARD; older women working for an SLF-funded organization, these nurses had been invited as delegates. As a powerful and highly emotive event, the Toronto Gathering raised a number of questions for them. They left wishing to conduct research into how older women in the Valley of 1000 Hills were being impacted by, and were responding to, the epidemic. Shortly after the gathering, they solicited my support. I agreed to help and, through extensive discussions with them, decided to dovetail my own questions – about why and how the Valley gogos were organizing, and how they might become linked to the budding Canadian Grandmothers Campaign – into their research plan. This is where the story I tell in this book begins. It was also the first time I had had the opportunity to engage in research that was, to a larger extent, community-driven.[4] Over the four years that followed, I worked most closely with one of the nurses, Noku, to articulate the HACT's research questions, establish appropriate methods, carry out fieldwork, analyze the findings, and decide how the knowledge produced should be used. I also continually tried to make the research accessible through presentations and reports, which the HACT drew on in instituting changes to its programming.

Personal relationships were pivotal in allowing me to carry out this work. Partnering with Noku, for instance, made it possible for me to connect with many of the gogos in the Valley. As an older Zulu woman from one of the Valley settlements, a trusted nurse with decades of community nursing experience, and a skilled counsellor and motivational speaker, she put the women at ease to share their stories. I cannot overemphasize the importance of her daily participation and presence in this research. In addition, working closely with three young women from HEARD's team as my RAs allowed me to engage and communicate sensitively with the gogos. All three were committed, skilled, empathetic, and hard-working;

their openness about their own experiences helped to build the rapport necessary to carry out the project. Through the course of our research together, and through hours of talking while driving the winding Valley roads to do home visits or to participate in the gogos' support groups, I developed close friendships with all four of these women. These friendships, and these conversations, have profoundly informed my analysis.

As with my earlier research with S'fiso, it is impossible to disentangle these relationships, the research process, and the knowledge produced from the emotional and ethical dimensions of this work. Because of the trusting relationships we were able to form with the gogos, they regularly shared some of their most traumatic experiences – stories, for example, of abuse, murder, illness, insecurity, and death. I realized that my questions would require them to relive these stories and I had many moments in 2008 when I considered stopping the research early for this reason. It was clear to me in these instances that I simply would not have been able to carry through with this work if it had not been for Noku, who offered counselling, assisted with accessing community services, and led the gogos' groups in healing prayers. I also felt responsible for Noku (though such activities seemed to be a regular part of her work) and my RAS (who were quite disturbed by what they were witnessing), and I was well aware of my own emotional stress. I made sure that Noku, my RAS, and I regularly had time to air our feelings and acknowledge the emotional intensity of the work, and I offered to find my RAS a counsellor through HEARD (although they did not feel this to be necessary). For me, it was not until after S'fiso's death, and with much personal and professional support, that I started to process this experience. I do not shy away from these emotional encounters in the book but instead seek to situate my analyses within the ever-shifting relationships – with all of their emotional and ethical complexity – that informed them.

A number of factors, then, came together to shape this research, including timing, external events, and chance encounters, alongside my underpinning philosophies, evolving academic interests, and personal and professional positioning. When the SLF launched its Grandmothers to Grandmothers Campaign, I had already committed to undertaking research that would bring visibility to the gogos, and I had well-established community relationships with SLF-funded groups; I was also looking for some way to reconnect my work to the Canadian context. The request for research support from the HACT nurses then presented an opportunity, finally, for me to try to engage in a more community-driven model of research, in line with what had drawn me into this work in the first place. I was fortunate to have the institutional support of HEARD, a team of dedicated RAs, and funding[5] that allowed me to live in Durban for periods of time and to travel back and forth between there and my home in Ottawa. In Canada, I was introduced to the SLF by the director of HEARD, who was a long-time friend and colleague of Stephen Lewis. Among the Canadian grandmothers, I also had a number of points of personal connection: the mother of one of my close friends co-founded one of the first grandmothers' groups in Ottawa, while, on the other side of the country, my mother-in-law soon joined the active Nanaimo group.

I embarked on this research in what was clearly a dynamic environment. Much of what I did was document, and analyze, a story as it unfolded; the story, however, has continued, and indeed outlived, its writing. This kind of research has required openness on my part – to the unexpected, to situations that left me feeling self-conscious, to the need to regularly revisit my own motivations, to the complex ethics and emotions involved, and to the uniqueness and fluidity of each research relationship – as well as a commitment to academic rigour.

S'FISO'S QUESTIONS (REVISITED) AND THIS BOOK

This book's content, goals, and form cannot, in my view, be separated from the philosophies, encounters, and relationships discussed throughout. With this in mind, I would like to return to S'fiso's two questions and offer my response. Would he find a place in this book? Would it be written in such a way that he could understand it?

S'fiso is not formally part of the story I tell – a story about why, how, and to what effect in the first decade of this century grandmothers in South Africa and Canada were organizing and joining forces in the struggle against AIDS. Yet I believe he warrants a central place in this preamble as someone who is integral to the broader story of my engagement in South Africa. Without his guidance and input, I am quite certain my work in and around Durban would not have extended over most of the past decade, nor would it have achieved the depth that it did. His was the first of several crucial relationships – with RAs and research partners – that greatly influenced my understanding of South Africa's HIV/AIDS epidemic. As such, he represents the intersubjectivity of the knowledge produced in this research and presented in this book; he is a reminder that what I have come to understand about HIV/AIDS and about its effect on people's daily lives is a result, first and foremost, of a series of significant relationships.

I have also felt a responsibility to write this book in a way that S'fiso would have been able to understand had he lived to see its publication. S'fiso metaphorically held a mirror up to me, requiring me to struggle with the differences in privilege bestowed on us as a result of our different skin tones and birthplaces. His question of whether he would be able to understand this book was just one such instance: it highlighted that, while I was a well-funded PhD student, he had never had the opportunity to attend university. In the decade since my earliest encounters in South Africa, I have earned two graduate degrees, had two healthy babies, and secured fulfilling employment. This stands in stark contrast to the experiences of so many of my friends and colleagues in South Africa, who, across differences in language, nationality, skin colour, generation, class, education, and more, participated in the production of this book. I am conscious, furthermore, that one of the ways in which, as a scholar, I continue to exert this privilege is through my writing: by being committed to paper, my interpretations gain further credibility and epistemic value. Thus, given my political and ethical positions, it makes sense that, while this is undoubtedly a scholarly book informed by theoretically nuanced questions and based on rigorous research, I have deliberately attempted to write it for a wide readership. My hope is that it will prove readable, compelling, and useful not only to other scholars but to my RAs, the HACT nurses, other practitioners, activists, junior researchers, students, and grandmothers as well. Writing accessibly while engaging in scholarly analysis and theoretical production is, clearly, a challenging task, but it is a task necessitated by the convictions that have shaped my entire journey: my desire to share ownership of the research and make the knowledge produced accessible, my commitment to remaining critical of how power operates in all research encounters, including through the writing process, and my attempt to apply an ethics of care to the relationships forged through this work.

I have chosen to write in a very personal way, narrating the book in the first person and adopting an intimate tone. Like other scholars before me,

I have written myself into the story: I have sought to acknowledge my own positions and to explicitly tell the story of *my* encounters with grandmothers in South Africa and Canada. I have deliberately inserted myself in small ways throughout the book to remind readers that what follows are not the "authentic voices" of grandmothers but my interpretations, which have been informed both by my experiences and relationships and by my formal academic training.

I start each chapter with a scene or two from my fieldwork in order to ground my analysis within the particular places, times, and encounters that are so central to this work. These vignettes serve to contextualize my questions and reveal my own shifting positions within these exchanges. They emphasize that the story I tell hinges on a series of personal relationships that were always in flux, shifting as trust built, as political and economic circumstances changed, and as participants' views of me changed, depending often on events in my life or theirs.

Finally, I avoid lengthy and exhaustive reviews of the literatures that have informed my work. Instead, I attempt to start from and emphasize the conversations, experiences, and observations that have most shaped my understanding. This does not make this book atheoretical. Rather, it is informed by a number of scholarly conversations, which I draw on substantively in chapter 1 to situate the book's central concepts and questions. I then focus on women's lives and relationships, moving from the particulars of their experiences to a discussion of what these mean, more broadly, for thinking about transnational solidarity, grandmotherhood, and global AIDS response. In other words, I take these experiences as sites of theoretical production, with the possibility for the details of the women's lives and associations to disrupt certain existing assumptions. Because my questions, directions, framing, and conclusions have all evolved as an iterative process between personal experience and scholarly reading, I would argue that such a grounded approach is both appropriate and necessary. However, I recognize that different readers will read this book in different ways; for those interested in further scholarly connections, I have included extensive endnotes throughout, especially in chapter 1.

This is a story, then, about the strength of older South African women who, amidst inconceivable grief, poverty, stigma, and violence, cared for their families and mobilized their communities, and about their intricate, often unknowing, alliances with women across the globe. To a growing body of scholarship on the politics, practices, challenges, and implications of building solidarities across distance and difference, this book contributes a detailed analysis of the everyday lives and diverse perspectives of older women and their particular relationships across North-South divides. To existing texts on the HIV/AIDS epidemic in southern Africa and on the global AIDS response, this work adds a unique focus on the South African gogos and their Canadian allies. To other feminist scholars interested in anti-oppressive methodologies, this story reveals some of the imperfect realities, intricate relationships, and daily dilemmas involved in doing engaged research. To Noku and all the others who courageously shared their stories with me, this work stands as a testament to the many ways in which their insights and relationships shaped my understanding of how tens of thousands of older women from across two continents organized and linked up to change their own lives and the lives of innumerable others. And for S'fiso, this book is written to honour his memory and to be a bridge between the academic and the everyday.

1 | THE UNEXPECTED

Inchanga, South Africa
July 2008

The slow, melancholic harmonies were barely audible from behind the small building, where I sat perched on an overturned pail. My research assistant and I watched in silence while Ntombi, a strong Zulu woman, carefully sorted a stack of photos. Inside, the energy intensified as a steady stream of women arrived to join the grandmothers' opening prayer circle. An active member of this group, Ntombi would usually be inside as well. But today she wanted to proceed straight to our interview. The previous week we had given her a disposable camera and asked her to try to capture what was motivating her to attend these weekly meetings; to "show us" the stresses in her life and the ways in which she was responding. She had waited all week to see the photos she had taken, which we had developed for her.

Leaning toward me, she placed a photo in my hand and asked quietly in isiZulu, "Can we start?" I nodded. "When I step outside my home," she explained, "this is what I see." She paused. The photo showed her small grassy yard set amidst the rolling terrain that characterizes this area, known as the Valley of 1000 Hills, in the province of KwaZulu-Natal, South Africa. The distant slope was speckled with small brick houses and tin shacks. "These are my children's graves."

To an undiscerning eye, the four coffin-shaped forms, each rising a few inches above the ground, outlined in small stones, and with grass growing overtop, could almost be mistaken for unused garden beds – except for the small wooden cross marking the largest of the sites.

"I am fifty-one years old," she continued. "All my children have died – all nine of them – and they left me with grandchildren and great-grandchildren. I have many kids at home who need food." Her voice was strained. "I do not even have a place to have a garden now because my home is clustered with graves. These [graves] are my daily reminder." Her eyes filled with tears, and I looked away. She was not the first in our research to photograph a burial ground beside her home, or to reveal the tragedy of premature, often preventable, death. This image was becoming something of a motif in our interviews – one that would emerge as vitally important to telling these grandmothers' stories.

The women's voices grew louder and stronger, escaping the confines of their cramped quarters and projecting across their settlement of Inchanga. Again and again, they repeated the prayer's simple verses, as if the words and the melody filled them with courage and determination.

Let us thank Him, let us thank Him,
He, who has such mercy, let us love Him,
Let us worship Him each day.
Hallelujah, the Lord Jesus, whose mercy is great,
We are called to Him today.

We can see Him in the innocent, in those who are child-like,
He will lead them home.
Hallelujah, the Lord Jesus, whose mercy is great,
We are called to Him today.

Let us thank Him, let us thank Him,
He, who has such mercy, let us love Him,
Let us worship Him each day.
Hallelujah, the Lord Jesus, whose mercy is great,
We are called to Him today.

Amen
(Translated from isiZulu)

Traditionally a simple prayer of gratitude, these well-rehearsed verses, unequivocally equated with Saturdays – the day of funerals – now punctuate the weekly routines of many South Africans. They have been appropriated to uplift and accompany the many hours spent digging and filling graves.

But these grandmothers (or "gogos" in isiZulu) were not gathered for a funeral; not today. On this chilly Wednesday morning, they had come together to speak, share, and learn, to try to generate livelihoods, and to pray for guidance. These women were confronting extreme poverty, grief, violence, and illness. Burying their children had become part of their everyday lives, associated with such frightening and mysterious phenomena as HIV/AIDS, witchcraft, and murder. Funerals, particularly those of young people, were simultaneously normalized and stigmatized. Yet, these gogos did not shy away from letting their voices reverberate with this prayer. They were not put off by its connotations. They were not silent from acceptance, or shame, or fear. Instead, they stood, asserting their dignity, acknowledging their mutual experiences, and seeking divine intervention.

In July 2008, their group was one of seven such groups affiliated with the Hillcrest AIDS Centre Trust (HACT), a non-governmental organization (NGO) located forty kilometres inland from the major city centre of Durban, in the Valley of 1000 Hills. The HACT supports families affected by AIDS across the Valley's 250 square kilometres of hills, plateaus, and ravines, providing care, help with income-generation projects, HIV testing and counselling, treatment monitoring, distribution of food parcels, and assistance with school fees.[1] Situated on the border of the former Bantustan of KwaZulu and province of Natal, this area is characterized by profound class, race, and gender inequalities. At its edges, closest to Durban, lie several affluent rural-suburban communities, inhabited primarily by "white" and some "Indian" South Africans,[2] and distinguished by mansion estates, shopping complexes, and tourist resorts. Most of the Valley's 100,000 residents, however, inhabit the nearby rural and peri-urban settlements – such as the settlement of Inchanga – where the transition to democracy seventeen years ago brought continued violence and poverty, formal employment is practically unknown, and some forty percent of women attending antenatal clinics are estimated to be HIV-positive. These areas are almost exclusively "black" and isiZulu-speaking; they remain extremely under-resourced, with poor housing, inadequate sanitation, and limited social services.[3]

Across the Valley's poorer settlements, the idea of gogos coming together to support one another spread rapidly in the early part of this century. Ntombi's group in Inchanga was the first, starting in 2007, and by late 2010 the HACT was working with twenty-six gogos' groups across four different settlements, with an estimated 900 older women involved. These groups became a lifeline for the gogos and for the thousands of women, men, and children who depended on them for care.

The story of this mobilization – of why, how, and to what effect these grandmothers were organizing in South Africa's Valley of 1000 Hills in the first decade of the twenty-first century – is not by any account straight-forward, though at its core it is about women's collective struggles for physical, financial, emotional, spiritual, and intergenerational survival. Unraveling this story means understanding what "gogo" had come to sig-nify in this context, where one in three children was being cared for by a grandmother, and where grandmothers' pensions were often the most reliable, or the only, source of family income.[4] It means closely examin-ing the gogos' daily lives, perspectives, and discourses. It means grappling with the implications of the rapid societal change that was underway: plummeting marital rates, increasing mobility, declining employment opportunities, and changing gender and family dynamics – all associated with the country's democratization, economic change, and HIV/AIDS epidemic. It requires carefully tracing the origins of the gogos' groups, understanding their linkages within and beyond the Valley. It means fully engaging with the emotional and the visceral, with the intimacies of birth, death, hope, and devastation. It also commands a certain openness to the unexpected – a commitment not to gloss over that which is "messy," counter-intuitive, contradictory, or contested.

Toronto, Canada
August 2006

In small, intimate talking circles, the African grandmothers gathered to give their testimonials. From thirteen sub-Saharan countries, these women had come together to tell the world their stories – stories of un-fathomable grief, indomitable strength, and relentless struggle. For three days in August 2006, 100 African grandmothers and 200 Canadian grand-mothers assembled alongside 25,000 delegates attending the XVI Inter-national AIDS Conference in Toronto. This inaugural Grandmothers' Gathering provided the African women with a long-overdue opportunity to raise their voices on the world stage. It was organized by the Toronto-based Stephen Lewis Foundation (SLF), which funds community-based

AIDS projects in sub-Saharan Africa, focusing on supporting "grassroots" initiatives that address the needs of women and children. The SLF was founded in 2003 by its current director, Ilana Landsberg-Lewis, a human rights lawyer, and her father, Stephen Lewis, the former United Nations (UN) secretary-general's special envoy for HIV/AIDS in Africa.[5]

Intimate conversations took place in the quiet privacy of grandmother-led workshops, while larger events – marches, speeches, dinners, and receptions – drew the media out en masse. On the final morning, 13 August 2006, two grandmothers – one from each continent – stood side-by-side in the atrium of the Canadian Broadcasting Corporation (CBC) building. With all cameras on them, they delivered their Toronto Statement, culminating with the following closing address:

> Africans and Canadians alike, we arrived at our grandmothers' gathering with high expectations, but also with nagging apprehensions. We worried that the grief – our own and our sisters' – would be overwhelming. We harboured fears that the language barriers would separate us. We Canadian grandmothers worried that our capacity to help might be reduced to fundraising alone; we African grandmothers worried that our dire straits might cast us as victims rather than heroes. But we were motivated to make the trip by the special love that every grandmother knows, and we were emboldened to face our fears by the wisdom of our years. Our courage paid off. The age-old African ways of speaking without words broke down our communication barriers. We gestured and nodded. And we sang. We danced. We drummed. We laughed and clapped and wept and hugged. Through our new discovery – grandmother to grandmother solidarity – we carried ourselves and one another through the grief to where we are this morning.
>
> May this be the dawn of the grandmothers' movement.[6]

They pledged to create and sustain a transnational network of grandmothers.[7] The African women would continue to do what they do – raise children, care for the sick, generate incomes, and organize within their communities – while the Canadian women would support them by raising funds, building solidarity, and mobilizing more Canadians to join their growing Grandmothers to Grandmothers Campaign.[8]

I felt privileged to stand among them that morning, both as a volunteer with the SLF and as a strong supporter of their efforts. Yet, as an academic and researcher, I was also filled with critical questions. Would this energy be sustained over time in Canada and, if so, to what end? Would the Canadian grandmothers be able to negotiate meaningful relationships with their African counterparts, and what role would the SLF play? How would the African grandmothers feel upon their return home? How would they be perceived by their communities? What would this "solidarity" mean for them in practical terms? What impact would it have in their communities? I was immensely hopeful about the possibilities but I could not have predicted the extent, reach, or intricacy of what these possibilities would mean in practice. In August 2006, I could not have guessed that two years later Ntombi and her group in Inchanga would be elaborately – and unknowingly – tied to a vibrant and sophisticated movement of nearly 10,000 Canadians.

Understanding the development of the Canadian Grandmothers Campaign and its complex, often unpredictable, interactions with the lives and associations of older women in the Valley of 1000 Hills is my focus in this book. I take one South African organization – the Hillcrest AIDS Centre Trust – as my entry point and through it connect with grandmothers from four communities in the Valley: Inchanga, Molweni, Lower Molweni, and KwaNyuswa. I ask why, how, and to what effect grandmothers in South Africa and Canada were organizing and linking up between 2006 and 2010, and what it meant for them to build solidarity across geographical distance and social difference. With careful attention to the specificities of time and place, I explain what brought Ntombi and the other women to that prayer circle in 2008 and show how their group drew on, even if unintentionally, resources, ideas, and networks generated in Canada.

GLOBAL AIDS RESPONSE

Two-thirds of the world's 33.3 million people infected with HIV live in communities in sub-Saharan Africa.[9] In this region, young adults are falling ill and dying, leaving older women to care for the sick, vulnerable, and orphaned. HelpAge International estimates that forty to sixty percent of orphans in several sub-Saharan countries live in grandmother-headed households.[10] While policy makers and development agencies have long focused on "orphans and vulnerable children," those caring for these children have received much less recognition.[11] As well, there has been limited scholarly analysis of older caregivers' diverse lived experiences, forms of association, support networks, and potential roles in global AIDS response.[12]

In the years following the Toronto Gathering, the global financial crisis (2007 to 2012) resulted in, or perhaps justified, the "flat-lining" of funding by many international organizations that, as part of the global response to AIDS, had pledged to sustain an increasing influx of resources to African countries for treatment and prevention programs.[13] Access to life-saving drugs, prophylactics, counselling, food, and education, among other things, became increasingly tenuous for many, while economic recession made their lives and livelihoods even more precarious.

While "global AIDS response" most often refers to funds, initiatives, and targeted programming provided by powerful international organizations and private foundations (for example, the Bill and Melinda Gates Foundation, the Global Fund to Fight AIDS, Tuberculosis, and Malaria, the President's Emergency Plan for AIDS Relief (PEPFAR), UNAIDS, and so on), many other individuals and groups across the globe – including the grandmothers described in this book – have also been engaged in this struggle. Though not nearly as prominent or as visible, these actors' lives, tactics, and perspectives clearly merit attention.

By recording the contributions of South African and Canadian grandmothers, this book expands the notion of what and who should be considered part of the global AIDS response. In so doing, it also responds to a broader need for critical scholarship on older women's roles in working for social change. Over the next forty years, the global population of people over the age of sixty is expected to triple, so that by 2050, for the first time in history, there will be more people worldwide over the age of sixty than under the age of fifteen. Life expectancy is higher for women than it is for men, with populations over sixty estimated to include two to five times as many women as men.[14] While different regions are experiencing this transition along different timelines, the emerging picture is that population aging is unprecedented, pervasive, and feminized. This transition is converging with growing transnational mobilization around global justice issues, including not only the uneven effects of HIV/AIDS but also unfair labour practices, growing social and economic disparities, the inequitable impacts of climate change, the ongoing dispossession of indigenous peoples, and systemic violence against women and children.[15] In this context, and by drawing on critical feminist understandings of agency, social mobilization, and global connections, this book seeks to expand current thinking around global AIDS response, transnational solidarity, and old age.

OLDER WOMEN'S AGENCY

Choosing to focus on older women's collective responses as opposed to, for example, their vulnerabilities[16] was both an academic and a personal-political decision. At the core, it is a conceptual shift away from casting older women as victims toward understanding their agency: how do older women act, gather, and assert themselves? In making this shift, I align with other scholarly efforts to unveil not only the *challenges* faced by older women, including, for example, economic strain, discrimination, impaired mobility, abuse, and health decline, but also their *contributions* in working for social change.[17] I do not mean to downplay the trauma and devastation experienced by the gogos in the Valley of 1000 Hills as a result of longstanding and interlocking forms of oppression and abuse, nor do I wish to suggest that these women exhibited superhuman strength and resilience to the point where they required no external support. Rather, I seek to understand the ways they were organizing, how they understood their own associations, and what their mobilizations were producing or challenging. Like Frank, "I do not want to tell another anthropological story of Africans as victims, nor am I content with a story of innovative survivors in the face of incredible odds. Neither story captures the devastation that the AIDS epidemic is causing throughout southern Africa or the everyday acceptance and dignity with which the local populations adjust their lives to catastrophic circumstances. The story I need to tell is somewhere in between and yet beyond both of these meta-narratives."[18]

I draw specifically from theorizing around agency that has been undertaken by feminist and postcolonial scholars, often under the rubric of studying "resistance."[19] I do not intend to generate a theory of agency, nor to embark on an exhaustive review of the extensive feminist writings on this topic. However, two key themes in these writings are especially helpful for understanding grandmothers' mobilizations and for challenging certain simplistic categories: (1) the importance of listening to women's own accounts of why they gather in certain ways, without assuming that their actions reflect certain pre-prescribed politics, intentions, or identities; and (2) the idea that, with each action, women participate in either upholding or destabilizing various norms, and thus their agency is tied to the instability of such norms.

Writing on women's agency first became common in the 1970s in feminist scholarship. Women who appeared to uphold "feminine" virtues were no longer viewed as having internalized some sort of patriarchal consciousness. Instead, the focus turned to seeking to locate sites of resistance or sites of women's agency; these were often "hidden" or subtle resistances that were believed to involve women subverting entrenched patriarchal practices and redeploying them for their own interests.[20] This scholarship greatly expanded debates about gender, reframing women as more than submissive victims of patriarchy but instead as active agents whose lives were far more complex than had previously been acknowledged. In this work, agency was understood as the capacity to realize one's own interests against the weight of customs, traditions, political-economic structures, and so on.[21] However, as Mahmood[22] pointed out with reference to Boddy,[23] some scholars in this school may have been overly guided by their own political projects: even when an explicit feminist agency was difficult to locate, there was a tendency to look for expressions of resistance that appeared to challenge male domination.

It was not until the 1990s that leading scholars began to critique this potential "romance of resistance" and suggest that tying agency to the feminist political project might misattribute forms of consciousness or politics to women in cases where these were not actually part of their experience.[24] The critique was particularly salient among certain postcolonial scholars working closely with women in the Global South, many of whom felt that, in the name of some universally defined "feminism" and in the quest to demonstrate that women everywhere were resisting global patriarchy, the actions of many so-called "Third World women" were being regularly misunderstood.[25] Abu-Lughod, who was prominent in this debate, raised the question of how to recognize instances of women's resistance without assuming some universal political project.[26] As she explained, "The problem has been that those of us who have sensed that there is something admirable about resistance have tended to look to it for hopeful confirmations of the failure – or partial failure – of systems of oppression. Yet it seems to me that we respect the everyday resistance not just by arguing for the dignity and heroism of the resisters but by letting their practices teach us about the complex interworkings of historically changing structures of power."[27] Her intervention recognized multiple forms of resistance and sought to move beyond ascribing a "feminist consciousness" to those for whom this was not a meaningful category.

Mahmood took this one step further, challenging the use of the term "resistance" itself. She asked whether, even when care is taken not to assume a feminist consciousness, the category of "resistance" imposes a certain progressive politics, eliding a whole range of actions that might not have any intention of opposing hegemonic norms. What about women whose actions are underpinned by other reasons, histories, and motivations?[28] Did the Valley gogos, for instance, view their associations as resisting or subverting certain forms of oppression? In order to respect other possibilities, other realities, and other forms of consciousness, Mahmood argued that it is necessary to detach notions of agency not just from the feminist political project but from goals of progressive politics in general. This means putting aside certain assumptions, as much as possible, and beginning one's analysis with grounded realities, stories, and perceptions. Viewed in this way, "agency" denotes not only acts that *resist* norms but also multiple ways of *inhabiting* norms: "the terms people use to organize their lives are not simply a gloss for universally shared assumptions ... but are actually constitutive of different forms of personhood, knowledge, and experience."[29]

Most recently, some scholars (Mahmood included) have drawn on Butler's works[30] to further nuance their ideas around agency. Butler broke with many feminist scholars before her, borrowing two key insights from Foucault: first, that power is not something that can be possessed and redeployed but rather continuously operates to produce relations, discourses, and desires; and second, that subjectivities (the ways in which people identify and are identified) do not precede power relations but are instead produced through these relations. From this perspective, "agency" is not seen as a byproduct of some undominated self that existed prior to the operation of power; by contrast, it is is understood as produced through that operation. In Butler's language, social norms do not merely exist, but rather are "performative": they are made and become dominant through repeated actions. However, the "reiterative" structure of norms (which means that they are made through repetition) can serve not only to consolidate a particular regime of discourse/power but also to provide a means for its destabilization. In other words, norms are understood to be made (and unmade) through the repetition of certain actions: with each repetition, norms can be entrenched, stabilized, secured, challenged, re-appropriated, or re-signified. Agency is grounded in this openness, this possibility for change.[31] This view further opens up agency beyond emancipatory politics, suggesting that acts of re-signification are context-specific, fragile, and unpredictable.

My focus on older women's agency in the face of HIV/AIDS is, in part, about dispelling victimizing narratives of older women's frailty. It is also about trying to understand whether and how the daily actions of grand-mothers in South Africa and Canada might have functioned to entrench or reconfigure certain norms. I do not seek to tie the agency of these women to a particular progressive or feminist politics in an abstract way. Rather, I aim at understanding their associations and linkages on their terms, with-out expectation that these women all shared common or pre-determined motivations or politics. In addition, I do not see their agency as exist-ing outside of their daily practices. Instead, I conceptualize it as their moment-to-moment actions that, through their repetition, function to produce, consolidate, challenge, or destabilize norms: I view these "per-formances" as always imbued with openness and possibility for change. It is from these ideas that one of the book's central questions emerges: what was being produced, consolidated, or re-signified through grandmothers' mobilizations – in the Valley of 1000 Hills, in Canada, and through their interlinking – and what were the consequences for the various women's lives and social practices? I revisit this question often throughout the book.

MOBILIZING GRANDMOTHERHOOD

Unpacking this question raises a series of other critical areas of inquiry. What, for instance, do I mean by "grandmothers' mobilizations," and what was actually being mobilized? How do I conceptualize "grandmother to grandmother solidarity": what did this mean and how was it practiced among the women in this alliance?

Of particular significance – both practical and conceptual – is that I explore the mobilizations *not only* of people and resources *but also* of identities and discourses.[32] I do not view identities – that of "grandmother" is central to this book – as essential, biological, static, or pre-prescribed: like Cooper,[33] Bernstein,[34] and many others, I recognize that people can deploy identities differently, *often strategically*, depending on context and social-political objective. I draw again on Butler's concept of performativity,[35] suggesting that identities are produced through their enactment and thus are always fluid, dynamic, and in the process of "becoming" (or of being produced). I also draw again on Mahmood[36] to probe how certain social locations can be mobilized or deployed as discursive categories and to unpack the assumptions, truth claims, and silences embedded within their dominant understandings. In other words, I ask how "grandmother" and "grandmotherhood" were perceived, practiced, and *deployed* in Canada and in the Valley, and I consider what "grandmotherhood" meant in these different contexts, what it made visible, and what it might have obscured.

This approach clearly wades into longstanding and diverse debates over the naturalness or socialization of "motherly" (or "grandmotherly" in this case) love, bonding, and care. Like Scheper-Hughes,[37] Lewis,[38] and many others, I frame "motherly" (or "grandmotherly") emotions and practices as historically, socially, economically, and culturally produced, not as part of a universal "womanly" ethic or ethos of maternal care. Much as I do not associate old age with stereotypes of frailty, disengagement, or marginality, I do not assume that there is some universal experience of being a grandmother based on the idea that all grandmothers feel a similar kind of love for and bond with their grandchildren. Instead, I investigate experiences, expectations, meanings, images, and emotions associated with grandmotherhood as contingent on time and place. I seek to understand how these are embedded in complex histories, geographies, and political economies.

It is useful to contextualize this view of "grandmotherhood" – and of identity more broadly – within the theoretical shift that is often associated with the transition from the "second wave" to the "third wave" in feminist scholarship; this has important implications for thinking about what the

Canadian Grandmothers Campaign calls "grandmother to grandmother solidarity." The "second wave" feminist movement refers predominantly to feminist activity that took place in North America and elsewhere in the Global North in the late 1960s and 1970s. Building on the successes of the earlier "first wave" women's movement, which won certain legal protections and the right to vote, "second wave" feminism fought for substantive equality for women. The movement is frequently depicted, often with reference to "the sisterhood," as based on the idea that all women are subject to oppression because of the ways in which patriarchy pervades families, workplaces, and society at large.[39] Feminist solidarity, from this perspective, pivots around a fixed identity group, "women," whose members are assumed to share similar experiences of exclusion and to have equal parts to play in subverting patriarchal structures.[40]

However, a number of postcolonial feminist scholars, many of whom identified as "women of colour" or "Third World women," opposed these assumptions of sameness.[41] These proponents of "third wave" feminism argued that not all women share comparable social positions within the so-called "sisterhood" and drew attention to the material and symbolic differences (and inequalities) in power and privilege that exist among women. In so doing, they urged an intersectional approach to the analysis of power, recognizing that skin colour, geography, class, and sexuality also shape how different women identify and how they experience oppression.[42] Queer theorists further complicated matters by calling into question the very category of "woman," suggesting that gender and sexuality are continuously performed in a multitude of ways and thus binary and static approaches to gender are insufficient.[43] By the early 1990s, feminism's "third wave" – now shaped by a much more vibrant North-South dialogue and more reflective of the struggles of women from diverse communities[44] – was faced with rethinking what had been the basis of feminist solidarity. For some, the very concept of "solidarity" seemed impossible without recourse to identity politics, while for many it remained an important concept and goal, and one that would need to grapple explicitly with social difference. For those in the latter group, what was required was a shift – from a collective struggle based on identity politics to one based on the shared goal of disabling longstanding, entrenched, and routinized practices that uphold discrimination and oppression.[45] In thinking about "grandmother to grandmother solidarity," I specifically investigate whether and how, in the context of this movement, solidarity was perceived and enacted by the different women involved, and how my findings align (or do not align) with contemporary debates around identity politics and social difference.[46]

GLOBAL CONNECTIONS

In addition to recognizing older women's agency and contributions in mobilizing for social change, this book is part of a growing scholarly effort to contest simplistic understandings of "globalization," "development" and, more broadly, "the global." There is an extensive and multi-faceted body of critical scholarship on development and globalization, certain threads of which inform how I conceptualize "the global" – a term I use often with reference to "global AIDS response" and "global connections." The scholars with whom I align recognize the historical basis of our uneven and inequitable global political economy, but they challenge assumptions that "global connections" – social, economic, political, and cultural linkages across distance and difference, often framed as North-South, transnational, or translocal relationships – are shaped by all-consuming, homogenizing, inevitable, imposed, or predictable forces, or by some universal aspiration.[47] They argue, and I concur, that these assumptions do not adequately grapple with how relationships are actually perceived and practiced.[48]

Gibson-Graham,[49] for example, suggests that organizations that accept funding from governments or international agencies are not necessarily going to be co-opted. Rather, she sees each funding relationship as contingent upon specific personal, institutional, historical, and economic contexts. Just as Mahmood[50] and others stress the importance of understanding women's agency on their own terms in order to avoid false ascriptions of feminist politics, Gibson-Graham stresses the importance of investigating how each North-South relationship is negotiated: "As we begin to conceptualize contingent relationships where invariant logics once reigned ... the economic certainties and generic stories of development discourses are effectively dislodged, as are the macronarratives of capitalist development (including most recently globalization) that loom in the vicinity of most social theorizing."[51]

Such work directly informs how I view "the global," and thus what I mean when I refer to "global AIDS response" and "global connections." I recognize that "the global" has implied a certain imaginary (or way of imagining the world) and has been used in scale-making projects to justify neoliberal practices and policies. Yet, like Tsing,[52] I reclaim the term, not to imply some homogenizing or constraining force but rather to refer to a variety of everyday encounters. Doing so opens up "global AIDS response": instead of thinking about it as some unified force, I recognize the many different efforts, participants, and initiatives involved in the transfer of resources and ideas in the context of an uneven epidemic. I contend that each actor – whether Bill Gates, Stephen Lewis, UNAIDS, or an individual African grandmother – should be subject to critical inquiry, rather than all being assumed to work in predictable ways.

Informing my approach is what Gibson-Graham calls a "politics of possibility" – a conviction that, despite existing inequalities and injustices, there is always the possibility that any dominant discourse or norm can be destabilized through the complex actions that people take in their everyday lives.[53] This politics is, again, framed by Butler's theorizing on agency and norms, where norms are understood to be made (and unmade) through their repeated enactment. From this perspective, each action, or each encounter, carries the possibility of producing, consolidating, challenging, or re-signifying norms. Such acts of re-signification, according to Butler, tend to appear in complicated ways that regularly confound and befuddle expectations.[54] In the case of this book, I ask whether and how the particular Canadian–South African encounters I document might reinforce or challenge patterns of imposition and exploitation, leaving open the possibility that certain critiques of development and globalization might prove overly simplistic or even inappropriate in this context.

This focus on "possibility" does not, however, mean glossing over contest or contradiction.[55] Instead, by closely examining certain "zones of awkward engagement," as Tsing calls them,[56] I provide a nuanced analysis of how Canadian and South African women were mobilizing and linking up in the first decade of this century. I specifically ask how the "friction" within their network – that is, the productive negotiation of contrasting goals, objectives, perceptions, and positions – might have generated possibilities for new arrangements of power. I explicitly investigate the heterogeneity within this transnational network, examining different participants' fluid perceptions, positions, ways of identifying, motivations, emotions, and experiences. In so doing, I again align with feminist scholars who probe the social differences and intersectional workings of power that condition how and why people organize.[57]

I refer often to "global connections," by which I mean grounded daily encounters across distance and difference, which are contingent on particular people, contexts, and conditions. These connections include all of the interactions that worked to link the women in the Valley of 1000 Hills to the Canadian Campaign, including exchanges of ideas, resources, and discourses between actors from the SLF and the HACT, and among the grandmothers themselves; these relationships, framed by the Canadian Campaign as building solidarity, were based on, among other connections, the provision of aid, moments of direct contact, the mobilization and re-mobilization of particular ideas, and engagement in advocacy. I look at how these encounters functioned without assuming pre-determined outcomes. Viewing agency as repeatedly enacted through all encounters and interactions, I also investigate how each enactment might have worked to consolidate or destabilize certain norms.

FEMINIST ETHNOGRAPHY AND THIS BOOK

This book traces a series of South African and Canadian relationships, taking the HACT as its entry point. The research was not intended to be a perfectly parallel process between South African and Canadian participants: it delves into greatest detail in the South African context, drawing on this to nuance certain assumptions embedded in the Canadian Campaign and in academic and popular discourses more broadly. A feminist ethnography of global connections,[58] the book's fieldwork involved negotiating intricate relationships with grandmothers, community health workers, research assistants, SLF staff, AIDS activists, and many others. I reflect on these throughout the book in order to contextualize and situate the stories I tell.

Most of the book's fieldwork was carried out between 2006 and 2010, and it involved my living and working intermittently in South Africa and Canada. On the South African end, I was based at the Health Economics and HIV/AIDS Research Division (HEARD), a vibrant and internationally renowned research unit at the University of KwaZulu-Natal in Durban. I helped the nurses at the Hillcrest Centre to develop, carry out, and analyze their questionnaire, which they administered to eighty grandmothers. I documented the life histories of these nurses, regularly interviewed other HACT staff, and participated in the centre's daily activities. With the help of three RAs, I carried out intensive research – repeated focus groups, in-depth interviews, participant observation, and the production of photo journals and family trees – with approximately one hundred gogos from the four Valley settlements of Inchanga, Molweni, Lower Molweni, and KwaNyuswa. Throughout, I tracked the growth and development of the HACT and its affiliated gogos' groups. On the Canadian end, from my base at Carleton University in Ottawa, I documented the growth and development of the Grandmothers to Grandmothers Campaign from its inception through to the writing of this book. This involved participating in key events, interviewing SLF staff members, interviewing Canadian grandmothers, and carrying out archival research. In 2009, with the help of a fourth RA, I also administered a survey to 167 Canadian grandmothers from fifty-three groups across the country. All of my research was a back-and-forth process, geographically and methodologically, with no clear start or stop date – one set of research activities would often necessitate additional research, either nearby or across the globe.

What emerged was that in Canada thousands of older women derived new forms of community, new ideas about solidarity, and a renewed commitment to social justice through their engagement in this transnational effort. Meanwhile, in the Valley of 1000 Hills, the Grandmothers Campaign resulted in access to new forms of support for some 900 caregivers, extending benefits to an estimated 9,000 people. While the book focuses primarily on one part of South Africa, it suggests that similar effects were also transpiring in communities across the southern Africa region.

This is a story of hope – of the possibility for older women to alter their lives through collective actions and of the ability of transnational solidarity to effect positive social change. As echoed throughout this chapter, however, it does not gloss over that which is unexpected or contested. Instead, by closely examining the diverse and contingent encounters, relationships, conditions, and perspectives that propelled this mobilization, it explains how, across two continents and an ocean of difference, Canadian and South African women mobilized and joined forces. It shows how "friction" within this network generated important openings for change and how these women's daily actions worked to destabilize certain norms and to reconfigure their lives, spaces, and associations. The analysis thus hinges on these central themes: "friction" (the importance of diverse perspectives and unexpected shifts of power within this transnational alliance), contingency (the ways in which such mobilizations depend on particular social histories, political economies, personalities, and relationships), and possibility (the potential for this kind of organizing to change lives).

The specific argument I put forward is three-fold. First, I suggest that this transnational network was driven not only by strong leadership, institutional support, and resources but also, and most significantly, by the ways in which key interlocutors (those who influence discourses) from the two continents strategically produced, deployed, and mobilized "grandmotherhood" as a discursive category. Second, I argue that the power of "grandmotherhood" as a rallying discourse – the multiple meanings attributed to it and the deep emotion it evoked – was contingent on time and place, conditioned by major social, political-economic, demographic, and historical shifts that played out in localized ways in Canada and South Africa. Third, by exploring the often-contrasting ways in which "grandmotherhood" was understood, lived, and mobilized in each place, I conclude that the multiple actors in this network did not require identical perspectives or motivations in order to achieve their common goals: their "solidarity," in other words, did not depend on some unified understanding or fixed way of identifying.

Through this work, I have witnessed the internal workings of a small number of organizations and the lives of a relatively few women. This kind of ethnography has, at times, been critiqued as so steeped in context and detail that it offers little by way of contribution to broader knowledge. I disagree. Like Abu-Lughod, I am convinced that this kind of understanding – this appreciation of the flux and contradictions of lives lived in particular times and places – can be brought to bear on, and can potentially destabilize, universalizing discourses and representations.[59] This book is not intended to make generalizations about how all (or even most) African grandmothers are organizing around AIDS, nor does it claim to show the impacts of the Grandmothers Campaign across all (or even most) of sub-Saharan Africa. It does, however, not only contribute to a better understanding of the lives of the Valley gogos and their connections to Canadian solidarity efforts but also, by bringing detailed analysis to bear on a host of wider assumptions, work to nuance current thinking in a number of key areas. It extends conventional notions of "global AIDS response" and disrupts simplistic narratives of development and globalization as forces exerted in predictable ways by large international organizations on communities in the Global South. It contests lingering assumptions that solidarity requires a sameness of motivation, identity, and social position. Finally, it clearly challenges stereotypes of older women as frail, passive, disengaged, and apolitical.

Nokuthula (Noku) and Kholiwe attended the 2006 Toronto Grandmothers' Gathering as two of the "African grandmothers" representing the HACT. Professional nurses in their sixties, both women had left positions in government clinics to work more directly in community outreach and HIV/AIDS care as part of the HACT's dynamic nursing team. They had both lived and worked most of their lives in the Valley's settlements, and they understood the daily struggles of gogos in the area as well as anyone could.

I visited them at the Hillcrest Centre two months after the Toronto Gathering. "It was a great experience," Noku began. "We had no idea that in other African countries they are talking about grannies like this." She paused. "You see, we already help grannies through our home-based care program, but we didn't identify the problem as being about *grannies* as such."

Kholiwe nodded. "We saw the other grannies from Africa and it was an eye opener ... we know that grannies are suffering, but we never thought of doing something especially for them." She looked down. "In Toronto, we thought, of course we need to work with the gogos who are caring for orphans, just like they are doing in other parts of Africa. We just hadn't thought of it as such. And you need to understand, it is also about us ... We never thought of ourselves this way [as gogos] because we are professional, employed nurses. But we are gogos too, with many of the same problems in our families." Both women were silent.

Then Noku spoke. "But it is not enough just to say we know there is a problem. We need to know *how much* of a problem, and *where*. We need proper information. *How many* families are headed by grannies? What do grannies need support with *exactly*? *How many* children are they caring for? We can't do anything until we have this knowledge."

"We made up a questionnaire," Kholiwe continued, "and we plan to visit every home. We will find out what grannies are doing and what their needs are ... then we can start support groups, we can get organized." They exchanged a long look. "Stephen's organization talks about a social movement," she explained, "but I don't know about that. Right now the gogos are just suffering individually in their homes. We will have to start small, maybe with support groups. Maybe the groups will come together. Maybe they will infiltrate other communities. We have to hope."

"Women are strong, you know," Noku added. "They are strong *already* and even now they belong to certain organizations, like certain churches. Mobilizing won't be difficult. But we need to hear from them. What are their issues? Who are they?" She took a deep breath. "We are not trained for this – we have never done this before – but we *have* to start with research. We thought maybe you could help us, maybe you could have a look at our survey."

More than any other early exchange, this conversation with Noku and Kholiwe played a pivotal role in shaping my research practice and the stories I tell. It was in this discussion that I first came to recognize the potentially profound influence that the Toronto Gathering could have in the Valley of 1000 Hills and the ways in which "grandmotherhood," as identity and discourse, was being deployed by different actors engaged in building this transnational network. Prior to the Toronto Gathering, for instance, these nurses had not thought of AIDS as an issue affecting "grannies" per se, they had not identified as "African grandmothers" who shared similar life experiences with many others from AIDS-affected communities, and they had not yet begun working explicitly with groups of gogos in the Valley. For them, the Grandmothers' Gathering resulted in three significant changes: (1) a change in discourse, so that, for the first time, they began naming HIV/AIDS as an epidemic that specifically impacted "grandmothers"; (2) a change in self-perception, in which they began to identify as part of an international solidarity movement, speaking about themselves as grandmothers who shared attributes with other grandmothers across the Valley, South Africa, the region, and the world; and (3) a change in activity, where they initiated research and began mobilizing gogos' support groups. Moreover, not only did this early exchange

make me aware of the catalytic power of the Toronto Gathering in mobilizing people, resources, and discourses, but the invitation to assist the
nurses with their own research also provided the basis for the engaged and
community-sanctioned approach I undertook and the close partnership
we formed in the years that followed.[1]

The Toronto Gathering in 2006 is, therefore, where the story I tell officially begins. It is the first in the series of "global connections" – grounded
encounters that link the gogos in the Valley of 1000 Hills to the Canadian
Grandmothers Campaign and movement – that I explore in this book.
My exploration culminates in May 2010 with another key global encounter: the Manzini Gathering. Organized by a SLF-funded Swazi group,
Swaziland Women for Positive Living (SWAPOL), in conjunction with the
SLF, the Manzini Gathering brought together nearly 500 grandmothers
and project staff from SLF-funded organizations across fourteen African
countries with forty-two SLF-selected Canadian grandmothers as witnesses and observers. This gathering, which was influential in shaping
international discourse and mobilization, was carefully named the first
"African Grandmothers' Gathering"; it was the second major international
gathering of the Grandmothers to Grandmothers Campaign and the first
major meeting to take place on African soil. Its strategic positioning – as a
gathering organized by African grandmothers for African grandmothers –
became pivotal to the way many in the Canadian Campaign viewed the
evolving dynamics of the international movement.

This chapter tells the story, in its simplest form, of the developments
that took place in Canada and South Africa in association with the Grandmothers to Grandmothers Campaign in the four years bookended by
these two gatherings. It introduces the actors, events, encounters, and
ideas most central to the story in order to seed the analysis of friction,
contingency, and possibility that occurs throughout the book. It also provides a preface to the more detailed, contextualized, and nuanced discussion of what was being mobilized in each context, who was involved, how
alliances were formed, and why these particular developments took place.

THE CANADIAN STORY: PREVIEW

The SLF officially launched the Grandmothers Campaign on the eve of
International Women's Day, 7 March 2006, but it was the Toronto Gath-

ering that marked "the dawn of the grandmothers' movement."[2] The most rapid mobilization in Canada took place in the period immediately following the Toronto Gathering, when the Grandmothers Campaign grew from 6 Canadian grandmothers' groups in early 2006, to 40 groups by the time of the Grandmothers' Gathering, to more than 100 groups by the end of that year. Four years later, when the Manzini Gathering was held, there were approximately 240 groups across Canada and the Grandmothers Campaign had raised more than C$9,000,000.

The Grandmothers Campaign emerged as a diverse, flexible, and dynamic network comprised predominantly of women from across Canada. It was made up of individual grandmothers' groups, which included not only grandmothers but many non-grandmothers (or "grandothers," as they were called).[3] These groups were affiliated with, and coordinated by, the SLF, but each group organized on the initiative and with the vision of its own members. All of the groups did some combination of fundraising and awareness-raising, and many of the members were also involved in advocacy. There was, however, no standard format, size, or set of activities to which the groups were required to adhere, as this grandmother articulated:

> All of the groups are different. Each one has its own personality. These are grassroots groups. No one is telling us how to organize, what our priorities should be, who should chair the group, whether we should keep minutes. One group might raise C$100,000 in a year, another might raise C$100. The groups are all fairly informal, flexible, small, and very dynamic. (Grandmother, January 2009)

The earliest priorities included building relationships in Canada and coming to agreement on the campaign's three official goals: (1) to raise awareness in Canada about the impacts of HIV/AIDS on grandmothers in sub-Saharan Africa, (2) to build solidarity among African and Canadian grandmothers, and (3) to actively support groups of grandmothers in Africa.[4] One of the early negotiations (and an ongoing source of "friction") had to do with balancing many Canadian grandmothers' desire for direct, personal contact with African projects with the SLF's underpinning values and philosophies. From the outset, the campaign was not based on "twinning" relationships (direct one-to-one contact between Canadian and African groups) or on Canadian grandmothers volunteering with, or raising funds for, individual African groups. SLF staff explained that such direct relationships can be unduly burdensome for grassroots groups operating in contexts of poverty because members can end up diverting their limited time and resources to the task of communicating with their overseas counterparts or risk jeopardizing those relationships, which they often depend on for survival. As well, SLF staff raised concerns that a twinning model of support would not provide mechanisms for new community projects to access resources, nor would it ensure that funding to recipient projects remained relatively stable. While there had been lively debate, most of the grandmothers involved in my research accepted that Canadian groups should forego such contact and instead fundraise for the SLF, allowing the SLF to transfer resources (and facilitate any contact) between Canadian and African grandmothers.

As part of its mobilizing strategy, the SLF has, however, fostered personal connections between individual grandmothers from Africa and Canada, and, according to the grandmothers I interviewed, these connections were pivotal in building the campaign and maintaining its momentum. They were forged at larger events, such as the Toronto and Manzini Gatherings, as well as during SLF-supported visits of African grandmothers to Canada and, less frequently, of Canadian grandmothers to Africa. These points of contact embody the grounded encounters or "global connections" that are central to the story I tell.

This way of operating positioned the SLF as an important mediator in most of the relationships and encounters between African and Canadian women. It vested the SLF with a certain ability to control who Canadian grandmothers met and what they saw and, by extension, reinforced the SLF's position as a powerful interlocutor and shaper of international discourse. Despite a widespread desire for more personal relationships with their African counterparts, most Canadian grandmothers accepted the SLF mediation, largely because of their trust in the SLF. Some Canadian grandmothers, however, challenged this model by opting to embark on their own, unmediated, relationships with African groups. One example, of particular importance to this book, is Rosemary, who worked directly with the HACT: while identifying as part of the Canadian movement, she chose to visit the HACT and work with Noku to mobilize gogos in the Valley of 1000 Hills. In subsequent chapters, I explore her story as a salient example of diversity and "friction" within the Canadian movement.

Between 2006 and 2010, the SLF worked to keep Canadian grandmothers engaged and to support their activities in a number of ways: by sending out a regular bulletin in Canada, facilitating "call-ins" (where campaign members listened in on conference calls with Lewis), dispatching staff members to grandmothers' events, employing a Grandmothers Campaign coordinator to oversee the campaign,[5] maintaining the campaign website, disseminating outreach materials, and providing tax receipts for those making charitable donations via the campaign or otherwise. Furthermore, the SLF worked closely with regional grandmother liaisons (volunteer campaign members) in order to stay connected with the campaign's diverse needs and dynamics across the country.

By 2008, the rapid growth of the Grandmothers Campaign had begun to plateau, although the sophistication of the campaign continued to develop. Four key changes took place. First, as the campaign grew, it also regionalized, with groups in different areas of Canada increasingly coordinating their work through regional organizing bodies. By this time most major cities in Canada were hosting multiple groups and cities such as Ottawa, Vancouver, Toronto, Edmonton, and Halifax started to coordinate efforts for fundraising and public outreach. The campaign also developed a national listserv, maintained independently by a volunteer grandmother, and some groups and members developed their own websites and blogs. Second, by two years into the campaign some groups were beginning to disband as a result of burnout or the illness or death of key members. According to Pat, campaign co-ordinator at the SLF at the time, attention thus turned to sustaining the campaign: this involved efforts on the part of the SLF to re-motivate and renew existing groups, as well as initiatives to draw in younger members via school outreach and an increasing focus on intergenerational solidarity. Third, as the campaign matured and individual Canadian grandmothers became more knowledgeable, many members and groups focused more energy on advocacy. Between 2007 and 2010, this was coordinated through a nationwide initiative called the National Advocacy Committee (NAC). As part of their advocacy work, Canadian grandmothers lobbied the Canadian government in an effort to change Canada's Access to Medicines Regime (CAMR) to enable countries in the Global South to access lower-cost medicines.[6] Fourth, four years into the campaign the first African Grandmothers' Gathering was held in Manzini, Swaziland. This gathering was an attempt both to sustain and energize the Canadian Campaign and to mark a shift, according to SLF staff, to a more African-centred movement, in which African grandmothers would become more fully recognized as experts and key actors in global AIDS response.

In Canada, the growth of the campaign was accompanied by the growth of a broader (less easily defined) grandmothers' movement that mobilized alongside, and connected to, the Grandmothers Campaign, supporting, building on, and intensifying its momentum. Throughout the book, I use "the campaign" to refer to the initiative coordinated by the SLF (i.e., the grandmothers' groups that were registered with, and fundraising for, the SLF) and "the movement" to refer both to the campaign and to a larger mobilization of Canadians who were not directly involved with the SLF but who supported (or advocated for) grandmothers in sub-Saharan Africa in other ways. The larger mobilization includes groups and individuals who had taken up a similar cause but operated differently and did not direct funds via the SLF; it incorporates independent Canadian grandmothers who had volunteered in projects in sub-Saharan Africa (of whom Rosemary was one) and other groups and independent actors who engaged in the movement in a number of ways.

In summary, between 2006 and 2010 Canadians organized quickly to raise funds and awareness in support of grandmothers affected by AIDS in sub-Saharan Africa. Propelled in large part by the high emotions and energy conjured during the Toronto Gathering, Canadian grandmothers' groups came together, at first within their own communities and then through regionally and nationally coordinated efforts, as they sought to build solidarity with women on the other side of the globe. How did their solidarity play out on African soil? What was happening among their African counterparts over this time? What meaning did their efforts have in particular African contexts? What change might they have sparked? I turn now to an overview of what was happening at the HACT and in the Valley of 1000 Hills during the period from Toronto to Manzini.

THE STORY OF THE VALLEY GOGOS: PREVIEW

In 2006, the HACT was not offering support programs explicitly designated for "grandmothers," although gogos from the area were coming into contact with the centre via its home-based care program. The Toronto Gathering was not only central to the early Canadian mobilization: it was also a defining event in the lives of the two HACT nurses who attended and, by extension, it shaped the mobilization that ensued in the Valley. As Kholiwe later reflected:

> We hadn't thought of it before, like exactly about how HIV and AIDS affects gogos. But then after Toronto we decided to start up this research, as you know. And we were thinking about what the other African groups we met were doing, and we decided we have to do this too, these support groups for gogos. So that is where we got the idea. So the first trip to Canada really changed what we are doing and how we think about the epidemic as being an issue for the gogos, and it changed the way we think about ourselves as grannies also: just the same in many ways as the grannies from across Africa and even Canada. So we see that this is a struggle that we all share and we have to stand together. (June 2008)

The seeds were planted in Toronto, but it was not until mid-2007, when the SLF invited the nurses on a second trip to Canada – a speaking tour to further rally Canadians – that mobilization in the Valley started. Their impending return to Canada gave the nurses renewed energy and, in the months leading up to their trip, they began meeting with home-based carers (trained lay outreach workers affiliated with the centre) to assess needs, resources, existing groups, and potential meeting places within the communities they served. They then worked with the carers to invite gogos to initial meetings, where they explained their idea of, in their words, "support groups for gogos caring for orphans." Their proposal was met with overwhelming interest.

They officially started the first "gogos' group" – Ntombi's group – in the peri-urban settlement of Inchanga in September 2007. Later that year, they began working with another support group in Molweni; this group had been started many years earlier by the Durban Association for the Aged (DAFTA) but had become fairly inactive. In early 2008, they spread their efforts to a third group in Lower Molweni and a fourth group in KwaNyuswa; like the Molweni group, both these groups had existed pre-viously in different formats. They undertook these early activities as part of their regular outreach activities with the HACT, fitting the community meetings in with their weekly home visits.

The nurses initially conceptualized these groups as providing support to "gogos caring for orphans" from families affected by AIDS – very much in line with the discourses circulating at the Toronto Gathering. This idea resonated strongly in the Valley of 1000 Hills for a number of reasons, which I discuss in more detail in chapters 4 and 5. For instance, the idea of generating support for grandmother caregivers validated ongoing struggles rooted in a migrant labour system in which older women historically cared for children in remote and rural communities while younger adults migrated for work. It also recognized the profound (and often overlooked) strains imposed by the epidemic on these caregivers and tapped into the localized power of "gogo" as discourse, identity, and institution. Despite this deep resonance, however, group members soon expressed a desire to open their doors to anyone in need. This led to a broadening of the groups: although still predominantly composed of grandmothers, in a few cases younger women and older men joined, usually as caregivers of vulnerable children. As a first order of business, the groups expressed eagerness to start income-generation projects, particularly sewing, crafts, and gardening. They requested, above all else, materials and training. The nurses assisted wherever possible, soliciting donated materials from local businesses and seeking out opportunities for free training sessions.

Kholiwe retired in July 2008, after which she was no longer active with the gogos. By this time, Noku was working with four additional groups in the geographically large area of KwaNyuswa. By late 2008, Noku was regularly meeting with some 250 women from eight different groups (the four original and the four additional KwaNyuswa groups). Described by many as their "lifeline," Noku helped the gogos start income-generation projects, connect with other NGOs, and access training and materials; she also provided support, spiritual counsel, information, and food. Within months, the groups were helping not only the grandmothers but also the large, extended networks of adults and children for whom these women were responsible. In late 2008, Noku estimated that there were between 2,000 and 3,000 people benefitting from the mobilization.

Yet, this was still a "shoestring operation," as one of the HACT staff described it. Noku was working with the groups in addition to her full-time nursing duties, buying basic items for the meetings, like tea and sugar, with her own money, and scrounging to pay for gas and to arrange her own transport. The groups had yet to secure any funding. The SLF continued to fund the HACT's home-based care program, as it had for several years, but in late 2008 this funding did not extend to the grandmothers' groups. Thus, much of the early mobilization took place in a spontaneous and piecemeal fashion, riding on Noku's energy and leadership, and on the minimal resources provided by her and certain key volunteers, including Rosemary.

In 2009 and 2010, a major reconfiguration took place in terms of both support for the gogos' groups and recognition for Noku's work. By mid-2009 the gogos were being profiled as the centre's "Grandmother Project" on its website,[7] and when the HACT's 2008–2009 Annual Report was released in early 2010, they were given a three-page spread. The Grandmother Project received significant local media attention in late 2009 and early 2010, and, as a result, private donations earmarked specifically for the gogos' groups began trickling into the HACT. A petty cash fund was established for Noku to cover her costs and make it feasible for her to continue working with the groups. In late 2009, the local Robin Hood Foundation came through with food sponsorship for the grandmothers, which meant Noku had regular access to food supplies for the groups' meetings. Meanwhile, Noku reported ever-increasing excitement and support for the project from the HACT administration.

When the HACT submitted its annual proposal for funding renewal to the SLF in early 2010, it made its usual request for continued support for its home-based care program only. However, the SLF knew about the gogos' groups and, with the Manzini Gathering impending and the SLF's continued commitment to supporting grandmothers, the SLF approached Jennifer, the HACT director, with the possibility of extending its funding to the gogos.[8] As Jennifer explained in May 2010:

What happened was we submitted our annual report and the proposal we do every two years to renew our funding, but I didn't ask for anything to cover the grannies initially; I asked the SLF only to renew our care funding. Frankly, I just couldn't risk jeopardizing funding to our care program and the respite unit, because these still have to be our first priorities. You know, we have people dying that need to be cared for, and this is our primary mandate. The SLF has been so generous and the relationship is so important to us, I didn't want to put anything at stake. But then, with the Gathering coming up in Swaziland, and you know, Stephen Lewis was here himself visiting the grannies' groups, and the Canadian grannies who have been here were probably talking about it, they [the SLF] came back to me and said, "We'd like you to submit a second proposal to ... support the grandmothers' groups." So we scrambled to write the proposal ... and the SLF accepted it. The money coming in for the gogos is going to be in addition to our core funding. We are so blessed.

New SLF funding for the HACT's Grandmother Project commenced in February 2010. By April that year, the HACT had bought each group two sewing machines, organized several training sessions for the grand-mothers, and hired a part-time Grandmother Project staff member to work with Noku.

By late 2010 there were twenty-six groups affiliated with the HACT's Grandmother Project, involving an estimated 900 women (and a few men), with benefits being felt by some 9,000 people across the Valley. As Noku explained in May 2010:

> The idea of support groups for gogos is just spreading from one ward to the next, and every month we have another group that wants to be part of the project. It's not just about gogos any-more, like when we started up, but really it's about rural women's empowerment.

As Noku's words reflect, the original focus of the groups on grand-mothers, orphaned children, and HIV/AIDS gave way rather quickly to a much broader focus on "rural women's empowerment" – training for income-generation projects with hopes of increasing economic security – which I explore later in greater depth. Between 2008 and 2010, many grandmothers underwent training in sewing, gardening, financial management, and/or bereavement counselling and, with the new funding in place, these activities were set to increase. Groups had gained access to fabrics, sewing machines, seedlings, and fencing, and to services and opportunities provided by local NGOs and government clinics. Noku explained that, going forward, the centre intended to focus on assisting the groups to participate in "train the trainer" programs: bringing members from different groups together to train them in various skills that they could then teach others in their groups and communities.

In May 2010, Noku was invited to present this "success story" at the Manzini Gathering. She spoke at length about our research and about the mobilization that had taken place in the Valley settlements. In so doing, she was transformed from a nurse who had only worked in one part of South Africa to a leader and mobilizer in the international sphere. Just as profound change had taken place in the grandmothers' movement in Canada between 2006 and 2010, these had also been years of change for the HACT, the nurses, and the gogos in their network.

GLOBAL CONNECTIONS: PREVIEW

While the Toronto Gathering was clearly a watershed moment in the mobilizations in Canada and South Africa, the changes that took place in both contexts in the years between the Toronto and Manzini Gatherings were influenced by a series of other such global connections as well. I use the term "global connections" here to refer to particular grounded encounters – specific exchanges based in resource transfer, solidarity building, and discourse sharing – that linked the gogos in the Valley to the Canadian grandmothers' movement. Unlike many well-known narratives of failed development efforts based on the assumption that all North-South relationships predictably impose North-centric ideas, policies, and practices on communities in the South, I view these connections and their outcomes as contingent on the particular people, exchanges, places, and circumstances involved.[9] I also view each encounter as imbued with the possibility of either consolidating or challenging certain norms.[10] While I have described some of these connections already, the following is an itemized overview of the eight encounters that are most significant to understanding the mobilizations and alliances that took place between the Valley gogos and the Canadian movement:

1 *The Toronto Gathering* As discussed, in 2006 the HACT nurses attended the inaugural Toronto Gathering. This event changed the way they thought about HIV/AIDS and grandmothers and, ultimately, was the catalyst for their initiation of the HACT's Grandmother Project. In Canada, this gathering sparked a mass

mobilization of grandmothers' groups across the country and marked "the dawn of the grandmothers' movement."

2 *Subsequent visits of the HACT nurses to Canada* In 2007, the nurses were invited to Canada twice on SLF speaking tours (Kholiwe went both times, while Noku travelled to Canada only once that year); this energized them and drove them to start their work with the gogos' groups. In Canada, the personal connections fostered when the SLF deployed African "grandmothers" to Canadian communities fuelled and maintained the campaign's momentum. The HACT nurses' visits were among such encounters.

3 *Direct involvement of Canadian grandmothers in the Valley* In 2007, Rosemary started making annual visits to the HACT, assisting Noku with finding materials for the fledgling groups and providing her with transport to and from the groups' early meetings. Rosemary brought resources and funds raised in Canada, which were particularly important between 2007 and 2009, when there were no resources allocated to the gogos' groups. In her later visits, Rosemary worked with the HACT communications team to increase the visibility of the Grandmother Project. Rosemary was one among several Canadian grandmothers who opted for this kind of direct involvement. In Canada, some of these grandmothers, Rosemary included, remained connected with the campaign, often taking on public speaking engagements to raise awareness and encourage further mobilization.

4 *"Grambassadors'" African tour* In mid-2008, twelve Canadian grandmothers and one SLF staff member were selected to visit several SLF-funded African projects, including the HACT. In Canada, these women became ambassadors (calling themselves "grambassadors"), pledging one year of public speaking to further educate and mobilize Canadians. The four Canadian grambassadors who visited the HACT were taken to meet the Inchanga and Lower Molweni gogos' groups. These women listened to the gogos' stories, expressed excitement over the growth of the support groups, and offered the gogos 10-kilogram bags of rice.[11]

5 *Stephen Lewis's visit to the HACT* In 2009, Lewis and several of his colleagues visited the Hillcrest Centre and were taken to meet some of the gogos' groups. Their visit increased the visibility of the groups

both locally and in Canada, as highlights of the visit were filmed and posted on the Internet.

6 *Administrative links and relationships* An ongoing relationship was nurtured between the SLF program officers responsible for administering funding and the HACT director. It was in the context of this relationship that funding was extended to the Grandmother Project in early 2010.

7 *The Manzini Gathering* In mid-2010, Noku, accompanied by two gogos from the Valley, attended the African Grandmothers' Gathering in Manzini. This opportunity allowed them to share their successes and learn from other groups in the region. It provided another well-timed boost of energy and support; for Noku, it also renewed her sense of connection to a broader solidarity movement. As discussed earlier, the Manzini Gathering was intended to build new momentum in Canada, where the selected Canadian grandmothers would later share their observations, as well as to shift the framing of the movement to be more African-centred.

8 *Research* Finally, my own connection to the Hillcrest nurses and the gogos – starting before the Toronto Gathering and continuing past the Manzini Gathering – functioned to keep Noku abreast of (and feeling tied to) the Canadian Campaign. I regularly wrote reports and gave presentations in Canada and South Africa, which assisted in making their efforts more widely known and understood (e.g., my 2009 report detailing the gogos' mobilizations and their need for support was circulated widely). As both researcher and volunteer, I was an interlocutor in the mobilizations in Canada and South Africa: for example, I assisted with documenting the Toronto and Manzini Gatherings, spoke regularly at community events in Canada, and provided information, analysis, and support towards the building of the HACT Grandmother Project.

I return to these eight encounters periodically throughout the book, examining them at varying levels of detail as I attempt to elucidate some of the contingency and possibility involved in this instance of linking across distance and difference. In keeping with earlier discussions, it is the particulars of these encounters that constitute how I conceptualize "global connections."

SUMMARY AND CONCLUSIONS

Just as the first four years of the Grandmothers Campaign – the period from Toronto to Manzini – saw extensive mobilization in Canada, they also entailed widespread reconfiguration for the gogos in the Valley of 1000 Hills. The HACT's engagement with the gogos' groups was propelled, at least in part, by linkages to the Grandmothers Campaign, which motivated and supported Noku and Kholiwe to become key community organizers. The magnitude of change that took place as a result of these global connections must not be underestimated, but this is only one part of the story. In fact, in order to more fully understand the developments that took place in both Canada and South Africa, as well as their interconnections, a more detailed, nuanced, and contextualized analysis is required. Such an analysis must begin well before Toronto and extend beyond Manzini: it must unpack the potentially contrasting motivations, discourses, and perspectives of those involved and the complex histories and geographies of their movements. The remainder of the book delves into these details.

It was a quiet evening in downtown Ottawa. On the radio, Stephen Lewis delivered the second lecture in the annual Massey Lectures series. While I had heard him speak many times and knew his stories well, his brilliant oration never ceased to draw me in. I turned off my car engine and leaned back to listen:

> It leads me to want to say a word about grandmothers. They have emerged as the heroes of Africa. The physical ravaging of extended families ... means that grandmothers step in when there's no one else to tread. I wonder if such a situation has ever occurred before in the history of organized society?

I rummaged through my purse for my notebook and pen. Was there something new in his discourse tonight?

> In the instance of Africa today, these old and unimaginably frail women often look after five or ten or fifteen kids, enduring every conceivable hardship for the sake of their grandchildren, alongside additional numbers of other abandoned waifs who wander the landscape of the continent. The trauma of the grandmothers equals that of the orphans; in fact, every normal rhythm of life is violated as grandmothers bury their own children and then look after their orphan grandchildren. I remember, vividly, sitting under the trees, outside the Alex/Tara Children's Clinic in Alexandra Township in

Johannesburg, with about twenty grandmothers as they told their heartbreaking stories of personal loss, one by one. I could barely imagine how they were functioning; every one of them had made that heart-wrenching trek to the graveyard, many more than once, and yet they spoke with a spunk and resilience that was positively supernatural.

I could picture the scene. I pulled my coat around me and continued to listen.

Save one. There was one woman, seventy-three years old, sitting slightly apart from the rest, who refused to speak. No amount of encouragement or cajoling would do, until the women collectively, in an incredibly moving show of commiseration, sang a soft song of solidarity and love.

And then Agnes finally spoke. She took no more than a couple of minutes: her story was wrenchingly brief, ghastly in its simplicity. She had buried all five of her adult children between 2001 and 2003 – all five – and was left with four orphan grandchildren. That was it. She wept.

I learned as I left that every one of her four grandchildren is HIV-positive. How much can one grandmother endure?[1]

My mind raced. What was it about this story? I knew why it was so painfully important, but what about it seemed so different – so *new*? I turned the volume down and stared out the window.

Admittedly, Lewis's words came as a relief. At that time, prior to embarking on the research for this book, I had spent the previous two years working with older women in Durban and writing about their struggles, at a time when older women were barely discernible in the global AIDS response and had little status in scholarly or public conversations. Lewis had now named and legitimized this forgotten group – whom Marais calls the "reverse orphans"[2] – in a venue that would reach not only the Canadian public but key international actors as well. He had captured the injustice, the horror, and the urgency in a way that felt, even to my critical ear, unquestionable. I was hopeful that his words might increase the visibility of these indomitable older women.

But there was more. It was not only *what* Lewis was saying, but also *how* he was saying it. He was not, it occurred to me, naming these women as "the elderly" or as "older caregivers." He was not defining them by age and gender, as was the norm in most research and policy circles. Instead, he was calling them "grandmothers" and thereby producing them according to a subjectivity based on position, identity, status, and, most importantly, their highly emotive relationships to the children in their care. An injustice borne by one "grandmother" would surely seem more reprehensible than decades of discrimination borne by all of the world's "older women." Would the Canadian public notice, I wondered? What about the hundreds (maybe thousands) of international organizations concerned with AIDS orphans – would this reach their directors' ears? Would they catch on? In this chapter, I examine the Canadian mobilization that occurred between 2006 and 2010, considering why it took place the way it did, exploring its central mobilizing discourses, asking what propelled and sustained its members, and discussing its emerging challenges and points of "friction."

MOBILIZING GRANDMOTHERHOOD PART 1: KEY INTERLOCUTORS AND CATALYSTS

Even in the years prior to the launch of the Grandmothers to Grandmothers Campaign, "grandmother" was never a value-neutral term in the international AIDS arena or in any other context. It was mobilized by certain actors and organizations according to their goals and objectives – and, in the same way, it has become imbued with certain meanings and discourses in contemporary AIDS response. Long before Lewis delivered the Massey Lectures or the SLF launched the Canadian Campaign, many international organizations, especially HelpAge International (HAI) and Global Action on Aging (GAA), were advocating for "elderly people" affected by HIV/AIDS. Reports dating back at least to the late 1990s mention the impacts of AIDS on "the elderly," the roles of "older caregivers," "grandparent caregivers," "older people as carers," and the "gender dimension of caregiving" in the face of the epidemic in Africa.[3] A number of international declarations were also signed that committed governments to addressing the needs of older people in communities with a high prevalence of HIV/AIDS. However, specific reference to "grandmothers" in this early advocacy work was rare, if not non-existent.

The change in discourse came somewhere between 2004 and 2006. While it would be too simplistic to attribute this shift entirely to one person or one organization, Lewis and the SLF were pivotal in generating, spreading, and legitimating international concern for "grandmothers" affected by AIDS. In 2004 and 2005, Lewis began speaking in venues across Canada, the United States, Europe, and Africa about the "plight" of Africa's "grandmothers," referring to these women as Africa's "unsung heroes."[4] His experiences in African communities as well as his use of personal anecdotes and visceral descriptors lent urgency to his words, and what had previously been a marginalized issue pertaining to "the elderly" rapidly became much more widely visible. Lewis's ability to affect discourse was attributable, in part, to his position as the UN secretary-general's special envoy for HIV/AIDS in Africa, and to the fact that he had long been an iconic voice of justice and compassion in Canada.[5] He was invited to deliver the prestigious Massey Lectures in 2005. These were aired nationally on the CBC, published in his best-selling book *Race Against Time* and, whether intentionally or not, laid the groundwork for how "Africa's grandmothers" came to be framed by AIDS advocates around the world. As will become evident in this chapter, they also seeded the mobilization that followed in Canada.

The excerpt from the second lecture, cited earlier, is significant and its messages were regularly deployed in the far-reaching changes that followed. Four elements are particularly noteworthy and reverberate throughout this chapter. First, Lewis spoke not only of immeasurable tragedy, wrenching grief, and ravaged families but also of heroism and resilience, trying to balance the horrors faced by African grandmothers with the hope emanating from their collective strength. He attempted to move beyond victimizing representations of African women, a shift that, resonating with early feminist ideas around locating women's "agency," later became central to the mandate of the Grandmothers Campaign. Second, he suggested a certain newness or novelty in the phenomenon taking place as a result of HIV/AIDS in sub-Saharan Africa, asking whether the situation of grandmothers raising children in such large numbers had ever occurred before. This question connected the emerging "grandmother narrative" with the idea that radical and unprecedented transformation was underway on the African continent. Third, by virtue of focusing unapologetically on women, he set the "grandmothers" squarely within a feminist agenda, noting the disproportionate caregiving burdens on women and viewing these women as agents of change. Finally, Lewis *named* the African women as a group of "grandmothers." Regardless of whether these women identified themselves this way (an issue I explore in detail throughout the book), this label transformed them into people international audiences could more easily relate to; it produced them as women who were "enduring every conceivable hardship for the sake of their grandchildren," drawing on a "universal" love and altruism that "all grandmothers" presumably feel for their grandchildren. Lewis framed the tragedies taking place in sub-Saharan Africa within the highly emotive discourse of grandmotherhood – a discourse that was then key to mobilizing the Grandmothers Campaign.

While the Massey Lectures clearly laid the groundwork, the 2006 Grandmothers' Gathering in Toronto was a watershed in the international production of "African grandmothers" and in the mobilization in Canada. Media coverage of this event was extensive[6] and images of the grandmothers were centre stage at the closing ceremony of the International AIDS Conference, where 10,000 delegates watched filmed conference highlights. The Toronto Statement, cited in chapter 1 and examined in some detail later in this chapter, echoed the messages previously articulated by Lewis. The Toronto Gathering made the struggles of African women increasingly visible and named the women as "grandmothers" on a whole new scale, infusing them with humanity and transforming them from "elderly victims" into strong, nurturing, altruistic, and heroic agents of social change.

Together, these images, texts, and events functioned as a catalyst for international organizations; post-2006, the language employed in *Race Against Time* and in the Toronto Statement was regularly reproduced in other advocacy-oriented writings.[7] This is certainly not to claim that all organizations uncritically adopted identical perspectives, nor to suggest that there have not been other influential interlocutors or actors. It is intended to highlight that the "grandmother narrative"[8] that is now well known in the AIDS field did not always exist: it was produced in Canada at the start of the twenty-first century. It was generated, moreover, alongside and co-constitutively with the Grandmothers to Grandmothers Campaign, as part of the movement's call to action. The campaign reflected these discursive interventions, while also becoming a powerful force in its own right – a force that then reproduced and altered the narrative in the years that followed. It is against this discursive backdrop that I look at the details of why, how, and to what effect the Grandmothers Campaign developed the way it did between 2006 and 2010.

THE CANADIAN GRANDMOTHERS AND GRANDOTHERS

Who are the "Canadian grandmothers"?[9] Clearly, grandmothers in Canada, as in any country, are a diverse group of people, differentiated by, among other characteristics, age, class, ethnicity, sexuality, education level, political leaning, affiliations, and geography.[10] The great majority of Canadians who participated in my research, however, shared certain characteristics: they tended to be well-educated, professional, worldly, and highly engaged women, who were willing to work hard in the struggle for justice. They also tended to be middle-class, white women in their sixties, new grandmothers, and long-time advocates and activists involved in feminist struggles. One grandmother aptly described the Canadian movement as follows:

> This movement is built on people like me: educated, maybe taking early retirement, middle class. We grew up in the '60s and had to fight for our rights as women. Many of us were activists, you know. We're used to marching, demanding, and seeing change happen. So you can understand why demographically and sociologically this is happening right now. (November 2008)

While the Canadian grandmothers who participated in my research represented only a small, self-selected subsection of campaign members, one of the campaign coordinators noted that the trends and patterns I documented reflected what she had observed more broadly. Of the 167 campaign members I surveyed, all were women;[11] eighty-five percent were from urban areas and fifteen percent from rural areas. Most were from the province of Ontario, followed by (in decreasing order) British Columbia, Saskatchewan, Quebec, Alberta, and the United States. Two-thirds of the women were originally from Canada, while the rest had been born elsewhere, most often in England or the United States. Most joined the campaign in 2006 or 2007, although some indicated that their involvement started as early as 2004 (they would have been part of the handful of groups in Canada doing this work independently and prior to the launch of the SLF's Campaign), while others joined only in 2009.

The average age among the women in my research was sixty-five years; the oldest was eighty-nine and the youngest thirty-two. The median and mode ages were also sixty-five; most participants were between sixty-three and sixty-seven years of age. The importance not only of age but of generation (that is, of being "early baby boomers") was highlighted repeatedly. Nearly all of my participants were mothers (ninety-six percent), and eighty percent were grandmothers. Of those who were already grandmothers, eighty-four percent were new to the role, having become grandmothers for the first time in the previous ten years. Among the "grandothers" (the women who were not grandmothers), the majority considered themselves "grandmothers-in-waiting": they had adult children and hoped to become grandmothers in the near future. It was clearly not necessary to be a "grandmother" in order to be a leader in this campaign; members did not need to embody grandmotherhood in a biological sense in order to identify with, and remobilize, this powerful and emotive discourse.

Ninety percent of the women in my research had completed post-secondary education: teaching was the most commonly represented profession, followed by nursing. Many had pursued second and third careers after working as teachers and nurses, and some had undertaken graduate-level education. All except one had worked outside the home in paid employment; twelve percent were still working, while the rest were retired or semi-retired. More than half (fifty-six percent) had travelled outside of North America, forty-one percent had previously been to Africa, and forty percent had either worked or volunteered in the Global South.

Most of the participants in my research indicated longstanding and present-day engagement in a variety of activist, advocacy, and volunteer activities: seventy-eight percent described themselves as "active volunteers," thirty-six percent described themselves as "activists," and forty percent noted that they were actively involved in social issues through their churches. Seventy percent indicated a history of involvement in advocacy, most often citing the women's movement, human rights work (with a large number involved in Amnesty International), and anti-war activism, while ninety-six percent indicated involvement in other forms of voluntarism, most often in the areas of education, health, and community development. As the following description demonstrates, many saw the campaign as an extension of their longstanding feminist advocacy and felt that their mobilization was actively contesting not only gender inequality but also ageist stereotyping of grandmothers as women who are old, frail, and apolitical:

> We are probably not what most people expect when they hear "grandmothers' movement." We're the early boomers, the women who fought for women's lib, the women who juggled raising families and having careers in a male-dominated world. We're educated, we're skilled, and we now have some time on our hands to re-engage in a struggle that clearly isn't over yet. And many of us, myself included, have recently become grandmothers. We understand what this passage means and what responsibility it brings. We are continuing our feminist struggle, now resisting age discrimination too. (November 2008)

Thus, the "Canadian grandmothers" to whom I refer throughout the book were, for the most part, educated, professional, engaged women, many of whom had either recently entered grandmotherhood for the first time or hoped to become grandmothers in the near future. Many had recently retired from paid work and identified strongly with feminist struggles. These characteristics are crucial to understanding why the campaign developed the way it did.

THE CAMPAIGN'S GROWTH AND DEVELOPMENT

The idea for the Grandmothers Campaign came in 2005, the year Lewis gave his Massey Lectures and only two years after the establishment of the SLF. Its growth, therefore, needs to be understood as taking place alongside and intertwined with the growth and development of the SLF itself. From its inception, the SLF's mandate was to fundraise in Canada in order to support community-based projects dealing with the effects of AIDS in sub-Saharan Africa. Started at the kitchen table of its director, Ilana Landsberg-Lewis, in 2003, by mid-2010 the SLF had grown to include over twenty full-time staff and fifty volunteers, and it had funded more than 300 projects in fifteen sub-Saharan African countries. Its work involved mobilizing Canadians through a variety of initiatives, including, but extending well beyond, the Grandmothers Campaign.[12] In discussing the campaign's trajectory, the majority of participants in my research described several overlapping "phases," which roughly group as follows: "seed-planting" (2004–05), rapid mobilization (2006–07), organizational development and maintenance (2008–09), and "African voices"/Canadian advocacy (2010–). As I examine each in more depth, many of the campaign's central (and shifting) discourses become increasingly apparent.

"Seed-planting": 2004–05

From the launch of the Grandmothers Campaign in March 2006 to its first anniversary in March 2007, the number of grandmothers' groups across the country grew from 6 to 150. This rapid growth was possible only because of a "well-seeded and fertile terrain," as one grandmother described it, which had been cultivated over the previous two years by Lewis's speeches (including his Massey Lectures). As he neared the end of his longstanding post with the UN (it ended in 2006), Lewis began speaking more frequently and more candidly about what he had seen in communities across southern Africa. Among the participants in my research, seventy-five percent had read or listened to *Race Against Time*, and ninety percent had heard Lewis speak in the year prior to the campaign's launch. His message and public (and media) presence primed Canadians for what was to come.[13]

His seeding messages fell on a "fertile terrain" in Canada, which many grandmothers felt had much to do with timing: a particular convergence of people, place, and demography. Many indicated that the campaign came at a pivotal time in their own lives: as they were entering grandmotherhood (or hoping to), as they were retiring (or preparing to), and as, for the first time in their lives, they had time and resources to spare:

> The success of this movement? I think it really is about the timing. If it was ten years earlier, it just couldn't have happened. We wouldn't have yet related to being grandmothers like we do now, and we wouldn't have had time. You know, we're the cusp of the baby boom.

We've gone through this life as trail blazers in a sense. We know about working for social change, but we've also had our hands full all of our adult lives – until now. (Grandmother, December 2008)

As another grandmother noted:

This movement has grown on some kind of a magic combination that involves skills, talent, and timing. It is largely built on a cohort of early boomers. We're talking about a unique period in time: we were the first generation that had birth control, and the first generation where a critical mass of women went out to work professional jobs. Our kids are having children later for the most part, so many of us are now becoming grandparents for the first time, just as we are also retiring." (September 2009)

Part of the timing also had to do with Lewis's readiness to take on the role of champion. His impending departure from the UN provided an opportunity for him to speak openly, at times quite critically, about the UN system, while simultaneously emphasizing the power of the "grass-roots" and the global importance of "grandmothers."

Lewis's role in this movement should not be underestimated. His personal stories, his ability to publicly express grief and rage, and, importantly, his message that every Canadian can do something, have been crucial for drawing in supporters, as this campaign member revealed:

Every movement has its champion, and clearly, Stephen is it for us. He has integrity, humanity, vision. I don't even remember when we last had a Canadian leader with any of those qualities ... Stephen is a real leader, and he's given us a real, tangible, concrete way to make a difference. He's got passion and charisma. And most of all, he believes in us – we're not a burden to society in his mind, we're society's best asset! (Grandother, September 2009)

But what made Lewis decide to focus so much attention on older care-givers and to name them as "grandmothers"? And how did the SLF know that the timing was right and envision this campaign? In fact, Landsberg-Lewis has been credited with the idea for the Canadian Campaign and with anticipating the receptiveness of Canadian grandmothers. According to a discussion with her in 2006, her vision came from direct contact with those at the centre of the epidemic: she had observed a pattern among the community projects the SLF was funding in which older women (whom she recognized as "the grandmothers") appeared to be at the centre of family and community response, though she recognized that they were not always being named as such. In our early conversations, she alluded to the SLF's challenge of trying to "stay grassroots" (i.e., not wanting to make any assumptions about the projects it funds or risk changing the projects' own priorities by re-naming them or channelling funding to new issues), while also wanting to know whether "grandmothers as caregivers" was indeed a pattern and whether there was need for more intentional support in this area. In 2011, she clarified that the SLF had always worked in a way that was responsive to the groups it supports. In the years prior to the campaign's launch, she explained, she heard regularly from her father about his meetings with groups of older women in Africa; at the same time, she was reading proposals from projects about the need for "elder support, parenting workshops, and support with caring for HIV-positive grandchildren." She then consulted with a number of these projects to investigate who the caregivers were that required such support; the answer she received was that these were, for the most part, the children's grandmothers. It was from these conversations that the idea of building "grandmother to grandmother solidarity" emerged.

Thus, the Grandmothers Campaign probably came about through some combination of observing what was taking place in African communities and having the foresight to name it anew at the right time and in the right context. The seeds were planted in the years leading up to the campaign's launch, when a receptive, available, engaged public collided with the presence of a charismatic champion, a compelling idea, and a talented team of mobilizers.

Rapid Mobilization: 2006–07

The most rapid mobilization in Canada took place in 2006 and 2007. Some grandmothers described the campaign at this time as having an air of "magic," "spreading like wild fire," and being "highly contagious." The 2006 Toronto Gathering and the Toronto Statement were pivotal to this rapid growth. Written on the last night of the gathering, the Toronto Statement quickly became one of the most important texts in mobilizing the campaign; it has been widely read, referenced, and circulated. It was so profoundly important to the development of the campaign that key excerpts merit inclusion here:[14]

As grandmothers from Africa and Canada, we were drawn together in Toronto for three days in August 2006 by our similarities: our deep love and undying devotion to our children and grandchildren; our profound concern about the havoc that HIV/AIDS has inflicted on the continent of Africa, and in particular on its women and its children; and our understanding that we have within us everything needed to surmount seemingly insurmountable obstacles. We are strong, we are determined, we are resourceful, we are creative, we are resilient, and we have the wisdom that comes with age and experience.

From one side of the globe we are African grandmothers ... In the short-term, we do not need a great deal, but we do need enough: enough to safeguard the health of our grandchildren and of ourselves; enough to put food in their mouths, roofs over their heads and clothes on their backs; enough to place them in school and keep them there long enough to secure their futures ...

We grandmothers deserve hope. Our children, like all children, deserve a future. We will not raise children for the grave.

From another side of the globe, we are Canadian grandmothers, arriving at the end of our gathering enlightened, resolved, humbled and united with our African sisters. We stand firm in our commitment to give of ourselves because we have so much to give – so many resources, such a relative abundance of time, so much access, so much influence, so much empathy and compassion. We recognize that our African friends are consumed each day with the business of surviving, and so we have offered – and they have accepted – the loan of our voices. We pledge to act as their ambassadors, raising the volume on their long-suppressed stories until they are heard, understood and acted upon ... We will not rest until they can rest.

Africans and Canadians alike, we arrived at our grandmothers' gathering with high expectations, but also with nagging apprehensions ... We Canadian grandmothers worried that our capacity to help might be reduced to fundraising alone; we African grandmothers worried that our dire straits might cast us as victims rather than heroes. But we were motivated to make the trip by the special love that every grandmother knows, and we were emboldened to face our fears by the wisdom of our years. Our courage paid off. The age-old African ways of speaking without words broke down our communications barriers. We gestured and nodded. And we sang. We danced. We drummed. We laughed and clapped and wept and hugged. Through our new discovery – grandmother to grandmother solidarity – we carried ourselves and one another through the grief to where we are this morning.

May this be the dawn of the grandmothers' movement.

Like the earlier Massey Lecture passage, the Toronto Statement's themes shaped the campaign's central narrative: actively resisting the victimization of African grandmothers, focusing instead on their strength, expertise, and resilience; framing AIDS as disproportionately impacting women and children; depicting African grandmothers' burdens as unprecedented and resulting primarily from the epidemic; and legitimizing "grandmother to grandmother solidarity" according to a shared experience of grandmotherhood.

Looking back, Pat, one of the campaign coordinators, reflected in 2008 that the early growth of the campaign was also propelled by constant media coverage. Each new "jump" in growth, she explained, could be linked to specific media coverage:

There were six groups when it was launched and it went to forty groups by the time of the gathering. By the time I started, the end of October 2006, there were nearly eighty groups, so it almost doubled in a month-and-a-half after the gathering. We had another jump that same year when CBC's *The Nature of Things* aired 'The Man Who Couldn't Sleep" [which profiled Stephen Lewis]. That was December sixth and I remember the next day the phone rang off the hook. Then things flattened for a bit, until Stephen stopped being UN envoy, and then another little spike. Things that brought media attention brought new groups.

Finally, during the campaign's early and rapid growth, its top priority was to build relationships and establish trust – between emerging grandmothers' groups and the SLF in the first instance, and then between and among the groups themselves. This period was described by some as a time of "growing pains," as members got to know each other and groups "gelled," as certain cities and regions realized that they would have multiple groups operating in close proximity, and as the SLF grew and tried to keep pace with the dynamism of the ensuing mobilization.

Organizational Development and Maintenance: 2008–09

By 2008, the growth in the number of Canadian grandmothers' groups had started to flatten out. According to the SLF, there continued to be steady growth, with new groups forming regularly, but the net growth evened out because some groups were becoming inactive, often when key members fell ill. With this flattening out, 2008 marked the beginning of the campaign's next phase, characterized by efforts in two areas.

First, there was a need for organizational development as the campaign became more sophisticated, more networked, and more regionalized:

> At first, it was all-growth-all-the-time, but very quickly, we were thinking about regionalizing, creating networks, newsletters, websites, linking together, national committees. We know how to organize, you see. Most of us have been doing it all of our lives. (Grandmother, December 2008).

A number of developments took place in 2008 and 2009: regional networks were solidified (for example, around Toronto, Ottawa, Vancouver, and Edmonton), the SLF increased its number of grandmother liaisons (volunteer grandmothers who assist with communications between the foundation and the groups), and, according to several grandmothers, fundraising, outreach, and advocacy activities became increasingly co-ordinated, resourceful, and creative. Some grandmothers reflected on the emergence of diverse regional "flavours" (i.e., noticeably different politics and priorities expressed in different parts of the country), the rethinking among some groups of their own mandates, and the quest among many members to better understand what was happening in African communities.

Second, according to Pat, this was also a time of maintenance, with activities dedicated to sustaining interest, nurturing members, and fostering long-term commitment. In 2010, another campaign coordinator, Jill, further reflected this sentiment:

> This is a mature campaign and it has a mature movement that
> surrounds it. So it has challenges that come from being around for a
> long time: some loss of connection, some loss of momentum ... we
> are working hard to keep members connected to what's going on on
> the ground, so we don't lose the idea that the centrality of their work
> is the African grandmothers. It's hard to be in a group for three years.
> People get tired of each other; they get tired of doing the same things.

A couple of years into the campaign, some groups and members were indeed beginning to experience burnout. To maintain the momentum, in 2008 the SLF sent twelve Canadian grambassadors to visit recipient projects in sub-Saharan Africa (four of whom visited the HACT), with the stipulation that these women would then spend a year publicly sharing their experiences in Canada. The SLF also continually brought African grandmothers to Canada to meet the Canadian groups and undertake speaking engagements. These connections, very much mediated by the SLF, were invaluable in sustaining the Canadian groups, as this campaign member clearly articulated:

> For me, the most motivating moments have been meeting the
> African grannies – when the Foundation has brought the grannies
> to Canada and sent them to speak in communities. Every visit from
> a grandmother from Africa has been a watershed moment for me
> ... I know it's hard to bring the grandmothers, it's hard for them to
> leave their communities, but it sustains us here in Canada. I can't
> stress enough how motivating it is to actually meet and hear their
> stories. (Grandother, September 2009)

This focus on sustainability, along with the levelling off of the number of grandmothers' groups, also brought attention to the need to attract young people to the movement in order to fortify it in the context of its aging membership. With this came increased emphasis on school outreach and intergenerational activities.

"African Voices"/Canadian Advocacy: 2010–

By 2010, another shift was underway. In late 2009, SWAPOL announced the upcoming African Grandmothers' Gathering, which was likened to an African version of what had taken place in Toronto several years earlier: an opportunity for project leaders and grandmothers from SLF-funded groups to meet on African soil, share their experiences, successes, and challenges, and articulate their needs for the future. It was co-organized by SWAPOL and the SLF and funded by the SLF. It brought together nearly 500 grandmothers and project delegates from fourteen African countries with 42 Canadian grandmothers, who had been selected by the SLF to be observers and witnesses. According to the SLF, the idea and genesis for the Manzini Gathering came from SWAPOL, and the SLF played a supporting role in its organization.

Not only did this gathering bring a well-timed energy boost to the campaign in Canada, but, in the view of several SLF staff members, it also marked the start of the movement's next phase – a phase that would be characterized by African women "finding their voices in the global arena." As Jill explained in 2010:

> Swaziland represents a really significant shift for the African grand-
> mothers, in their understanding of their own roles, the value they
> place in each other, and the recognition of their own expertise,
> which is really the next step. This is not an issue that is going to go
> away: countries are poised to be dealing with HIV/AIDS into the
> future – look at China and India. The African grandmothers are
> the first and the most experienced in what it means to work in the
> grassroots and build community connections around this epidemic.
> So now it's about trying to position their voices, not just as the
> heroes of the pandemic but actually as the experts globally. There's
> a compelling reason to listen to these women and learn from them
> and apply what they can teach us elsewhere – this is really the next
> step for the campaign.

On the final day of the gathering, 8 May 2010, several thousand grand-mothers (many bussed in from rural Swaziland) marched in the streets of Manzini, congregating at the end to listen to the culminating Manzini Statement. Like the Toronto Statement, the Manzini Statement was written on the last night of the gathering to reflect its mood and content.[15] Less about building grandmother to grandmother solidarity and more focused on the needs and demands of the African grandmothers, the Manzini Statement reflected an important shift in discourse – a shift that was already underway at the SLF and one that was quickly adopted by the Grandmothers Campaign. Key excerpts from this text are as follows:

We are gathered here in Manzini, Swaziland – 500 grandmothers from fourteen countries, sharing our experience and knowledge, and celebrating our progress in beating back the ravages of HIV and AIDS ...

In 2006 we were battered by grief, devastated by the deaths of our beloved sons and daughters, and deeply concerned for the futures of our grandchildren. We stand here today battered, but not broken. We are resilient, and stand unwavering in our resolve to move beyond basic survival, to forge a vibrant future for the orphans and grandmothers of Africa ...

We have lived through the enormity of AIDS in our communities, and have played our part in helping our nations survive the devastation. Without us, the toll on orphans and our communities would have been incalculable. Equal urgency and passion must now come from our Governments around the provision of services, and the guarantee and delivery of our rights. Urgent action must be taken in these priority areas:

1) Violence against grandmothers. These egregious acts, whether domestic violence, elder abuse, or accusations of witchcraft, must cease and be censured.
2) Grandmothers must have meaningful support in the form of pensions and social security.
3) Laws must be passed and implemented ensuring the safety and rights of grandmothers and their grandchildren.

In considering the shift that was taking place, two points are particularly noteworthy. First, while still recognizing the central role of the SLF in the gathering and in the writing of this statement, the Manzini Gathering was a much more deliberately African-focused event than the Toronto

Gathering. Held on the African continent with a much higher ratio of African to Canadian grandmothers, it did not concentrate to the same extent on building transnational solidarity but rather focused on what African governments must do to support and protect grandmothers. The Manzini Statement was not co-read by an African and a Canadian grandmother, as the Toronto Statement had been. Instead, the picture was one of African women standing on their own feet, on their own soil, making their own demands. The idea that this event was, for the most part, led by African women was of great importance to many in the Canadian Campaign who believed that their solidarity should support such a shift in power, and this point was emphasized repeatedly in Canada by the SLF. Second, the Manzini Statement suggested that there had been significant change in the four years since the Toronto Gathering: African grandmothers were no longer "battered by grief"; they were now feeding their families, and they stood "unwavering in [their] resolve to move beyond basic survival, to forge a vibrant future for the orphans and grandmothers of Africa."

The message that rippled through the Canadian Campaign was that, with basic needs beginning to be met (through grassroots initiatives, many funded by the SLF), African grandmothers were now organizing, becoming stronger, and making demands for larger-scale and longer-term change. Four years after the start of the Grandmothers Campaign, African grandmothers had apparently moved beyond their struggles for basic survival and were working, as advocates and global actors, for the longer-term changes needed to ensure that their families could thrive. This was a message of hope and accomplishment – one that I revisit in later chapters alongside the Valley gogos' own perceptions of their mobilizations.

Many Canadian grandmothers felt that there was also another important shift in 2010: an increase in the prominence of advocacy within the campaign. Many described 2010 as the "year of granny-advocacy," as more grandmothers gained experience on the African continent, educated themselves about key political issues, and felt prepared and confident to speak out. Many also felt that sustained advocacy, in which they would commit to working for changes that could benefit African grandmothers through activities in the places where they held some power, such as lobbying for changes to Canada's international policies, was an important dimension of their solidarity practice. This emphasis on advocacy coincided with a simultaneous peak in a longstanding movement among other Canadian AIDS activists to redefine Canada's Access to Medicines Regime (CAMR) and thereby make medicines more accessible in the Global South. With momentum growing in Canada around CAMR, many grandmothers not previously engaged in formal advocacy work connected with what was then the National Advocacy Committee as well as other advocacy organizations and actors outside the SLF (including, most prominently, the Canadian Legal AIDS Network). When a new bill (Bill C-393) was passed in the Canadian House of Commons in 2010, laying the groundwork for the long-proposed changes, "the grandmothers" were publicly recognized as key mobilizers in this process; they had written letters, signed petitions, called politicians, and regularly packed the House of Commons to make their presence felt.[16]

Thus, the Grandmothers Campaign grew and developed rapidly in Canada as a result of a "well-seeded terrain" and the skills, motivation, empathy, and leadership of women in the SLF and across the country. Evidence from the African Grandmothers' Gathering (and the shift in discourse that followed) also suggests that some material change, mobilization, and consciousness-raising took place on the African continent over this time, although it is impossible to determine the extent of this change except as it effected those women fortunate enough to have attended the Swazi Gathering and to be regularly supported by the SLF. Throughout the chapters that follow, I explore some of the effects of the campaign in the context of the Valley of 1000 Hills and the ways in which these narratives reflected (or did not reflect) the realities of certain gogos there. Regardless of its impact in Africa, however, there is no doubt that, in Canada, the campaign's first four years were highly successful in terms of raising awareness, engaging older women, and mobilizing people, funds, and powerful discourses.

MOBILIZING GRANDMOTHERHOOD PART 2: CANADIAN GRANDMOTHERS' PERSPECTIVES

I have elucidated the ways in which "grandmotherhood" was first mobilized in global AIDS response by Lewis, the SLF, and certain key texts – connected with notions of an unprecedented social injustice, a relentless feminist struggle, and the need for alternative or "grassroots" solutions. I have also examined common characteristics among campaign members and the way their mobilization unfolded. Why did this campaign gain such purchase among Canadian grandmothers? How was it understood by them? What propelled and sustained them in their mobilizations? To answer these questions more fully, I turn to a more detailed examination of Canadian grandmothers' perspectives on what motivated and underpinned their commitments. What emerges is that, in the years following the campaign's launch, many of the key messages and discourses first mobilized by Lewis and the SLF were remobilized in various, often contrasting, ways by Canadian grandmothers. Indeed, connecting with the threads already interweaving this chapter, these women discussed their engagement as deeply intertwined with powerful discourses of grandmotherhood, exceptionality, alternativeness, and connection.

Solidarity in Grandmotherhood

When asked why they joined the campaign, the most common response I heard from Canadian grandmothers had to do with their deep love for their own grandchildren and their empathy for the African grandmothers. Evoking the notion of "sisterhood" with their African counterparts and an identity politics reminiscent of "second wave" feminism (based on women's supposedly shared experiences of patriarchy and oppression), many suggested that their solidarity was based on a bond that exists between African and Canadian grandmothers because they share the experience of grandmotherhood:

> At our core, we all know, Canadian and African grandmothers alike, what it means to love our children and give of ourselves. That's what our solidarity with our African sisters is based on. (Grandmother, December 2008)

Canadian grandmothers frequently described their perceptions of the universal attributes of all grandmothers, based on their love for their grandchildren, their wisdom, their sense of responsibility for future generations, and the idea that, under "normal" circumstances, grandmothers should feel less constrained by family and workplace commitments than they had at earlier points in their lives. This grandmother's words are revealing:

> I think this movement works because we can, in a sense, relate to each other as grandmothers: any grandmother would step in if they had to. Once you watch your own children have children, it's like you go through the motherhood passage all over again: the responsibility to see the next generation grow, the love, the pain, the putting your own needs last, you know. But when I see what our sisters, the African grandmothers, have to do, how they have to become parents all over again, I feel lucky to be able to enjoy my grandkids. I love them, I spoil them, but I still have my own life and free time … I can't imagine how hard this is for the grandmothers in Africa who never get a break and who are dealing with so much grief. They deserve to be cared for as they get older. (November 2008)

Many lamented that the African grandmothers deserved rest and retirement but instead were saddled with childrearing responsibilities. Some expressed this "denial" of their retirement as an injustice:

> What motivates me? It's a justice issue. Here we are enjoying our retirements, enjoying our grandkids, with time on our hands and resources to spare. If it weren't for this epidemic, the African grandmothers could be retiring too. As grandmothers, we all feel responsible for the next generation, for leaving behind a better world than we came into. But they are grandmothers; they shouldn't be parenting, they should be cared for at this time in their lives! (Grandmother, January 2009)

Some grandmothers went on to explain that part of being a grandmother is coming to understand the importance of intergenerational links and taking responsibility for future generations, and that this is something they share with their African counterparts. Moreover, several grandmothers expressed the profound, even spiritual (broadly defined), connection that comes with the passage into grandmotherhood.

While such invocation of the spiritual dimensions of grandmotherhood departed significantly from the SLF's early messaging, it was evident that part of the success of the campaign was its ability to tap into what many grandmothers described as an intensely meaningful life passage:

> There's something about the nature of the movement that speaks very strongly to our desire, our need, our searching to make a connection with something larger than ourselves ... There is something about becoming a grandparent for the first time and that whole maternal passage ... the intergenerational link, seeing yourself reflected in someone else, and in doing so, recognizing their need ... It's this spiritual connection that I believe has driven this movement and its success. (Grandmother, September 2009)

Mobilizing (and remobilizing) grandmotherhood – as passage, experience, identity, and discourse – was thus foundational to the Canadian Campaign and movement. It formed the basis of Canadian grandmothers' solidarity, rooting their commitment in a deeply meaningful passage in their own lives.

Exceptionality: An Unprecedented Situation

Canadian grandmothers also linked their mobilizations to notions of exceptionality: the ideas that a fundamental change was taking place in the lives of grandmothers in sub-Saharan Africa as a result of AIDS and that the stresses they were experiencing were unprecedented. Just as Lewis wondered whether "such a situation has ever occurred before in the history of organized society,"[17] many Canadian grandmothers suggested that what motivated them was the fact that AIDS was radically altering the lives of African grandmothers. Many specifically referred to AIDS as "an unprecedented disaster," and quite often they described its impacts as "transforming Africa." This grandmother's words are illustrative:

> I am sure that life was not easy before the epidemic, but now AIDS trumps everything. It makes everything worse. Now the grandmothers are losing all of their children, one after another, in a way that no society has ever experienced. (December 2009)

Likewise, this grandmother clearly reflected these ideas, linking grand-motherhood to the idea of an unprecedented injustice:

> There just has never been an example where so many young adults
> have died and left behind kids. We have to step in. Doing nothing is
> not an option. These are our fellow grandmothers and they are deal-
> ing with a disaster of a magnitude that humans have not witnessed
> before. They are responsible for more orphans than any society has
> ever known. (December 2009)

Thus, perceptions of the magnitude and exceptionality of AIDS impacts propelled many Canadian grandmothers to get involved. Many described the stresses of AIDS in sub-Saharan Africa as fundamentally changing families and altering grandmothers' roles in a way that had never been seen before in any society.

An Alternative Form of Engagement

A third, strong theme running through my discussions with Canadian grandmothers was the idea that the campaign provided them with an "al-ternative way to engage" in the world, remobilizing some of Lewis's re-flections about "grassroots" solutions and melding these with their own experiences of doing advocacy work in Canada. Many indicated that the campaign fulfilled their desire to be involved with something useful and meaningful in a different format from other forms of volunteering – they were not "stuck licking envelopes or selling products door-to-door." They explained that they were seeking a way to engage that was less prescribed and less paternalistic than what they had previously experienced:

> The thing about the grannies movement is that it's quite a unique
> way of going about things. It's very feminist in a way. I think
> that a lot of charitable organizations have adopted a typically
> male-model of doing business: top down, hierarchical ... But the
> granny movement is exactly the opposite: it's bottom up; it's a
> female model. It operates under totally different principles: it's
> collaborative, it's nurturing, it's understanding, it's creative, it's
> flexible. And so, if you're going to attract women, especially older

women, who are from our generation and have been through all the male domination crap already, you need to find a whole different way. We're redefining what political involvement means. We're rewriting the book on how volunteerism can work. (Grandother, September 2009)

Many described the most compelling characteristics of the Grandmothers Campaign as grassroots, feminist, and accountable. By "grassroots" they meant they were bypassing the kind of heavy bureaucracy and conditionality associated with government aid and larger international development organizations, and their money was going directly to organizations serving African grandmothers. Part of this was that they felt they were supporting "grassroots" mobilizations in sub-Saharan Africa, meaning that they were not imposing their own agenda but, resonating with the SLF approach, supporting efforts already underway. This was expressed succinctly by one of the grandmothers who attended the gathering in Swaziland:

This [the gathering] solidified what I already knew made our campaign different from efforts to "develop" Africa. We can see that the African grandmothers are organizing of their own accord, we can hear their demands, and we are here to support them. We are supporting from the grassroots to the grassroots, not imposing, not developing, not changing their paths. (June 2010)

Many Canadian grandmothers also described the campaign as a "feminist" movement or "female" model of engagement. These women explained that, for them, this not only meant that they were engaged in a struggle for women's equality globally but also referred to the way they were organizing – for women, by women, done in a collaborative, caring, and non-hierarchical way. This sentiment resonated in this grandmother's statement:

The grandmothers' movement is different ... It's the magic, I think, that comes from building relationships among women, from challenging the way things are done, from recognizing grandmothers as valuable members of society, from getting the right people together at the right time ... It appeals to us as grandmothers, as feminists, and as people who are still ready to fight the fight, even if our government is not. (January 2009)

Moreover, the notion that the campaign could provide a more "accountable" venue for their efforts than many other fundraising options was raised by many in my research. These members felt a high level of trust that the funds they raised were going where they were supposed to be going, largely because of their respect for the Landsberg-Lewis family. Some pointed to "development horror stories of the 1980s and 1990s," referring to instances when development funding was grossly misused, and they felt that the SLF was one of the few viable alternatives to these. One grandmother expressed these ideas like this:

When I aligned with the Stephen Lewis Foundation, I was confident that the money I raised was going to where it was supposed to be going. I liked their approach of grassroots right to grassroots. I didn't want to have government intervention and have to be aligned with our government's goals and objectives. I also wanted to do something that felt real, where real people would see benefits, where it wouldn't be endless door-to-door campaigns and who knows if the money ever went anywhere ... and as much as I wanted to get involved, I just couldn't see working for "the man," literally or figuratively. So this is just right for me. (December 2008)

Personal Connections

Finally, much of what motivated Canadian grandmothers was the sense of intimacy they felt within the campaign: the personal connections, meaning, and community that were generated through their mobilizations:

For me, the most motivating moments have been meeting the African grannies – when the foundation has brought the grannies to Canada and sent them to speak in communities. And hearing the stories of the Canadians who visited the projects. You see, it is really about personal connection. We need to know real stories about real people. (Grandother, September 2009)

They described the sense of community the campaign was creating in Canada, as well as the motivation they derived from meeting with, and hearing about, grandmothers from sub-Saharan Africa. Many were also driven by their own quest for meaning and desire to be connected to something larger than themselves. As this campaign member reflected:

> I would suggest that the success of this movement has to do with meaning – making meaning. Finding meaning in our own lives; connecting the way we engage in volunteering and in politics to real issues impacting on motherhood and grandmotherhood; finding meaning in being in the world and being engaged citizens of the world. It is more than just volunteering – it is a spiritual quest. (Grandother, September 2009)

These connections were especially important for many Canadian grandmothers who were at turning points in their own lives. Pointing again to the role of timing in this mobilization, many explained that not only were they in the process of retiring and/or becoming grandmothers but they also were dealing with serious illnesses and/or going through divorces. The support, connection, and meaning associated with involvement in this movement are thus crucial to understanding what drove this mobilization and what it produced.

CONTINGENCY: MOBILIZATIONS IN CONTEXT

What emerges as central to understanding the Canadian mobilization – including the way grandmotherhood was mobilized, the meanings it held, and the reasons why the above themes resonated so deeply – is the concept of contingency. The success of this campaign and movement can only be understood by examining the socio-political context within which they developed. Two trends are particularly salient and worth exploring (or re-exploring) here: (1) Canada's large cohort of socially and politically engaged aging women and (2) recent political trends associated with a narrowing of spaces for justice-oriented engagement.

As noted earlier, many Canadian grandmothers referred to themselves as "early baby boomers." Canada, like many countries in the Global North, experienced economic prosperity and an associated population expansion (or "baby boom") in the years following the Second World War. Women from the earliest cohort of this generation – the majority of campaign members – were born in the late 1940s, came of age in the 1960s, had children in the 1970s, and turned sixty in the first decade of this century, coinciding seamlessly with the campaign's launch. Many of these women identified with North American feminist struggles of the 1960s and 1970s, or "second wave" feminism. Starting in the 1960s, this "wave" of feminism tends to be associated with struggles for full equality: building on the successes of the earlier "first wave" women's movement, which won certain legal protections and the right to vote, this movement called for a profound transformation of patriarchal structures that were seen to systemically subordinate women. It emphasized a broad range of social equality and justice issues, including equal rights to education, equality in the workplace, an end to violence against women, women's reproductive rights (and rights to safe contraception and abortion), and the equal rights of all women, regardless of skin colour, class, sexuality, ability, marital status, and so on.[18] As a result of this movement, by the late 1970s radical changes were felt in every part of Canadian society as women's subordination came to be understood as systemic and political.[19] It was amidst this social transformation that many of the Canadian grandmothers in my research entered the Canadian workforce, negotiated their marriages (or other life partnerships), and raised their children. "Baby boomers" now comprise the largest cohort of Canada's aging population and, in a context where life expectancy is approximately eighty years of age, many "early baby boomers" remain active and healthy as they near retirement and enter grandmotherhood.[20] This demographic trend certainly helps to explain who the campaign members are and why discourses of grandmotherhood, feminism, and social justice have resonated so deeply with them.[21]

Contemporary politics have also shaped how the SLF is perceived by Canadian grandmothers and the Canadian public more widely. The SLF was founded two years after the 11 September 2001 attacks on Washington, DC and New York City: a time when neoconservative politics were gaining ascension in North America and across much of the world. With the start of the subsequent "War on Terror," development agencies in many countries emphasized the potential links between development and security, increasingly framing development not in terms of improving lives in the Global South but as part of an effort to appease and contain potential threats.[22] The UN system was also experiencing a retraction of global influence and many social justice actors – particularly those critiquing US foreign policy or the general inequity of global power structures – felt silenced.[23] In Canada, the Canadian International Development Agency's (CIDA) 2005 international policy statement, *A Role of Pride and Influence in the World: Development,* reflected dominant security discourses and deeply ensconced practices of tying aid to economic or ideological conditions, while the newly elected (2006) neoconservative government increased security and military spending and re-opened debates over controversial social policies (e.g., the legalization of same-sex marriage and abortion). In this political climate, the liberal values of the Canadian Charter of Rights and Freedoms – which, in 1982, had enshrined gender equality as a core principle – and the feminist struggles (and victories) of the previous decades, were, once again, being called into question.[24] In the latter part of the century's first decade, Canada saw a further tightening of economic policies and the retraction of development funding (including the retraction of resources committed to global AIDS response), attributed largely to the global financial crisis of 2007–12. The Canadian government was systematically defunding (and in other ways disabling) numerous Canadian social justice organizations, including many women's rights and global justice groups.[25] The result, coinciding with the SLF's first eight years of operation, was an increasingly tenuous and tense working environment for feminist and justice-oriented organizations operating in Canada.

The SLF was thus born in a neoconservative political climate, in Canada and globally. While the SLF has not had to navigate the precariousness of being defunded (because it is not funded by the Canadian government), the fact that it depends on private donors means that maintaining public support and its legal status as a charitable organization (which allows donations to be written off as tax deductions) is essential to its functioning. To this end, according to several SLF staff, it is crucial that the SLF be viewed as non-partisan, non-political, and engaged predominantly in activities that are not deemed to be activist.

In this politically charged environment, maintaining this status has required a careful balancing of its mandate with its affiliations, guiding values, and approach towards mobilizing Canadians. Indeed, the SLF is officially non-partisan, but, when asked what drew them to the Grandmothers Campaign, many of the grandmothers in my research explicitly discussed Lewis's (and his father's) links to Canada's social democratic and labour movements (and to the Canadian New Democratic Party); many also positioned themselves as "in line with the Leftist political leanings" of the Landsberg-Lewis family and many of the foundation staff. One grandmother explained that, because of these affiliations and leanings, the SLF "cannot help but be seen as a radical, lefty operation," but she also noted that "it is precisely this that makes it a good alternative to the status quo, conservative way of doing things" (January 2009). While the SLF does embody certain social democratic values, perceptions of it as being "radical" and "alternative" clearly need to be understood in the context of the contemporary shift in Canada to the political right. Other affiliations aside, even the SLF's language of "social justice" and "solidarity" might be viewed as contentious when placed in this context.

As Landsberg-Lewis pointed out in 2010, maintaining the SLF's approach requires challenging negotiations in the political and politicized context of HIV/AIDS funding and social justice work more broadly. She noted external pressures to conform to more prescribed and bureaucratic funding practices and to certain ideological frameworks that were not in line with her foundation's principles – pressures that were amplified during the financial crisis and the subsequent "flat-lining" of international funding to certain HIV/AIDS initiatives. Yet, she reinforced that, even if the SLF might be viewed as a "renegade organization" by some, she remained committed to funding "grassroots" and "feminist" projects, without placing ideological or economic conditions on recipients, and to listening to the needs expressed by women in Africa.

In a practical sense, this has meant infusing the Grandmothers Campaign with the objective of building solidarity based on a global responsibility to redistribute wealth, and with the image of African women as experts in their own lives and communities. As Pat explained in 2008, the SLF has tried to avoid paternalistic practices and overtones, discouraging, for instance, Canadian groups from "adopting" African groups, grandmothers, or children. It has attempted to develop genuine relationships with those in the projects it funds, respecting their autonomy, expertise, and integrity, and placing minimal obstacles before (or conditions on) them; whenever possible, it has taken a "project-driven" approach towards its funding, encouraging community groups to channel Canadian financial support towards meeting their own priorities. It has positioned its views on "twinning" and other forms of direct contact between Canadian grandmothers and African projects within these philosophies and values, actively resisting "charity models" of engagement. As Pat described this in 2009:

> I think that what we're doing with the campaign is about resistance in a lot of ways. We are trying to resist the whole charity model, to get grandmothers to engage in the struggle in solidarity with African grandmothers ... not "helping" or "doing good" but working for social justice as part of their responsibility as people with privilege ... We're also resisting all that old, colonial language, and the paternalistic overtones ... We see the African grandmothers as the experts, and this is the basis for how we go about funding the projects.

Overall, understanding the contemporary political climate in Canada helps contextualize why the SLF's philosophies and practices might be viewed as a resistance to the "mainstream" and/or as an "alternative" way to engage. These perceptions have contributed to the campaign's appeal, as evidenced by the many grandmothers in my research who described a narrowing of opportunities for social justice work in Canada and saw the SLF's campaign as one venue in which they could make a difference. It is worth noting that these grandmothers identified according to diverse (albeit never right-of-centre) political leanings.

To a group of women once connected to the largely progressive and liberal values of "second wave" feminism, and in an increasingly conservative political climate, the positions and discourses mobilized by Lewis and the SLF resonated strongly. Thus, in some ways, this grandmothers' movement re-mobilized certain dimensions of an ever-changing feminist/social-justice movement in Canada, while in other ways it emerged as a response to contemporary politics. The importance of this contingency echoes repeatedly throughout the book.

EMERGING "FRICTION" AND COMPLEXITY

The final section of this chapter highlights two emerging areas of "friction" revealed in my research. Following Tsing,[26] these "zones of awkward engagement" are crucial to driving the mobilizations and their possibilities; they reveal areas for critical thought, discussion, and debate.

Grandmotherhood: Grappling with Nuance and Difference

During my research, especially towards the end, it became apparent that some Canadian grandmothers, grandmothers' groups, and SLF staff were beginning to seek a more in-depth understanding of the issues around which they were mobilizing. Some expressed a desire to grapple further with the complexity and diversity of "African grandmothers' lives" and to begin to develop more nuanced ideas about building solidarity, moving beyond universally shared identities, experiences, and the passage of grandmotherhood – or what I have referred to periodically as the "grandmother narrative." This was not an overarching trend in my research, in that these concerns were noted by only a small proportion of the Canadian grandmothers with whom I had contact, yet the issues raised by these critical "outliers" are important because they suggest that some Canadian actors were beginning to ask key critical questions:

I think we now get that African women are not victims in the "dark continent." We are at the point where we're ready for more information and we need to understand the situation better. One of the things our group is doing now is dedicating some of our meetings for educating ourselves. We want to be able to answer the hard questions. (Grandother, September 2009)

A few grandmothers noted the need to refine their assumptions about "African grandmothers," without losing the powerful symbol of "grandmotherly love" (recognizing that this idea had been central to mobilizing the campaign). As indicated earlier, the discourse of grandmotherhood mobilized in Canada often assumed a shared grandmother experience, identity, or passage that was based on middle-class, twenty-first-century Canadian family norms. While most Canadian grandmothers in my research did not outwardly question this universalizing discourse, a few were beginning to ask how their African counterparts understood their own roles as grandmothers and whether these Canadian assumptions resonated with them:

An important question I think some of us are starting to ask is does this "grandmother to grandmother solidarity" make sense in Africa? What is it that we really share as "grandmothers"? What does being a grandmother mean in different communities there [in sub-Saharan Africa]? (Grandmother, June 2010)

According to some grandmothers, one of the campaign's key challenges was to develop more nuanced notions of "grandmother to grandmother solidarity" and to understand better how that solidarity was perceived and experienced by women in Africa. Such grappling with social differences – particularly those involved in transnational linking – and the question of what they mean for building solidarity reflect some of the central concerns of contemporary feminism; these tensions form the cornerstones of feminism's so-called "third wave."

For a few Canadian grandmothers, delving into these questions also meant reflecting more broadly on how the campaign had framed African grandmothers and what impacts this had had. One grandmother in my research discussed the importance of viewing African women as "heroes," applauding the SLF for challenging victimizing representations; she also wondered, however, whether this framing might be generating new stereotypes in which "we now all picture these lovely, strong, African grannies, drumming and singing and upbeat, but surely they cannot all be like that all the time ... surely we are ready to start to understand who some of these women really are" (March 2010). In August 2009, Pat poignantly captured this challenge:

Many of the Canadian grandmothers have now swung from thinking that aid had to happen in a certain way and that people had to go in and change their practices and teach them ... to believing that African grandmothers have all the knowledge they need, and they're the experts. This is really what we believe. But I guess along with this, there's a tendency to believe that they're all beautiful and fabulous; always singing, dancing, upbeat, generous, giving. I think what needs to happen to move beyond this stereotyping is to begin to see the diversity in any group of people. People are motivated by different things. The African women should be calling the shots;

they should have their agency recognized, but that means recognizing it when they do things well and when they mess up.

These concerns also reflect certain shifting ideas and tensions within contemporary feminist theory. They speak particularly clearly to the inad-
equacy of certain pre-prescribed conceptualizations of women's "agency,"
supporting Mahmood's assertion that women's motivations and actions
must be examined and understood from within the context of their own
lives and from their own perspectives.[27]

The campaign's representation of African grandmothers as heroes
and experts – like its use of the powerful symbolism of grandmotherhood – had clearly been important for building Canadian solidarity. What
emerged, though, for some in the campaign was the wish to more fully
grapple with difference and to better understand African women's own
perspectives and experiences. These critical voices suggested that an important future challenge for the campaign could be to recognize diversity
among African women and represent the complexity in their lives, while
also maintaining the simple, clear messages that had been so effective in
mobilizing Canadians.

Personal Contact: Balancing Differences in Approach

Another emerging area of "friction" was the issue of contrasting approaches among various actors within the Canadian movement. In my research this manifested itself most frequently as tensions between certain
groups (or individual Canadian grandmothers) and the SLF, with the most
common flashpoint being the desire on the part of some Canadians for
direct, unmediated contact with African grandmothers.

While SLF staff made it clear that the foundation could not, and did
not want to, control every Canadian grandmother's actions, they also held
firm to the position that the kind of relationships some grandmothers
wanted could inadvertently function to burden African groups and undermine their autonomy. According to Jill in 2010:

> The thing with having people go over [to Africa] or keep in touch
> is that we know from the African groups that this can eat up their

precious time and resources: letter writing, hosting volunteers, and so on ... But there's also the issue of the whole philosophy behind it. We're trying to get beyond this idea that what is needed is Canadian "help" or "expertise." We don't have to go over; we can trust that with resources and support, these groups have the capacity and expertise to change their own conditions. This is really an important foundation of the campaign. I think most of the Canadian grannies get this, but I guess to some it probably still seems unreasonable that we try to limit personal contact.

As she said further:

There are groups of grandmothers all over this country, and sometimes they are three degrees removed from the foundation ... It is really the joys and the frustrations of what something grassroots actually means, and what it's like to be in the midst of a movement. It's a tricky balance. How do we serve this campaign – the campaign itself, which is the SLF's campaign and which has a pivotal role to play in the broader movement? We don't want to control what these women do and how they do it just because they've come on board with the movement. But for what this campaign is about, it still really matters that people are on the same page ... because a lot of things get said out there in the name of the foundation and in the name of Stephen Lewis, which just don't resonate with what we do or our values. There's a question of what is our role, and what does our role continue to be as the campaign gets larger and larger? Because we have to be content with people finding their own voices and saying their own things.

Most of the grandmothers in my research appeared to support the SLF's approach, although, again, there were significant "outliers," who clearly revealed heterogeneity both within the campaign and the broader movement. Some noted, for instance, that they found the SLF's "no-contact policy too heavy-handed" (Grandmother, January 2009), and it was particularly difficult for Canadian grandmothers who had been selected either to visit African projects (the grambassadors) or to billet African women in their homes to forego any further personal contact. Despite the SLF's firm stand, some indicated that they were "keeping in touch, on occasion, in [their] own way" (Grandmother, April 2009) or that they intended to visit (or revisit) the African women with whom they had connected. Some also noted that allowing the SLF to mediate all contact between Canadian and African grandmothers gave it too much power in shaping what Canadians could see and how they understood the broader issues.

Furthermore, several Canadian grandmothers across the country had opted to distance themselves from the SLF's formal campaign and instead forge independent personal connections with certain African groups. Rosemary, introduced in chapter 2, is just one such example, but, given her connections to the HACT's Grandmother Project, the particulars of her situation warrant further attention. Indeed, her positioning as a key interlocutor between the Canadian movement and the Valley gogos made her role a pivotal global encounter in my research. According to Rosemary, in 2006 she fundraised for the SLF as a "grandmothers' group of one." She attended the Toronto Gathering, where she met Kholiwe and Noku, at a time when she was planning an imminent visit to Durban (where her daughter was then working). Keen to follow up on a potential volunteer opportunity, and taking her cue from the nurses' warm reception, she decided to visit the HACT in 2007. She then became integrally involved in working with Noku to build the Grandmother Project, and her initial visit developed into an annual commitment. She stopped raising funds for the SLF in 2007 and instead fundraised in Canada to support her work with the HACT. While she recognized the contrast in her approach from the SLF's, she could also see the difference her material contributions made in the Valley, and she began to separate herself from the Canadian Campaign. In her words:

I met the Hillcrest folks at the Toronto Gathering in 2006 and asked them if I could come volunteer with them and what I could bring ... Well, Kholiwe and Noku were just so thrilled, they said "yes!" and "everything!" and that was the beginning of our happy time together. I've been going back every winter – they have become more than just friends to me, they are like family. I know the SLF doesn't love the arrangement, but I can see how eager Hillcrest is to have me come, and how much we do for the gogos in the Valley ... They keep telling me how much they benefit from my support. They have accepted me as one of them. Working with them is now part of me; I am committed to do it each year as long as I possibly can ... in Canada, I guess my role is to raise awareness, share my personal experiences, and to educate others about what's going on. I support what the SLF is doing but keep some distance since I am now doing my own thing. (June 2010)

From the SLF's perspective, these kinds of relationships reveal the delicate negotiations required of it as both the coordinating body of the Grandmothers Campaign and a central mobilizing force in a larger grandmothers' movement that, by definition, must be allowed to take on its "own life," encompass multiple visions, and settle upon a variety of different leaders. From this "zone of awkward engagement," a number of important questions emerge: What do these differences of approach mean for the campaign? Are there instances when direct contact can benefit African projects? How, exactly, are various Canadian grandmothers engaging in these connections? How do various African groups perceive these grandmothers? While Rosemary was not the only Canadian who had opted to "do [her] own thing," in my research she embodied this complexity: she was the most direct, sustained, and intimate contact between the Canadian movement and the HACT, and she was a grandmother who has clearly identified an alternative approach to engaging in this struggle. Using her position as a window onto the implications of contrasting approaches among the movement's actors, as well as onto how power can operate within particular transnational encounters, I return to some of these questions in the chapters that follow.

SUMMARY AND CONCLUSIONS

Mobilizations in Canada between 2006 and 2010 exceeded all expectations, as the Canadian Grandmothers Campaign grew from 6 groups at the time of its launch to 240 groups four years later. In grappling with why it resonated and grew the way it did, two key factors emerged. First, the "grandmother narrative," which was mobilized by Stephen Lewis and the SLF (in a complex dialectic with African groups) in the years leading up to the campaign's launch, was crucial. Drawing on the powerful discourse of grandmotherhood, this narrative appealed to such strong emotions and desires as love, empathy, and the quest for meaning and connection. It embodied assumptions of a universal grandmother identity or experience: sharing the bond of "being grandmothers" motivated many Canadian women to build solidarity with, and care for, women on the other side of the globe. Re-mobilizing Lewis's central messages, Canadian grandmothers also sensed the injustice being borne by their African counterparts as a result of the unprecedented and exceptional impacts of the HIV/AIDS epidemic, which many viewed as denying African grandmothers the opportunity to retire and be cared for in their old age. Yet, as pivotal as this narrative was to mobilizing Canadians, it also revealed certain areas of "friction" for the campaign: most notably, its central ideas were interpreted within twenty-first–century Canadian perspectives on grandmotherhood. Reflecting contemporary feminist debates, this interpretation raised important questions about how women in particular African communities perceived grandmotherhood, the HIV/AIDS epidemic, and their roles within their families and communities.

Second, the Canadian Campaign developed and grew at a particular moment in time and in a particular place. It was pitched to a large and receptive audience: Canada's "early baby boomers," or women with skills, education, energy, and sympathies for feminist struggles, who were retiring and becoming grandmothers for the first time. This coincided with a time when Lewis, a highly trusted and compelling Canadian icon, had become available to take on the role of champion. Many Canadian grandmothers also felt that the campaign provided a meaningful and alternative way to engage in international issues at a time of narrowing opportunities, and they viewed this mobilization as a continuation of earlier struggles for women's equality. Thus, the Grandmothers Campaign was deeply emplaced in twenty-first–century Canada, contingent on certain historical, geographical, demographic, and socio-political trends and on the infusion of a particular vision, commitment, and leadership.

What has the campaign produced, challenged, or re-signified in Canada? These mobilizations were, for example, one way of resisting stereotypes of old age, frailty, and disengagement, and of positioning aging Canadian women as social justice actors. The campaign also generated new forms of community and meaning in Canada, while significantly raising public awareness about the African AIDS epidemic across the country. Moreover, while there were clearly differences in vision and approach, the Grandmothers Campaign sought to challenge certain ways of engaging in HIV/AIDS and development work in Africa, actively contesting, through language and practice, models based on charity, conditionality, and imposition.

....

Inchanga, South Africa
August 2008

The ground, which had been frosty just hours before, now baked in the midday sun. I leaned against the warm car listening to the conversation between Noku and Sihle, one of the gogos from the Inchanga group. They spoke in hushed tones in isiZulu; I could understand only enough to know that Sihle feared for her life.

"Today my abusive son tried to butcher me with a machete," Sihle had told us in last week's focus group. "I was saved only by my grandchildren's crying and screaming. If the children were not at home I could have been dead now ... He said he was going to burn me with boiling water." Thinking back, I shuddered.

Noku looked nervous. I slipped into the car and glanced at my assistant, Mbhali, who was anxiously watching out the window. We sat in silence. Finally, Noku and Sihle hugged, Sihle wiped her eyes, and we were off.

"It is not so good to talk like this, where the neighbours can see us," Noku said, glancing back as we pulled away. "Her son thinks she is bewitching his girlfriend, making her sick," she explained. "He is threatening her. She is in real danger."

By this time, I had witnessed many similar stories, yet I still could not quite believe what I was hearing. I had not anticipated the extent to which violence – murders, accusations of witchcraft, theft of pensions, intimidation, sexual violence, damage of property, domestic abuse – would figure in my research. I was struggling to make sense of it.

"Um, Noku," I asked at last, "can you tell me more about the violence of the 1980s and 90s?"

Noku shrugged. "Those were scary days," she said. "You've heard the stories ... There were killings, first on one side and then on the other ... no one really knew who belonged to what, but they were killing each other out of vengeance ... And they would attack schools and children. You'd be scared to leave your children at the school, but then you'd be scared for them to be at home too. It was one side or the other, or the police ..."[1]

"But here in this community," I clarified, "like in these gogos' families, what side were they on? What exactly happened?"

She sighed. "You see all along there," she said, pointing to several burnt-out buildings along the roadside, "the houses are burned. This valley was one divide: that side was IFP" (motioning to the hill sloping up from the road on one side) "and this one ANC" (indicating the hill sloping upward on the other). "You'd see them coming, there would be waves of fires, homes burning, and then people running ... Some of them [the gogos] are still rebuilding their houses ... and they lost their husbands."

"Do you think there's a connection," I asked tentatively, "between that violence and what is happening now?"

"Probably," she nodded. "You know, it's like, once people lose their humanity, once they kill other people, then everything changes ... The children grow up with gunshots and houses burning and their fathers killed people or were killed ... It's hard for the boys to get away from this."

"Hmm," I reflected, "we hear a lot more about violence in these groups than we hear about AIDS."

"Yes," said Noku, "this is what the gogos deal with every day; it's a big part of why they come here."

"But aren't they afraid," I asked, "to speak so openly like this?"

Noku thought for a moment. "They have lived through a lot. They are very brave to tell these stories, but they need to also. Because if anything happens, at least some people will know the truth."

Sihle's words from last week sounded in my mind again: "At least when I come here and tell the others this, they will know if I am dead next week what happened."

Noku continued, "These gogos have been telling their stories like this for a long time. Even in the days of the violence, the only thing we could do as women was tell each other the truth of what was happening. This hasn't changed. Only now we have violence *and* AIDS."

This conversation with Noku reinforced two issues, which, in 2008, were emerging as central to my research: first, the gogos appeared to be organizing in response to the multiple, combined stresses in their lives, which included, but were not limited to, HIV/AIDS; and second, in order to explain these stresses and the gogos' organizations, my discussion would need to start much earlier than 2006. Our conversation revealed the ways in which the women's lives and associations were deeply embedded in complex histories, geographies, social practices, and daily struggles.

Hinting at certain discursive overlaps and disjunctures with the Canadian "grandmother narrative," in this chapter I begin to illustrate the intricacy and context of these gogos' mobilizations and the diversity of perspectives among those involved. In so doing, I set the context for chapter 5: the lives and perspectives of the gogos' themselves.

LOCATING THE VALLEY OF 1000 HILLS

In chapter 2, I provided an overview of the gogos' mobilizations, starting in 2006. Yet, prior to the Grandmothers Campaign in Canada, and even before the HIV/AIDS epidemic began in South Africa, older women in the Valley of 1000 Hills were gathering in various ways to respond to the stresses they faced. In many cases, these older associations – their forms and guiding logics – resonated more strongly with the gogos I spoke to than the idea of organizing anew around their shared experiences as grandmothers, either in response to AIDS or in connection with an international network. These women's profound stresses, their ways of organizing, and the community support available to them could not be detached from the Valley's complex history and geography, just as the roles played by the HACT (and by Jennifer, Noku, and Kholiwe) must be understood within this context. What follows, then, is a brief thematic history.[2]

Colonization and Apartheid: Impoverishment, Dispossession, and Family Fragmentation

The Valley of 1000 Hills (Kwadedagendladle) is characterized by extreme contrast and inequality. Approximately forty kilometres outside the major city centre of Durban (eThekwini), the rolling hills of the Valley straddle the former Bantustan of KwaZulu and province of Natal. The HACT is located on the main street of the affluent suburb of Hillcrest, although most of the centre's clients come from the surrounding under-resourced rural and peri-urban settlements, including the settlements of Inchanga, Molweni, Lower Molweni, and KwaNyuswa, where the gogos' groups are located. Understanding the Valley's inequalities requires some consideration of how the grip of colonization and apartheid lingers in this area.

The Valley of 1000 Hills was among the first tracts of land in present-day KwaZulu-Natal to pass into European hands. In 1824, the Bay of Natal (now Durban) plus ten miles to the south, twenty-five miles to the north, and one hundred miles inland were annexed as the first British trading post in the region. In 1843, the former Natal (all of present-day KwaZulu-Natal south of the Tugela River) became a British colony.[3] Lacking either administrative or financial resources, Natal was organized in a way that provided a model for later segregation policies. Africans were constituted into "tribes" and governed through chiefs appointed by the government.[4] Reserves were set aside for the sole occupation of black Africans, and relocations were common.

As the twentieth century approached, the black population[5] was squeezed onto smaller and smaller tracts of the colony's least fertile land, including KwaNyuswa, Inchanga, and Molweni. The first half of the twentieth century brought more systematic segregation, dispossession, impoverishment, and migrancy. The division of rural land by "race" was formalized in 1913: eighty-seven percent of the land was set aside for whites and thirteen percent (the least accessible and fertile parts) for blacks. Meanwhile, diamonds and gold had been discovered along the Witwatersrand and industrialization was underway; by 1911, more than 200,000 black Africans were employed in the mines.[6] Men in many families in the Valley of 1000 Hills began migrating further and further afield, beyond the nearby white-owned farms and Durban industry, to the industrial areas near Pietermaritzburg and Hammarsdale, and to the Johannesburg mines. Many women remained on the reserves, ever more dependent on remittances from men's wages.[7]

In some respects, this pattern of increasing male labour migration reflected and reinforced longer-standing social practices and gendered roles, where women remained at family homesteads (with younger women working the fields and older women raising the children) and men moved around herding cattle or trading. Male mobility and older women's (paternal grandmothers') responsibilities for childrearing were thus not new phenomena introduced by colonization.[8] In other ways, however, colonization and industrialization radically altered lives, economies, roles, and identities. Cattle and land were once the backbone of the economy in the Valley but this pattern was disrupted throughout this period: relocations to smaller tracts of less fertile land meant that many African women could no longer feed their families, while the introduction of taxes (paid to the colonial government) meant that many men gave up cattle herding in favour of (often unpleasant) wage jobs, which took them further away from their families and kept them away longer.[9]

This pattern of men oscillating between home and industrial centres and women remaining on increasingly impoverished reserves was further entrenched through the apartheid period, which started in 1948. Racial segregation became even more ideologically ensconced and brutally imposed. New "pass laws" meant that blacks were extremely restricted in their movements: except for purposes of formal employment, they faced serious penalties if they ventured outside their designated areas. Relocations and forced removals became even more common. The Homeland of KwaZulu (a "self-governing" territory also referred to as a Bantustan) was carved out of the former Zululand and Natal in 1972; it was a fragmented archipelago of land that strung together many already impoverished reserve areas, including the communities in the Valley where my research took place.[10]

The practice of children being raised by grandmothers in remote rural areas was further reinforced during this time, with gogos caring for children in impoverished Bantustans and ever more dependent on remittances in order to meet their basic needs. These relationships were increasingly described as "reciprocal contracts," where adults (mostly men, but some women as well) sent money to support their families, and in return grandmothers cared for the young children. Children were also viewed as "extra hands" and were meant to develop a sense of responsibility towards caring for the elderly as they aged.[11] Thus, in KwaZulu, as in Bantustans elsewhere, apartheid resulted in the entrenchment and deepening of existing gender divisions, family fragmentation, and institutionalized poverty.

The legacy of colonialism and apartheid is a crucial piece of this story. Shifting the gaze on grandmothers back in time, it becomes evident that grandmotherhood, in this context, has not necessarily been associated with retirement and decreasing childrearing responsibilities. Rather, older women in KwaZulu-Natal (and elsewhere in the region) have historically taken on important caregiving roles in their families. Kholiwe's words resonate strongly here:

I was raised by my granny. Noku was raised by her granny, at least for a while. Many of the gogos you've met, they were raised by their grannies too. This is not really new here. (July 2008)

Furthermore, not only have gogos in these communities provided care for children but, as a result of dispossession, deprivation, and restrictions, they have often done so in remote areas, with inadequate resources and few opportunities. Grandmotherhood in this historical context clearly contrasts with the concept of grandmotherhood that drove the Canadian mobilization.

The Introduction of Christianity: Implications for Women's Lives and Associations

With colonization came the introduction of Christianity into African communities. The first Christian missionaries arrived in the former Natal in 1835, and mission stations quickly came to play an important role in the region, providing jobs and education to many. By 1895, there were more than fifty mission stations in the areas around and between Durban and Pietermaritzburg (as a result, the Valley of 1000 Hills and some of its adjoining areas are sometimes referred to as a "Bible belt"); by that time, an estimated 40,000 "souls [had] professed the Christian faith."[12] The majority of present-day residents in the Valley (including all of the women in my research) consider themselves to be practicing Christians (of various denominations), although many simultaneously retain understandings and practices that might be considered "Zulu" or "indigenous."[13]

In addition to altering certain spiritual beliefs and ritualized practices, there is also some evidence that the shift to Christianity brought important modifications to women's and men's roles in society. According to Vilikazi, a "peculiar feature of early Christians was that they were all women."[14] He attributes this, in part, to the fact that women had no legal status at that time and so in joining churches they did not commit their families to doing the same (whereas if men converted, their families would automatically be converted as well). He explains that, whereas men were historically "the priests for their families" (in charge of appeasing their ancestral spirits), in Christianity (or particular sects of Christianity) every person was seen to be responsible for his or her own spiritual well-being. Christian women thus prayed for themselves and assumed greater responsibility for the spiritual lives of their families. They were responsible for the souls of their children, taught them to pray, and made sure they were baptized.

Moreover, Vilikazi also suggests that, prior to the introduction of Christianity, worship and ritualized practices tended to take place within the family homesteads, led by the male head of the family. Christian churches provided new meeting places and places of worship that extended beyond families. Christian women attended the churches (often without their husbands); they also began gathering in informal congregations and prayer circles, even in the absence of priests and preachers.[15] Gathering with other women to pray in this way may have generated new forms of associational life for women living on reserves (and later in Bantustans). Moreover, women's prayer circles, as these words of Noku suggest, continue to resonate in many women's lives in the Valley:

As Christian women, coming together to pray like this would not be new to these grannies. Probably their mothers and grandmothers were Christians too, and they would have grown up with the women doing these kinds of gatherings. (July 2008)

Thus it is somewhat paradoxical that, through the immense pressures associated with colonization and apartheid, Christian churches and Christianity (themselves introduced through colonization and likely sites of fierce contest) may have generated new spaces for women to gather, assert their voices, and receive support. There is indeed some evidence that participation in Christian worship and Christian churches served to open up new roles for many women within their families and new possibilities for their spiritual autonomy.[16]

Transition: Unemployment, Mobility, Violence, AIDS

By the late 1970s, the apartheid era was on the decline and a long period of transition was beginning. As Elder points out, while the first democratic election in 1994 was a transitional *moment* in South Africa, the *transition* was actually being lived as much as twenty years earlier and continues to be negotiated into the present day.[17] It has been experienced by at least two, perhaps three, generations. For people like Noku, Kholiwe, and the gogos in my research, their adult lives have been, to a large extent, conditioned by this transition period – its hopes, its successes, its insecurities, and its challenges. Jennifer's words capture this contingency well:

> What you need to understand about these gogos is that they spent their childhoods in the impoverished KwaZulu, they were married and having their children during the transitional violence, and now they're raising their grandchildren with the deepening poverty, high levels of domestic violence, and the AIDS epidemic. Just like all of us, they're responding to our brutal history – it's just they've lived the worst possible part of it. (August 2008)

There is little doubt that the transition in South Africa has brought positive changes. South Africa is frequently hailed as having one of the most progressive constitutions in the world and congratulated for having maintained continuous economic growth throughout its political and economic turbulence. Old-age pensions are reaching more households than ever before, and child and disability grants have been made available.[18] These are important achievements, and social grants were vital to the wellbeing of the gogos in my research. However, while the last two decades have seen some previously disadvantaged groups gaining power and wealth, the lives of others, including the gogos in this study, have remained extremely difficult. The transition has not been experienced evenly.[19] Again, Jennifer's words are revealing:

> The gogos here in the Valley have not been the ones to benefit from our democracy. If anything, life has become harder for them with HIV/AIDS. (July 2008)

Four processes, which converged with the political transition, are especially pertinent to understanding the daily struggles and forms of association in the Valley of 1000 Hills. First, the political transition was accompanied by economic change: the opening of South Africa's previously protected economy to global markets and market forces. While debates and critiques around the ANC's adoption of neoliberal economic policies abound, in the decade following the first election macro-economic change was clearly associated with a drop in formal employment, growth of the informal economy, increased levels of spatial inequality, and a growing income gap between rich and poor.[20] For many, hope and expectation gave way to the daily realities of deepening poverty.[21] Marais suggests that those most "left behind" by the transitioning economy have been older African women from the rural areas (the gogos); those who, under the apartheid regime, received limited education, were unable to move around freely, and depended on the wages earned by distant family members.[22] Rising unemployment levels have, furthermore, been linked to declining marriage rates, as fewer and fewer young men can afford to pay *lobola* (bride price); this has profound implications for families, responsibilities around childrearing and support, masculinities, and entitlements.[23]

Second, the transition period resulted in increased geographical mobility and increasingly fluid family arrangements. With the 1994 election came the formal redrawing of political boundaries and the abolition of legal segregation (i.e., KwaZulu and Natal were merged into the present-day province of KwaZulu-Natal). As apartheid declined through the 1980s, restrictions over where people could live and work were lifted and cities were deregulated. Patterns of oscillating urban-rural migration became increasingly common and increasingly feminized: growing numbers of women were now seeking informal work in cities, while keeping strong ties to their rural family homes.[24] Poverty and increased mobility led to an expansion of shack settlements in urban and peri-urban areas, and, as transport to the rural areas was expensive, many young women resided for longer and longer periods in urban shack settlements.[25] The picture from the early 1980s onward was one of rising (and increasingly feminized) urban poverty, as well as increased movement between urban and rural areas.

Third, as Noku alluded to at the start of this chapter, violence intensified in the transition period. The 1980s and 1990s were characterized by violence throughout South Africa, but in KwaZulu and Natal "political" violence took on a different order of magnitude. Between 1984 and 1994, an estimated 11,600 people were killed, some 25,000 were injured, and between 200,000 and 500,000 were made refugees. Warlords demarcated "no-go zones" for their rival groups, pitting families against each other and mounting violent onslaughts when their demands were not respected.[26] While it is beyond the scope of this book to delve into the complexities of this violence, it is important to understand certain present-day implications. For instance, according to Bonnin, the intensity of the transitional violence in communities surrounding Durban resulted in large numbers of men dying, becoming "numb," or being afraid to speak out in public, while young women lived in fear, as rape became a weapon of intimidation.[27] Many older women took over as the "heads" of their households, increasingly responsible for both income-generation and the handling of community affairs. Many also saw themselves as "witnesses," putting themselves in the streets in order to try to limit the violence around them and holding prayer vigils in public spaces from which they had previously been excluded. During this time many older women extended their "mothering" beyond feeding and caring for their children to trying to protect them from the violence; in so doing, they undertook new roles, responsibilities, and forms of associational life. In contextualizing the present-day violence in the Valley, it is useful to consider the possible connections, as Noku suggested, between this history of structural and political violence, and the domestic abuse, rape, gang violence, car-jackings, xenophobia, murders, home invasions, and muggings that remain part of everyday life throughout South Africa.[28]

Fourth, during the later part of the transition period, HIV was first detected in South Africa; the country has felt the implications of its HIV/AIDS epidemic largely since the first democratic election. The epidemic has coincided with, and in some ways been driven by, the rapid societal change, intertwined with the increased mobility, deepening poverty, entrenched gender inequalities, and general insecurity of life.[29] In 1990, national HIV prevalence was less than one percent. By 2009, approximately 29.4 percent of women attending antenatal clinics in South Africa, 39.5 percent in KwaZulu-Natal, and over 40 percent in and around Durban (including the Valley of 1000 Hills) were HIV-positive.[30] While treatment campaigns have made important headway in recent years,[31] for much of the first decade of this century the national government's responses to the epidemic were, at best, inadequate and, at worst, destructive.[32] AIDS (like violence) has now become part of everyday life in contemporary KwaZulu-Natal and it remains overwhelmingly stigmatized, with any discussion of it silenced. Moreover, as is the case for many in the Valley, those who are unable to pay for transportation to treatment sites, access regular health care, make sense of conflicting information, or secure adequate food for their families feel the compounding effects of AIDS among the myriad other hardships of daily life.[33]

It was amidst these lingering inequalities, fluid family arrangements, ever-shifting gender and generational dynamics, longstanding practices of gogos as caregivers, historical roles of prayer and prayer circles in women's mobilizations, struggles with violence, and challenges associated with AIDS response that the HACT was working to assist families. It was also amidst these converging processes that Noku was becoming a key community organizer and the gogos were finding new and renewed ways to support each other.

LOCATING THE HILLCREST AIDS CENTRE TRUST

Like many community-based AIDS groups across southern Africa, the HACT is a multifaceted organization that responds not only to the impacts of HIV/AIDS but also to the other pressures I have described as shaping life in the Valley, including unemployment, food insecurity, and violence. It supports AIDS-affected families across the Valley by offering a combination of HIV testing, counselling, and care, income-generation projects, gardening programs, assistance with school fees, distribution of food parcels, and community outreach programs.[34] Founded in 1991 in connection with the Hillcrest Methodist Church, the HACT is one of the oldest community-based AIDS organizations in South Africa. A flexible and dynamic organization, it has continually adapted its activities in response to changing community needs and to the evolving epidemic. As Kholiwe explained:

> The staff members at the Hillcrest Centre understand the needs of the communities here and are dedicated to meeting these needs, whatever that takes. It is unlike a hospital or a clinic. We are always

changing what we do. It is an organization that is creative, flexible, in touch with the communities. I think it is really unique too in the way it brings together people from all different backgrounds here in the Valley, in our collective struggle to care for those in need. (June 2008)

According to Jennifer, when the HACT started HIV levels had not yet reached epidemic proportions in South Africa, and so its initial focus was on preventative counselling and education. Through the 1990s, as the epidemic grew and there was little hope of treatment, the HACT focused on palliative care activities (assisting terminally ill people to die comfortably in their homes). Most recently, with the roll-out of anti-retroviral (ARV) therapies, the HACT has turned its focus to longer-term and respite care, treatment access and monitoring, and HIV-management strategies – that is, to helping people living with HIV remain healthy. Offering onsite testing and counselling services, CD4 counts, TB screening, and a fully functioning respite unit, in addition to a host of complementary outreach services, the HACT aims to alleviate some of the load HIV/AIDS places on the state health care system.[35]

A nurse by training, Jennifer led the HACT from 1996 to 2011, making the provision of quality care the centre's primary focus. During the course of my research, the centre also employed four other highly experienced, high-calibre nurses and trained hundreds of lay health care providers. For most of Jennifer's first decade as director, the centre specialized in home-based care. However, as the epidemic progressed and families lost their caregivers, Jennifer observed an increasing number of families pulling children out of school to care for their dying parents. In 2006, in response to these acute situations, the HACT opened a respite unit in a wing of a local hospital. Faced with the impending closure of this wing, in 2008 it fundraised for and built a twenty-four–bed respite unit on its own property. Its role in care provision in the Valley then shifted: rather than focusing on basic home-based care, it began specializing in more sophisticated medical care and advanced training. Jennifer explained the rationale as follows:

I call it a respite unit, not a hospice. The vision is that it is not just a place to die but a place to get medical care, start treatment, and hopefully recover enough to go back home. There is a major gap in our health care system here, so we are training our home-based carers to be able to provide proper nursing care in the unit. Meanwhile, there are so many small community home-based care groups now. We don't want to compete with them, and it's great that there's such a change. But now, with treatment available, the needs are different. We have medical expertise and are now functioning as a community resource. We offer specialized training, from our excellent nurses on staff. We can do a lot of primary care right here and we're training a team of volunteers to assist us. (April 2010)

The HACT's sophistication extends well beyond its provision of care to include its approach to funding. According to Jennifer, the centre strives to receive small amounts of funding from many donors in order to prevent "dependence on any one source, and because smaller amounts means less onerous reporting requirements" (May 2006). Over the course of my research, the centre received funding from multiple sources, including international donors,[36] the private sector, and, in the earlier years, the South African Departments of Health and of Social Welfare. In a conversation in 2010, Jennifer explained that the SLF had become its "number one donor, which is wonderful, amazing, generous, a blessing, and also a bit scary." With the SLF contributing more than one-third of the centre's annual income, she emphasized how important this relationship was to her and to all the families it supported, and how careful she was in nurturing it:

The Stephen Lewis Foundation is a gem. They are the best donor I've worked with. They are sensitive and committed and professional, and I'm very conscious of maintaining this relationship because so many families here now depend on it. (May 2010)

The location of the HACT on Hillcrest's main street is also important: it was built there to draw passersby with money into the vibrant craft shop and garden centre – two of the HACT's successful income-generation projects, which benefit hundreds of families struggling for their basic needs across the Valley. This location was also considered to be a more anonymous setting for HIV testing and counselling than the government health clinics that are located in the Valley's settlements. The staff and volunteers at the centre reflected the surrounding communities: they came from both the more affluent (and predominantly white) and the under-resourced (and predominantly black) communities. As members of a faith-based organization, their shared vision was, according to several staff members, their commitment to providing "unconditional love" and support to those in need, as part of being faithful Christians.[37]

The HACT had attracted and fostered a number of leaders over the years: the craft shop, the gogos' groups, the garden centre, and many of the other projects had grown as a result of staff or volunteers who had had the vision, energy, dedication, and skill to champion these initiatives. Jennifer's leadership had also been instrumental: she guided the centre's strategic planning, while also leaving space for individuals to exercise their own creativity, skill, and expertise in responding to community needs. Her ability to balance the building of the respite unit in 2008 with allowing the necessary space for Noku's and Kholiwe's work with the gogos is just one example.

Thus, the HACT's focus, location, approach with donors, and leadership all contributed to its success. The gogos' groups that linked into the HACT's Grandmother Project had connected with a sophisticated organization which had had a longstanding presence in the Valley – an organization that had been disseminating resources, providing care, and responding to community needs long before it started linking into international efforts to support "grandmothers."

LOCATING THE GOGOS' GROUPS

The gogos' support groups around which my most intensive research focused were much smaller and less formalized than the HACT – as of 2010, these groups were not registered as NGOs or charitable organizations but were considered to be loose neighbourhood associations. Located in the Valley's settlements, they operated both independently and with support from the Hillcrest Centre. Some of the groups were new associations that had been initiated by Noku, but a close look revealed that many were re-inscribed and renewed associations that had existed prior to the HACT's involvement. This gogo's insights are revealing:

We are just people from around this area who have come together for a long time. We have come to pray, and to sit under the tree here and do our beading, and we hope we will be able to sell our crafts. Now a group from within us is gogos, and with sister Noku we are forming this group to support each other as gogos. (Gogo, Lower Molweni, July 2008)

Each group was unique, yet all shared certain commonalities. Like the HACT, they all addressed not only the impacts of HIV/AIDS but also the daily stresses of poverty, unemployment, food insecurity, illness, and violence. To some extent, the history and origins of these groups shaped what they looked like and how they operated, as was apparent in my conversations with the groups' chairpeople. All appeared to blend various "models" or forms of community organizing. For instance, several of the groups drew on health care models of "support groups," which likely reflected their connection to the HACT nurses and, in some cases, to other community health workers. All of the groups had taken on the task of "income-generation projects" (e.g., crafts, gardening, poultry farming, and/or sewing), consistent with neoliberal-inflected discourses of entrepreneurship and self-reliance and in line with the broader economic climate around much community organizing in South Africa.[38] They were all working to establish "partnerships" with other community groups, churches, or private companies. All of the groups also came together in "prayer circles," and many undertook "communal projects" such as gardening, building projects, and quilting.

Their meeting formats varied from week to week and from group to group, but often followed a similar rhythm: they started with a prayer circle, then moved on to the "business of the day" (which could range from a business meeting with private sector partners one week, to a beading session the next, to a testimonial circle the next), and ended by coming together again to pray and eat. Frequently, when group members were in the acute stages of grieving or mourning, group meetings were given over entirely to prayer and song.

What follows is a closer look at the four groups that participated in my intensive research: what these groups did and where they met. These descriptions also touch on some of their particular connections to the

Grandmothers Campaign and other networks, as well as their key challenges, objectives, and aspirations.

Inchanga Support Group

As noted earlier, the Inchanga group was the first gogos' group started by the HACT nurses in late 2007, and it was one of the groups visited by the Canadian grambassadors in 2008. Meeting once a week, it operated out of the Eyetsu Community Centre, a drop-in centre that provided meals to children in need before and after school. It was located on one of the main roads in peri-urban Inchanga. The building itself was well maintained, with two sizeable rooms and a basic kitchen. However, in 2008, the group, with its forty-six members, had outgrown the main meeting room, and there were very few chairs; the women had to squeeze in and sit on the floor. In 2010, the group had located a new site and was making plans to move to a larger and more secure building.

This group was chaired by two dedicated home-based carers, who also cooked for the children attending the drop-in. One of these women (herself a grandmother) attended the African Grandmothers' Gathering in Swaziland with Noku in 2010.

By 2008, the Inchanga group had developed a number of important private sector and church partnerships, and members had participated in many training workshops. Several of the gogos had also participated in a bereavement counselling workshop, co-organized by Noku and a private clinic in Inchanga, with the aim of developing the women's capacities to counsel their orphaned grandchildren. They had received horticultural support from the Amalgamated Banks of South Africa (ABSA), which provided tree seedlings and pledged R8,000 towards homestead gardening projects; the group also began planning a poultry farming project and communal garden. In 2009, four of the grandmothers were selected to attend sewing training sessions and Noku was regularly delivering fabric to them, which they sewed into garments to sell at pension points.[39]

Molweni Support Group

The Molweni group was the second group with which the HACT nurses began working, also in late 2007. This group had been started nearly twenty years earlier by the Durban Association for the Aged (DAFTA), an NGO located in Chatsworth (a township approximately fifty kilometres from Molweni); as of 2008, it was still being visited periodically by a DAFTA social worker. The group had become fairly inactive by the time of Noku's first meeting with its members, but when she approached them with the idea of welcoming new members – grandmothers caring for orphans – she was very well received. Membership quickly grew from approximately ten to twenty-three active members, and one of the HACT-trained home-based carers began supporting the renewed organization. However, in August 2008, this home-based carer found paid employment elsewhere and group membership began dwindling once again.

Like the Inchanga gogos, the Molweni group was situated in a relatively accessible peri-urban locale. It met in what Noku described as an "abandoned tribal courthouse" adjacent to the Molweni clinic. It had one large room and a very small second room, as well as a small propane tank and burner on which the group prepared its meals. In 2008, the building was in poor condition, with many of its windows broken. In 2009, Noku assisted the group with obtaining materials from a local donor to paint the building and replace its windows.

The Molweni grandmothers tended a communal garden. They were also doing crafts and selling these at pension points, as well as receiving donated materials through Noku. In mid-2008, the group had completed a government-funded literacy course. In 2009, it partnered with a new home-based carer (also a local priest), who obtained sponsorship from the Imana Soup Company to develop the community's first soup kitchen.

Lower Molweni Support Group

In early 2008, the HACT nurses started working with a third group of grandmothers, in Lower Molweni (also called Umgeni). Before this, community members (older, younger, male, and female) had been gathering in a "beading circle" under the guidance of one of the HACT-trained home-based carers to make and sell beaded crafts. With Noku's input, a subgroup of grandmothers from within this beading circle formed a gogos' group. The home-based carer leading the group was a talented beader (and also a grandmother), who was part of the Hillcrest Centre's successful craft shop; she also accompanied Noku to Swaziland in 2010.

The most rural and remote of the four groups, the Lower Molweni group met at the very bottom of the Valley, at the base of the Umgeni River, at least a twenty-minute drive from the other Molweni group. In 2008, these gogos did not have a building in which to meet and so they gathered under a tree, sitting on grass mats, outside the home-based carer's home. In 2009, with Noku's assistance, they obtained materials from local sponsors and began constructing a building.

This group had also received some training in sewing, through a local Baptist church, and members had several donated sewing machines. They were tending a communal garden, having received fencing and seedlings in 2009 through the HACT. Like the Inchanga group, they were visited by the Canadian grambassadors in 2008.

KwaNyuswa Support Group

The fourth group, operating in KwaNyuswa, also began working with Noku in early 2008. Like the Molweni groups, this organization had existed prior to the HACT's involvement: established by a community health worker from the local clinic almost a decade earlier, its goal was to provide support to people with chronic illnesses. In early 2008, Noku approached the group to gauge interest in the issue of grandmothers caring for orphans; as it turned out, the vast majority of its members were grandmother caregivers, and they were keen to partner with the HACT and to shift their focus slightly.

This group met in a large, one-room "rondavel"[40] on the property of a local pastor. In this rural community, all members lived within walking distance of the meeting place. The group's members had a large communal garden on the pastor's property; in 2008, they were able to fence the garden to prevent livestock from eating their vegetables. With support from Noku, the KwaNyuswa grandmothers had started sewing, and in mid-2008 they produced their first major piece: a large quilt. As well, on their own initiative, they began pooling their pensions in order to jointly rebuild the houses of members living in inadequate conditions.

By 2010, KwaNyuswa had become an area of rapid mobilization, encompassing all twenty-two of the additional groups operating as part of the HACT's Grandmother Project. The community's enthusiasm was demonstrated as early as 2008, when a Women's Day gathering in KwaNyuswa brought together grandmothers and health care professionals to celebrate the strengths of grandmothers and to pledge support for their struggles. According to Noku, the high level of activity in this area had to do with its being geographically diffuse (thus requiring many smaller groups spread throughout) and the fact that there were many active community health workers in the area (paid outreach workers who had time and resources to assist with these groups). It was also noteworthy that this mobilization was taking place in the area where Noku had lived and worked since 1971, an area where she was highly active, well known, and respected.

In late 2008, a partnership was established between the KwaNyuswa groups and a local NGO, Embo Crafts. This NGO donated seven sewing machines to the groups in early 2009 and provided the grandmothers with training. In the same year the HACT pledged support for new gardening projects in this area.

Thus, all of the gogos' groups undertook a number of activities, including prayer, support, training, gardening, sewing, and crafts. Many had long been operating with little or no funding by drawing on evolving community networks and partnerships, of which the HACT was one. While none of the groups that existed prior to Noku's involvement focused on "grandmothers" or HIV/AIDS, most members were older women and caregivers, and thus Noku's ideas resonated with them. All were keen to be connected to the HACT, which was recognized as a longstanding care provider in the area. In all cases, once the groups partnered with the HACT, their membership increased and their members were afforded significantly more support.

LOCATING THE HACT DIRECTOR

Chapter 3 provided an extensive discussion of the perspectives and motivations of key Canadian actors. In moving towards an understanding of the multiple actors involved in the Valley, including their different roles, ideas, and visions, I turn now to an examination of the lives and perspectives of three women who played leadership roles in the HACT's Grandmother Project: Jennifer, Noku, and Kholiwe. Of the three, Jennifer had the least direct contact with the gogos' groups, yet her role in the mobilization was pivotal: as HACT director from 1996 to 2011, she made important decisions about staffing and resource allocation that impacted the Grandmother

Project, and she developed and maintained relationships with donors, including the SLF.

Jennifer is a university-educated, middle-class, white, Swazi-born woman. When asked why she worked for the HACT (and in community-based HIV/AIDS work more generally), her response was that, as a nurse, a Christian, and a person of privilege, this was her duty and her responsibility:

> HIV/AIDS is something I have no choice but to struggle with. I am a nurse, I am a Christian, I must provide care and love to those in need. I have skills that are needed here. And unlike the women across the Valley who are doing care work with nothing, I have a husband who is supporting me. I can't just sit back and watch while women suffer, caring for their dying families without anything at all, and I can't watch kids being pulled out of school to care for their dying parents. I can't pretend it's not happening. I don't see this as a choice. (October 2006)

She spoke of consciously working to break down South Africa's racial barriers and inequalities, and she suggested that AIDS care was one area where this work should take place. Working through the transition to democracy in the Valley alongside nurses and other staff from the former Bantustan, Jennifer's progressive politics, determination, and vision clearly served the HACT well.

In terms of supporting the mobilization of gogos, her role was predominantly concerned with fostering Noku's leadership and autonomy. This required careful consideration of the centre's priorities and a balancing of its limited human and financial resources, which was not always easy. It took nearly two years from the time the nurses first began working with the gogos' groups until the Grandmother Project was formally recognized by the HACT and profiled in its written materials. I also noted Jennifer's concerns about jeopardizing funding to the centre's home-based and respite care programs in the years when the respite unit was under construction. Discussing the challenge of balancing the HACT's priorities, she explained that, while she always supported Noku's work, in 2008 the centre's priorities were to complete the building of the respite unit and to ensure that the nurses could provide the necessary care and training to make it operate:

> The reality was, in 2008, that every one hundred rand that came
> in had to go to the respite unit. We couldn't afford to spread our-
> selves thin. We had people dying on our doorstep, and our primary
> mandate is care. Supporting caregivers and community outreach is
> really, really important, I'm not diminishing that, but as an organ-
> ization we have to balance being flexible enough to take on new
> projects with following through with what we start. We have to be
> careful not to over-extend ourselves. And we had to be careful in
> 2008 with human resources too. With retirements and not having
> posts filled yet, it was difficult to have Noku out of the centre
> regularly; it put some pressure on the other nurses. We needed to
> hire another nurse, which we have now done. So I was supportive
> of Kholiwe and Noku doing whatever they could within the con-
> straints of our situation, and I always felt it was important. We were
> all eager to see it work. We just couldn't easily put resources into it,
> or completely free up Noku, or dedicate one of the centre's vehicles,
> or anything like that. (April 2010)

In 2009, with the respite unit functioning and staffing concerns sorted out, the centre was able to turn more attention to the gogos. A petty cash fund was established for Noku, and the communications team at the HACT worked to publicize the growing mobilization to media and local donors. Jennifer later explained that she viewed this as extremely important both for the communities and for the centre's profile, noting the emotional appeal of "grannies" to both local and international donors. In her words:

> The granny project is really important. It's important for commun-
> ities, and that's our main concern … I also think it's important for
> the centre. Everyone wants to support grannies; it has emotional
> appeal locally and internationally. It's much more appealing to think
> about supporting grannies, you know, than to think about caring for
> people who are dying … Internationally there's a push for a grand-
> mothers' movement with the upcoming Gathering in Swaziland;

international donors are interested in grandmothers now. There's a
real opportunity ... to uplift women in our communities who have
suffered far too long. (April 2010)

When asked whether she felt there was a strong connection between the
groups operating in the Valley and the Canadian mobilization, Jennifer
suggested the following:

Well, no, not exactly. I don't really think that what's happening here
in the Valley is a "movement" in the sense of trying to effect some
kind of broader change. Sure, we are trying to offer psychosocial and
financial support to women who are struggling through community outreach, but it is more about mobilizing resources to provide
support really. I doubt the gogos understand what is happening in
Canada or how this is being spoken about, but you'd have to ask
Noku about that ... That said, I do see a connection between the
Canadian movement and the way Noku has grown and changed,
and Kholiwe too for that matter. Noku has really found her calling:
she feels connected to something larger and the work she does with
the gogos, she derives so much meaning from it. (April 2010)

Knowing the debates and tensions in the Canadian context, and curious
about Jennifer's perspective, I asked her in 2010 about the issue of direct
contact between Canadian and South African grandmothers, and in particular how she felt about Canadian grandmothers visiting the HACT. In
responding, she emphasized that the centre welcomes some visitors and
volunteers, while recognizing that others can become a significant drain
on the HACT. In her words:

Some volunteers and visitors are wonderful and others can be hard
work. We need to be careful it doesn't drain our resources or our
time. [Rosemary], for instance, is wonderful. She jumps in and isn't
afraid to get her hands dirty. We love her here. But I can't say the
same for all visitors or all volunteers that come through. (April 2010)

From Jennifer's perspective, then, Rosemary was an asset to her organization and to the gogos' groups, although she clearly saw the potential for
this kind of relationship to be otherwise.

Jennifer's view about the grambassadors further reflected her openness to visitors alongside her caution at not over-burdening her centre. She emphasized that she considered requests from visitors or volunteers on a case-by-case basis. In our discussion about the grambassadors, Jennifer expressed the following:

> I know it can seem like more AIDS tourism, but it hasn't been like that in this case. Generally we have felt that the Canadians who come through are respectful, and the SLF is extraordinarily respectful. I think the gogos liked having them [the grambassadors] visit – from what I gather, they got a kick out of the idea that these women came all the way from Canada to see them. Still, we have to be cautious about this kind of thing not taking up too much time, and we have limited resources. I believe it was [Rosemary] who ended up taking on much of the planning on that; I was away and we simply were too busy. (July 2008)

In other conversations, Jennifer also noted that the SLF, while one of the most sensitive and responsive donors she had ever worked with, was still a donor. She acknowledged that nurturing relationships with any highly valued donor meant negotiating a delicate power dynamic that made turning away requests from associated visitors or volunteers difficult.

An exceptional woman, Jennifer made an enormous commitment to working in an extremely demanding job, where many in her position might have opted to do less. Others at the HACT described her as a "natural leader" and a "woman of vision." While she played a less direct role in the gogos' groups than the nurses did, as longtime director of the HACT and its main link to the SLF, her views on the global connections that were being forged offer crucial insights. Her perspectives, indeed, illuminate some of the complexities involved in linking across distance and difference, raising questions about how personal contact was viewed in this context (not necessarily as burdensome, although clearly having this potential), about the delicate job of maintaining relationships with donors because of the inevitable dependence that is created, about how gogos perceived their groups (as connected or not connected with an international network), and about the ways in which organizations might choose to draw on certain discourses (like grandmotherhood) because of their donor appeal.

LOCATING THE HACT NURSES

Like Jennifer, Noku and Kholiwe are extraordinary women and tremendous leaders. While their backgrounds could not be more different from Jennifer's, they had long been partners with her in the struggle against AIDS and in their dedication to improving lives in the Valley. In keeping with this chapter's goal of portraying the contingency and complexity of lives lived in historical and geographical context, Noku's detailed life history (and the shorter discussion of Kholiwe's) helps illustrate what drove these women and how they perceived their work.

Lives and Life Histories

In 2008, at the time of my intensive research, Noku was a highly energetic sixty-five-year-old woman who had been living in KwaNyuswa since 1971. Between 1971 and 2003, she worked in a government clinic in Botha's Hill, near KwaNyuswa. In 2003, she retired from the clinic, but within a few months of retirement she was "bored" and "needed to get back into the community." She started working at the HACT later that year. In 2008, she was supporting her husband (who was in hospital following a stroke), her mother-in-law, and two of her husband's teenage grandchildren (children of her husband's daughter from a different mother).

Noku was born in 1943 in Kranskop, KwaZulu-Natal, north of the Valley of 1000 Hills, on the edge of the Tugela River that once divided Zululand from Natal and within what would become part of the Homeland of KwaZulu. One of five siblings (the only girl), she lived with her mother, paternal grandmother, and father's family, while her father worked away from the home in a commercial kitchen in Durban. When she was in grade five, Noku's father stopped paying her school fees, as he did not feel schooling was a priority for girls. However, her teacher was impressed with Noku's academic abilities and when she got married arranged to take Noku with her to assist with domestic chores (as was common practice among some more affluent isiZulu-speaking families). Noku lived with, and worked for, this woman and her husband's family for over a decade, without her father's knowledge, in exchange for having her school fees paid. Noku described her school years as follows:

In the mornings before I would go to school, I would go work in the [family's] fields. Then I would come back, prepare the porridge, wash myself, eat, and then go to school. And when I came back from school, I would eat quickly, and then go into the fields for some time. Then I would come back to prepare the family meal, or whatever was needed for the family. That's how I got my education. And at night, once everyone was in bed, I would study. I did very well in school. I had a lot of energy. (August 2008)

When Noku finished high school, the woman she worked for made arrangements for her to train as a nurse at one of the hospitals in Durban. She also completed certificates in midwifery and psychiatry and then worked for several years at a hospital in Zululand, north of Durban.

Noku met her husband in Kranskop in her final year of high school (his family was living there at the time, but was later relocated to KwaNyuswa). After dating for ten years, they were married in 1971. She moved to live with his family in KwaNyuswa, taking a job at the nearby government clinic in Botha's Hill. This, Noku explained, was when her life became very difficult. She described her husband as a "womanizer and very bad alcoholic," and her relations with her in-laws as strained and "abusive." She felt ostracized by his family and described him as "abusive" towards her and their children.

They had four children: a son in 1972, twin daughters in 1975, and another son in 1979. Noku worked two nursing jobs, one at the clinic and one at the hospital, so that she could put all of the children in boarding schools: this was her way of protecting them from her husband and from the political violence that ravaged the area in the 1980s and 1990s. All of her children excelled in school, receiving bursaries, and they all pursued post-secondary education. Her two sons became engineers, one daughter became a banker, and her other daughter became a doctor (and was working in Canada, but passed away in 2006 after a long battle with brain cancer). Although all of her surviving children had moved away from the Valley, taking jobs and raising families elsewhere in South Africa, she remained extremely close to them.

Noku described how, as an adult, she depended on her adult children for emotional support. She felt they were witnesses to her life, and she valued their insights and validation. She explained that, even when all her children were grown, her husband's abusive behaviour remained a major stress for her:

I mean it was bad, bad, bad before he was admitted to hospital. His alcoholic problem was a serious one because he was drinking every day. And he would be drunk every day and he wouldn't walk home, he would be dragged home. People would carry him from the road to home or they would dump him on the gate for us to help him in. And sometimes he would sleep outside. If someone put him inside our fence, we would just leave him to sleep there 'til morning ... and then he would come in the house angry. It was terrible, terrible, terrible. (August 2008)

She described a turning point in her life as coming when all of her children were grown and employed; she felt tremendous relief that they had succeeded despite so many obstacles. She felt particularly grateful that her boys had managed to break the cycle of violence in their own families. The following is an excerpt from one of our interviews in August 2008:[41]

I: You say things are better now than they were. When did it start to change?
R: I only got relief, even mentally, when my children finished school and started working. They started supporting me, not financially, but I would discuss problems with them. And another thing that was, like, they were witnesses. I mean they knew everything that has happened to me, and that affected them a lot. My in-laws never sided with me; they never acknowledged what was happening, but my children saw it just as it was. When they grew and started working, they even hated their father like anything because of the things they had seen happening to me. And witnessing that was hard on them. But they always supported me, even when my in-laws didn't.
I: Do they have a relationship with their father now?
R: Very little, they have only started now when he is sick. It has helped them to be religious and realizing that they have to forgive. I have begged them to try to forgive everything that has happened to them.

I: You said earlier that seeing them make the transition from children to successful, employed adults has been a major turning point for you.

R: Yes. In fact, it's more than just that they are employed. I was very scared that my children, like the boys, didn't have a role model. I was scared that they would copy. They had a hard life.

I: You worried that they would follow the same path as your husband?

R: Yes, they would follow the same. I worried for them. But they are very different. Even the way they are handling their families is quite different. They are dedicated husbands and fathers. They help their wives with feeding the children and changing nappies, and they don't drink alcohol ... I'm very grateful to God because I don't know how that happened to them: instead of copying what their father was doing, they have done the opposite.

I: They have broken the pattern?

R: Yes. The cycle that we see. I mean, at times children would just copy as males, boys would be just like their fathers. But they are quite different from that. They are so different you wouldn't even know he's their father.

In addition to her work at the HACT and much time spent with her family, Noku was very active in her church and community. In 2008, she started a women's walking group and a neighbourhood youth group, which met in her house. She was a lifelong learner: over the course of my research, she was also studying theology in order to be able to better spiritually advise the women with whom she worked.

Noku's strength, commitment, dedication, and energy were all clearly evident from a young age. But, while she worked hard her whole life and lived through extremely difficult circumstances and losses, it was only once she began to work with the gogos that she was afforded public recognition. The following excerpt from a prayer circle in Inchanga illustrates the magnitude of her contribution to the gogos' lives:

Our Lord, we pray to you, our heavenly Father. We thank you for our leaders and for this organization; for gathering us here. We ask you to keep our leader [Noku] safe; she has helped us so much to learn and to cope. She has helped us grow our group and gather here. She has given us comfort and changed our lives, helped us in our projects, given us a place where we can be free. We are very thankful for this woman who has come to us, who you have sent to us. We ask you to guide her with light as she travels back home, and to watch over her until she visits us again. (Inchanga Gogos, September 2008)

In 2010, Noku was awarded the Shoprite Checkers South African Woman of the Year Award for this work. In a conversation following her nomination, she emphasized how transformative this work had been for her and how she hoped her nomination might lead to more long-term support for the groups, so that, in her words, "when I die, these groups should live on." Indeed, the issue of sustainability was at the forefront of her mind, even as her own leadership and achievement were being publicly recognized.

Like Noku, Kholiwe had dedicated much of her life to community work and had persisted through her own challenging family circumstances. Born in Vryheid, also in northern KwaZulu-Natal, raised by her grandmother (her mother died of dysentery and her father worked away from the home), Kholiwe was sent to boarding school, after which her father insisted that she train as a nurse. She completed nursing and midwifery training in Johannesburg. Like Noku, she had endured difficult losses: first her mother, and then her first husband, who was murdered not long after they married (leaving her with an eight-month-old son).

After some pressure, she was remarried to a "priest"[42] who already had four young children. In an extensive interview in 2008, she told me how she had lived an extremely difficult married life: she worked to support a total of eight children (her first-born, her husband's four, and three they had together), surviving despite extreme poverty and her husband's "abusive and alcoholic behaviour."

Her life remained difficult even once her children were grown, and indeed violence and isolation continued to shape Kholiwe's family life in 2008. As she explained, her family had recently "turned" on her: her husband and his children had accused her of witchcraft and her husband was seeking a divorce. Feeling chased from her home, she was living with her cousin in a nearby township. She expressed humiliation and pain, feeling she had sacrificed her own life and the opportunities she could have given her biological children in order to care for her husband's family.

Yet, like Noku, Kholiwe was also an optimist, a lifelong learner, and a highly faithful and articulate woman. Her involvement with the Grandmothers Campaign had encouraged her to undertake public speaking and writing for the first time and she had discovered her significant talents in both areas. She, too, derived deep meaning from her work with the gogos and from her connections to the international arena. She retired, as noted earlier, from her position at the HACT in 2008, at the age of seventy, and thereafter was not involved with the Grandmother Project.

Complex Motivations

What motivated Noku and Kholiwe to become organizers among the Valley gogos at this time? What enabled their leadership? What sustained them? To some extent, understanding their backgrounds and life histories sheds light on these questions.

The most direct and immediate impetus for their work with the gogos came from their connections to the Grandmothers Campaign. The initial spark came from their experiences at the 2006 Toronto Gathering, where they first realized that support groups for "grandmothers" affected by AIDS existed elsewhere in the region, while their subsequent trips to Canada were the catalysts for their Grandmother Project. They both said that their encounters with Canadians (in Canada and at the HACT) were deeply meaningful for them – as their first opportunities to travel and establish relationships outside South Africa, and as connections that made them feel part of a transnational solidarity movement – and they recognized the potential of these connections to bring resources into the Valley to uplift the women most in need. Like Jennifer, they both saw the importance of maintaining these ties.

The Grandmothers Campaign, however, was only one part of the story of these women's careers and life courses; indeed, their global encounters functioned to steer their efforts in a particular direction, not to substantively alter them. Long before 2006, both Noku and Kholiwe had already proven their dedication to their communities. When asked why they were doing this work, both women expressed their desire to "see change." As Kholiwe explained, "If I can help somebody then my living shall not be in vain. This is my course" (June 2008). Noku similarly explained: "I want to see change and that is all. My wish is to help these gogos, to help these communities, and for these groups and this change to persist once I am gone" (May 2010). They both drew strength from their faith and from being of service to others.

Both women had experienced loss, pain, violence, poverty, and abuse in their lives. As will become clearer in the next chapter, these nurses had much in common with the gogos in my research. Kholiwe's words are illustrative:

> Our lives, mine and Noku's, I wouldn't say they have been so easy.
> But they haven't been so different from many women our age, even
> the gogos you have been meeting. In some ways we have been very
> lucky. (June 2008)

This commonality made them particularly adept at empathizing with the gogos' struggles. They drew heavily on their own life experiences in counselling them, revealing the intimate pain they too had felt in their lives. In Noku's case, I regularly witnessed her speaking openly about the grieving process she went through when her daughter died. Their interaction with the gogos became something of a two-way supportive relationship, where the nurses acted as counsellors but also derived support and healing from this work. As Kholiwe remarked, "not only can they be helped by hearing about our experiences, but we also get some personal support and healing from speaking openly about these things" (June 2008).

Finally, both Noku and Kholiwe felt that they had experienced "lucky breaks" in their lives (from their early schooling to their recent travels to Canada), and they both expressed their responsibility to "give back" for all that they had received. In this sense, much like Jennifer and many of the Canadian actors introduced earlier, they felt privileged and thus that it was their responsibility to try to improve the lives of women who had been less fortunate.

MOBILIZING GRANDMOTHERHOOD PART 3: PERCEPTIONS OF THE GOGOS' MOBILIZATIONS

In Canada, the Grandmothers Campaign was framed as a solidarity network based on the shared experiences of "grandmothers," the "unprecedented" burdens on African families, and the "exceptional" stresses posed by AIDS. At the HACT, Jennifer described the mobilization taking place in the

Valley as a form of "community outreach" or a way of providing "psycho-social support," and she viewed the Grandmother Project as drawing on an emotive "grannies" discourse that had both local and international appeal. Clearly, multiple ways of framing these mobilizations are beginning to emerge. How did the nurses perceive what they were doing? Did they view themselves as building solidarity between the gogos and the transnational network? How did they perceive the Canadian grandmothers?

The discourses employed by the nurses fluctuated over time. In 2006 and 2007, they drew heavily on language similar to that used at the Toronto Gathering: they spoke of supporting "grandmothers caring for orphans" and of the "unprecedented impacts of HIV/AIDS" on grandmothers. They also depicted grandmothers as "heroic" and as sharing certain commonalities across Africa and even overseas. Kholiwe's words are revealing:

We know now [since the Toronto Gathering] that we have to stand with our fellow grandmothers in Africa and even Canada, because we all understand what it is to be grandmothers, and we know that the ones here who are caring for their orphaned grandchildren are the heroes, and they need our support. (October 2006)

In 2008, however, the nurses framed the mobilization then taking place in the Valley as being less about AIDS and grandmothers, and more about daily struggles for survival. They suggested that the gogos were responding not to HIV/AIDS in isolation but to the combined stresses of the epidemic and existing poverty, violence, and illness. They also increasingly spoke about the spiritual dimensions of the groups, describing them as "prayer circles" with long histories, and emphasizing the spiritual impacts of trauma on the gogos and their need for spiritual counseling. In Noku's words:

The thing is that I would not describe these groups as just about gogos or HIV/AIDS. No, they are responses to many things, as you've seen. Like poverty, violence, not having houses. They are places where women are coming to get financial and spiritual help, and we are helping them to stand on their own feet and sustain themselves, to survive. We are not really talking about "grannies caring for orphans" the same way at this time. (September 2008)

In 2010, Noku further expressed that the groups were "not so much about gogos, or orphans, or caregivers" as about "rural women's empowerment" and "upliftment." Noku's focus was on training, capacity building, economic empowerment and security, and income generation. She explained that, with the number of groups growing so rapidly, she could not provide the same kind of regular counselling and spiritual advising as she had in 2007 and 2008, but she could still assist with developing programs that would build capacity to meet basic needs. By this time, discourses of grandmotherhood, orphans, and HIV/AIDS no longer entered into Noku's description of the groups, although, when specifically asked, she did affirm that the majority of the groups' members continued to be older women and caregivers. Moreover, when asked what the main reason was for these groups coming together, she answered: "Survival – physical, financial, spiritual – but we are focusing on the financial because without basic needs the rest is not possible" (May 2010).

While Noku acknowledged that the mobilization in the Valley was not just about "gogos and HIV/AIDS," she (like Jennifer) felt it was important to *call* the groups "gogo groups" and the mobilization the "Grandmother Project." This, she expressed, would keep them tied into the larger grandmothers' movement and would keep Canadians and others interested in supporting this work. In her words:

> It is much broader than gogos and HIV, we know this. It is, like, now we are talking about empowering rural women who have long been excluded. But we will continue to call them "grannies' groups" and the "Grandmother Project." It keeps the interest in what we are doing here. (May 2010)

In another conversation, she said:

> Whether it's about women's empowerment or grannies caring for orphans, we will call it the Grandmother Project because this is what it was originally, and it keeps people here and in Canada connected to us. (May 2010)

In discussing her connections with the Grandmothers Campaign, Noku expressed, as I have indicated already, that she felt "fuelled by knowing that across southern Africa and around the world there are others standing with [her] in this struggle" (April 2010) – the idea of "grandmother to grandmother solidarity," as introduced at the Toronto Gathering, resonated with her and validated her daily work.[43] She also frequently discussed the importance of Rosemary's assistance and support, and her gratitude to "the Canadian grannies" (especially those who had visited the HACT) for the resources and recognition they had infused into the Valley. Probed further, however, Noku did not perceive a substantive connection between the gogos themselves and the transnational solidarity network, other than the fact that, as of 2010, they were beginning to receive funds from the SLF via the HACT. Like Jennifer, she doubted whether the gogos were conscious of the campaign, even though many had been visited by Canadian grandmothers. As she explained:

> I don't know if they [the gogos] understand about the Canadian grandmothers or the solidarity. I don't think so. Even the ones who have had [Rosemary] or the Canadian grannies who were here to visit them, I think they probably see them as independent people who are visiting or volunteering with us. (May 2010)

A number of themes emerge. For instance, it is important to recognize the centrality both of having champions who can act as connectors, resources, and interlocutors (through their skill sets, education, positions, and access) and of creating spaces where gogos themselves can develop their own priorities, activities, dynamics, leadership, and initiatives. It is also clear that Jennifer, Noku, and Kholiwe were driven to engage in this work for profoundly personal and emotional reasons, including their feelings of responsibility and privilege, their sense of empathy, their spiritual connection to their work, and the meaning they derived from it. They also, in various ways, expressed the contingency of their mobilizations: a sense that the "brutal history" and lingering inequality underpinned their work and that this work with the gogos was part of their longstanding commitment to improving the lives and wellbeing of women in the Valley.

While the language they used in describing their motivations reflected, to some extent, the language used by some Canadian Campaign members (e.g., responsibility, empathy, meaning, spirituality), their perspectives on the gogos' mobilizations also denoted a diversity in discourse among the actors involved: unlike many of the Canadians, by 2010 Jennifer, Noku, and Kholiwe were not framing what was happening in the Valley as being about unprecedented stress, grandmotherhood, or radical changes taking place as a result of AIDS (although they always recognized AIDS as severely exacerbating existing stresses and the crucial roles older women played in AIDS response). However, given the deep meaning and resources associated with this transnational alliance, and given the emotional appeal of "gogos" both locally and internationally, they continued to draw on discourses of grandmotherhood and AIDS in naming their community outreach efforts.

This discussion also reveals complexities in other areas, especially contrasting views around the issue of direct contact between Canadian and African grandmothers and emerging questions around whether gogos themselves understood the "solidarity" being built (and, indeed, whether they needed to). I explore these areas of "friction" further in chapter 6.

SUMMARY AND CONCLUSIONS

While much of the impetus for the HACT's Grandmother Project came from the nurses' connections to the Canadian Campaign, the mobilization that took place in the Valley at the start of this century was, in fact, complex and contingent, conditioned by certain key places, people, and perspectives. A summary of three of my central findings is worthwhile here. First, in contrast to the discourses that propelled the Canadian mobilization, the gogos' associations were not responding to the stresses posed by HIV/AIDS in isolation but to the multiple and interacting stresses in their members' daily lives, including food and livelihood insecurity, violence, and illness. Second, because the gogos' stresses, their roles in their families and communities, and their ways of organizing were all embedded in particular histories and geographies, in order to understand their mobilizations, it was necessary to begin the analysis well before the launch of the Canadian Campaign or the start of the HIV/AIDS epidemic in KwaZulu-Natal. Third, as with the Canadian mobilization, this discussion revealed the importance of leadership and the complex, embodied emotions and motivations that drove the mobilization in the Valley. It also showed the way in which key mobilizing discourses changed over time and were actively deployed. Indeed, as the focus of the Grandmother Project moved away from supporting "grandmothers caring for orphans," the HACT staff continued to draw on the emotive "gogo" discourse in order to maintain local and international support. I expand on this further in the chapters that follow.

What, then, can be gleaned from this chapter about what these mobilizations have produced, consolidated, or re-signified? A number of possibilities have emerged. Importantly, connections to the Canadian Campaign generated deep meaning and validation for the nurses, empowering them to expand their roles as community organizers in the Valley and positioning them as experts in the international arena. The influx of support, ideas, resources, and validation they experienced fuelled their ever-growing Grandmother Project, thereby allowing them to extend support and counsel to some 900 women across the Valley. This linkage also provided them with their first opportunities to travel abroad and to be widely recognized for their exceptional work.

Much has been revealed in this chapter about the intricacies and context of lives and associations in the Valley, and about the ways in which certain South African perspectives began to nuance some of the assumptions embedded in the Canadian "grandmother narrative." Still, the whole story has yet to be told. I turn now to the last major piece of this story: the gogos' lives and perspectives.

Lower Molweni, South Africa
August 2008

Every Thursday morning, the gogos from Lower Molweni would walk from their rural homes, some travelling great distances, to meet at the well-kept property of Sibongile, home-based carer, gogo, and chair of this group. Sitting on grass mats under her tree, they would bead, pray, and talk.

Mbhali and I knew this group well. As we arrived on this cool morning, the familiar tune began:

> Let us thank Him, let us thank Him
> He, who has such mercy, let us love Him
> Let us worship Him each day
> Hallelujah, the Lord Jesus, whose mercy is great
> We are called to Him today.
>
> Translated from isiZulu

Sibongile ushered us to two chairs she had set out. "We welcome you this morning," she said.

We greeted each of the gogos as we made our way to our seats. When everyone was comfortable, Mbhali started. "Good morning, thank you," she said. "Thank you for coming to be part of this focus group today."

"Yes," the gogos answered in unison.

"This week we would like to ask you some questions about HIV and AIDS," Mbhali continued, "about how it is affecting you and your families."

Silence.

"Last week we heard many of you talk about caring for children who are very sick, and about grieving when they pass away. We also heard about violence and abuse, and about the stresses of having teenagers in your homes," Mbhali said slowly. "We would like to talk a little bit about this epidemic we are having in KZN. Do you know what I am asking about? Would it be okay to talk about this?"

More silence.

Then Sibongile cleared her throat. "May and Mbhali would like to talk about this disease [AIDS] today," she said. "We know about this here, do we not? Are we open to talking about it?"

"Yes, we know this disease," responded Thembe, a fifty-three-year-old gogo whom we had interviewed the previous week. Another long silence followed.

"We do not want anyone to feel pressured to speak if they are not comfortable," Mbhali offered, "but we know that in this community, it is very rare to find any family who has not been affected. It is like this all over KZN. I will tell you that I have seen it in my family. Why is it so hard to talk about this disease?"

Thembe spoke again: "People talk when you say you have this in your family. They say the person was sleeping all over the place and deserves this punishment. And we hear that once one person dies from this, the rest of the family will die too."

Nodding, Sibongile added, "But it is a problem we are all facing. We see it all over these parts."

"Would anybody feel comfortable sharing her experience with us?" Mbhali asked.

A third gogo, sixty-two-year-old Buyi, now uttered a few quiet words, and then began to sob. Sibongile put down her beading and started to sing, a gesture we had witnessed many times, yet one that never ceased to overwhelm me with its power and love. One after another, the other gogos joined in, surrounding Buyi with a gentle song of compassion, until she regained her composure and was able to speak. She proceeded to tell us the heart-wrenching story of her daughter, Nonhlanhla, who had been living in a shack settlement in Durban, where she was raped, became pregnant, and found out she was HIV-positive. When she returned to her mother, Nonhlanhla was four months pregnant, sick with TB, and depressed to the point of being suicidal.

Buyi took her daughter to the local clinic, where a treatment regime was started immediately; the regime, however, required monthly visits to a "treatment roll-out site" at a hospital some fifty kilometres from their home. The monthly cost of transport was more than their family income. With three young grandchildren at home, Buyi was forced to borrow money, sell off all her chickens, and call repeatedly on her neighbours for support. The situation quickly became untenable, while Nonhlanhla became increasingly reluctant to take her medications. With the treatment stopped, the last part of Nonhlanhla's pregnancy was extremely difficult. The baby, whom they named Dumi, was born in hospital, underweight, in distress, and HIV-positive. Unable to afford more than one night in hospital, they returned home and decided to consult a traditional healer to help mother and baby recover. Neither survived the week.

Weeping, Buyi described the pain she felt while she cared first for Dumi, and then for Nonhlanhla, as one after the other they died painful deaths in her home. She buried them together in her yard, next to the graves of her three other children.

When she finished speaking, Sibongile smiled warmly and addressed the group. "These are hard stories, but it is good for us to share them, so we don't hold it all inside. Is there somebody else who wants to speak?" The other women now told their stories, one after another, intermittently breaking into song, prayer, and sobs; each story was more horrifying than the previous one. When every gogo had spoken, we stood and sang until the energy of the group had been transformed.

"We thank you," I then said in isiZulu.

"We thank you," Mbhali reiterated. "You are brave to share these stories with us. You are strong women." She paused. "Can we ask you a few questions about your group? I mean, about whether your group is helping you deal with these stresses?"

"Yes," the gogos responded in chorus.

"It does," Sibongile offered, "but it is not just that. It is like we said last week, the pain we all share every day. The pain from the deaths, and from our children who abuse us, and from having nowhere to pray, and not being able to pay the school fees. And it is also the other illnesses, like TB and meningitis, and flu, and even road accidents. We are here to give each other advice."

"And here we can talk about things that we don't talk about at home," Thembe added. "When our Sister Noku comes we talk about this thing [AIDS] and we accept each other, even though other people might not accept us ... We stand together so we don't feel alone."

Now Buyi spoke again. "Sometimes, caring for kids who have this, or even if they don't, even if they have TB, it is so bad. People talk, they assume. And it is terrible to watch your children turn into skeletons. It exhausts you and you want to lock yourself in your house and hide away while you deal with this. This group helped me a lot when I was dealing with Nonhlanhla, not to be so alone."

"Would you describe this group as an HIV/AIDS group, like the Hillcrest Centre is an organization that responds to the epidemic?" Mbhali asked. "Do you see this group in a similar way?"

"No, no. It isn't," Buyi responded. The rest of the group concurred. "We come here to support each other and pray, to make these crafts so we can sell them. We need the group to survive. We gathered like this before this thing [AIDS] came into our families. We have prayed and protected each other and grieved together for a long time."

I open with this lengthy passage from my third focus group in Lower Molweni because it provides important insights into both how the gogos spoke about HIV/AIDS and how their groups were operating. It illustrates the complex issues surrounding the epidemic, such as, for example, how access to treatment was about more than the availability of medications in hospitals: it was also about whether families could afford transportation and whether they were able to manage concurrent conditions, like depression and tuberculosis (TB). In so doing, it elucidates two of this chapter's central themes: the intricate and subtle ways AIDS was exacerbating, and being exacerbated by, other factors, such as poverty, violence, lack of access to medical care, and other diseases and the fact that the gogos' associations were not necessarily AIDS groups but rather responses to these multiple and interacting stresses.

THE VALLEY GOGOS: CAREGIVERS OF VULNERABLE CHILDREN AND TEENS

The gogos in my research were a diverse group of women; while I highlight some key areas of diversity, I focus on certain overall themes and common characteristics among them. Most of them were "gogos caring for orphans," as per Noku's and Kholiwe's initial conceptualization of the groups. There were, however, some non-grandmothers among the members: of the one hundred participants in my study, to whom I refer collectively as "gogos," two were young women, two were older men, and the remaining ninety-six were grandmothers.[1]

Most of the gogos were between the ages of forty-five and sixty-five, with the oldest in her eighties and the youngest in her twenties. In 2008, the average age was estimated at sixty years (i.e., born in 1948, the year the apartheid government came to power). These gogos, then, were in an age cohort similar to that of the Canadian grandmothers, though their life experiences could not have been more different. Words like "boomers," "feminists," and "retired" held no resonance for these women, as will become increasingly clear. Most had been raised by their own grandmothers in the impoverished Bantustan of KwaZulu, with limited (if any) access to formal education. Most had had their first children in their late teens or early twenties (in the late 1960s), and had become grandmothers for the first time in their early forties[2] (in the late 1980s, at the height of the political violence). Many were not only grandmothers, but also great-grandmothers, an important conceptual distinction because each additional generation appeared to significantly increase their caregiving responsibilities. Most of the gogos were also widows who had lost their husbands in the political violence of the 1980s and 1990s. Looking back several decades, they told stories of trying to raise children under the immense insecurity of daily murders, home invasions, armed conflicts, and house burnings. They all described themselves as active Christians and as religious women.

Primary caregivers for their extended families, these women described their fluid family networks as ranging from one to more than twenty people, with an average family size of approximately ten. These included children, grandchildren, great-grandchildren, brothers, sisters, nieces, nephews, and neighbours. Caring for, on average, seven children each, they cited a number of reasons why children were ending up in their care: the parents had passed away, fallen sick, were working elsewhere, or had simply "left them." As one gogo from Lower Molweni noted:

I have a family of fifteen, including my two grandchildren who are orphans ... These children are not really orphans because they still have their mother, but she gave them away because she is sick. She has this disease and their father died. (August 2008)

Another gogo, this one from KwaNyuswa, explained:

I also have two grandchildren who were left by my daughter: she went and got married and left the children behind. They are not really orphans but I am still taking care of these children from my pension money. (August 2008)

Despite the original emphasis of the support groups on "gogos caring for orphans," these women emphasized that their caregiving stresses were not necessarily a result of the *orphans* in their care but rather the overall number of *children* in their care, their relationships with these children, and their lack of financial and emotional support. In some cases, gogos noted that orphaned children were easier to care for because (1) there was the possibility of accessing foster care grants for them; (2) the death of one or both parents often meant the end of long protracted illness in the family, which alleviated some of the associated financial stress and the trauma of watching a loved one suffering; and (3) it was easier to explain that a parent had died than that a parent had left or abandoned the family, which many gogos felt to be the case.[3] Moreover, many of the "children" in the gogos' care were teenagers and unemployed young adults, adding a different dimension to the nature of their caregiving: teenagers were reportedly more "unruly," "rebellious," and "promiscuous." As one gogo from Molweni lamented:

I have a problem with my granddaughter: she does not want to stay at home. She goes and stays with different boyfriends every night. She really hurts me because I would call her and beg her to come home until I cry but she does not like to stay at home. We all know what will happen next: she will have children, she will get sick, and it will become my problem. (July 2008)

Most of the gogos were supporting their families primarily with grants from the government:[4] old-age pensions, child support grants, foster care grants, and disability grants. More than half were receiving government old age pensions, available to women over the age of sixty, although it is noteworthy that just under half were receiving no pensions because they were not yet sixty. This gogo's words reflect this struggle:

I am fifty-six years old ... I am taking care of six orphans; three of them are my sister's children and the other three are my daughter's children. She [my daughter] passed away last year December and left me with her children. The oldest is four years, the other one is two years, and the last born is seven months old. Sometimes I do not even have food to give them and that stresses me a lot, especially for the last born because she still needs baby formula. I am usually forced to give her boiled water ... I am too young still to get a pension. I worry about these children's future ... I worry about what if I die? Who will take care of these children because I have no one now? (Gogo, Inchanga, July 2008)

Approximately eighty percent of the gogos were receiving other government grants (most often child support and/or foster care grants for children in their care), while less than twenty percent reported income from the formal or informal employment of any family member. The gogos did not perceive these grants as "belonging" to one family member but rather as contributing to their household income, to be used for basic expenses such as food, medicines, and school fees, and to be distributed as needed. These grants – while often difficult to access (because of missing identity documents, problems filling out forms, or lack of access to government offices), at times the source of resource struggles within families, and inadequate to support families comfortably – were crucial to the survival of the grandmothers' extended networks (as has been reported elsewhere in South Africa).[5]

Table 5.1 summarizes some of the information on the gogos' families and income sources, according to a questionnaire administered by the HACT nurses in early 2008. I have not presented these figures by community, age of the gogos (older or younger than sixty), or whether or not they were receiving old-age pensions, because there was, in fact, very minimal variation in these figures along any of these axes of difference. Where I have provided averages, I have also given the range of responses in order to depict some of the diversity that emerged. For instance, while it is important that the average number of children being cared for by each gogo was approximately seven, it is just as significant that some gogos were caring for only one child, while others were caring for as many as seventeen.

Many of the gogos joined their support groups in response to the multifaceted pressures associated with their roles as caregivers. The "household maps" we generated in 2008 provide a good visual snapshot of these

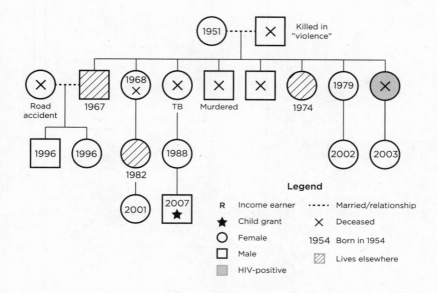

Figure 5.1 | Household map for Bongiwe, Inchanga, 2008

TABLE 5.1 | GOGOS' FAMILIES AND INCOME SOURCES (FROM PRELIMINARY QUESTIONNAIRE)

	Total (n=80)
Percentage of gogos caring for 3 or more orphans	46.3
Average number of orphans in care per gogo (min–max)	2.7 (1–8)
Average number of non-orphaned children in care per gogo (min–max)	3.7 (0–12)
Average total number of children in care per gogo (min–max)	6.5 (1–17)
Percentage of gogos receiving pensions	66.3
Percentage reporting pensions as only income	55
Percentage receiving child support and/or foster care grants	80
Percentage reporting income from employment, incl informal	18.8
Average number supported by income (min–max)	10.2 (2–20)

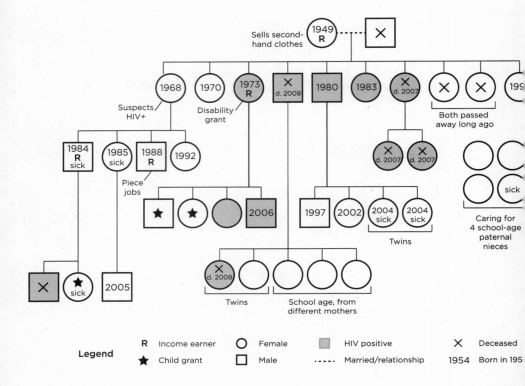

Legend

R	Income earner	◯	Female	▨	HIV positive	✕	Deceased
★	Child grant	☐	Male	·····	Married/relationship	1954	Born in 195

Figure 5.2 | Household map for Vuyelwa, Molweni, 2008

women's family networks and caregiving responsibilities, while further highlighting some of the diversity among their situations.[6]

Figure 5.1, for example, was drawn with Bongiwe from Inchanga and portrays a number of wider themes in my research. Bongiwe is represented by the circle at the top; she was born in 1951 and thus, at the time of the interview in 2008, she was fifty-seven. She, like many of the other gogos, considered herself to be the head of her household, having lost her husband in the political violence in the 1980s. Her family network, and thus her caregiving responsibilities, spanned four generations, with members living in multiple locations. The "children" in Bongiwe's care were diverse in terms of age (one grandchild was twenty-six, while Bongiwe was also caring for a two-year-old). Very few family members were employed,

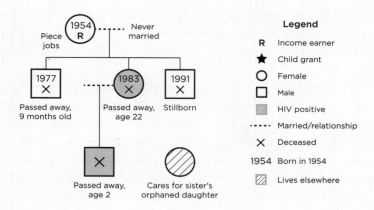

Figure 5.3 | Household map for Mandisa, Lower Molweni, 2008

and her family depended on government grants. Furthermore, many of the "middle generation" in Bongiwe's family had passed away as a result not only of illness but of violent crime as well.

While Bongiwe's household map highlights many overarching trends among the gogos, the contrast between Figures 5.2 and 5.3 brings some of the differences among these women into focus. Figure 5.2, the household map of Vuyelwa from Molweni, shows a woman responsible for six children, seventeen grandchildren, two great-grandchildren, and four nieces. In 2008, she was not yet eligible for a pension and thus relied on selling used clothing (received from the HACT). The family also received one disability grant and two child support grants. Vuyelwa's family had been in constant flux and in mourning continuously over a number of years. She had recently lost two children, three grandchildren, and one great-grandchild; with these deaths, she had also lost access to two foster care grants. She was dealing with extreme stress, grief, and exhaustion.

The story of Mandisa (see figure 5.3) from Lower Molweni paints a very different, though equally stressful, picture. Mandisa lived alone; she had never married but had three children. Two of her children passed away in infancy, the third passed away in 2005, and the grandchild from this child passed away shortly thereafter. In 2008, she was alone and felt extremely insecure, in part because she had recently been threatened with accusations of witchcraft. Although the huge caregiving burdens on many gogos, like Vuyelwa, have tended to be more widely recognized, the loneliness and fear that some gogos, like Mandisa, face have been far less well understood.

What emerges is that many (though not all) of the gogos were caregivers to large, extended families that were often (though not always) made up of four generations, dependent on government grants, living in multiple locations, geographically mobile, and losing middle-generation members. For the majority of gogos, caregiving responsibilities and the associated stresses had led them to join support groups and mobilize into a broader support network. Keeping in mind both these wider trends and the existing diversity among gogos, this overview of these women's families and income sources provides a context for a more in-depth look at the daily stresses in their lives and their complex motivations for mobilizing.

COMPLEX MOTIVATIONS FOR MOBILIZING

Unlike the motivations of many other actors in this story – for instance the sense of responsibility and profound meaning described by the HACT nurses and the Canadian grandmothers – the gogos regularly described their groups as their response to the multiple daily stresses they faced and as being about physical, financial, emotional, spiritual, and/or intergenerational "survival." As this gogo's words illustrate, much of the power of these groups came simply from women gathering together and from their sense of not being alone:

> Everything changed when I came here [to the support group]. Just to sit beside each other, to have tea and pray with other women, we know that we are not alone. We share our problems and give each other advice, and it helps to know that even the others are suffering like me. I am free when I come here. I leave all my stresses at home; for one morning a week, I am free. (Gogo, Inchanga, July 2008)

What follows is a more detailed examination of what drove these women to gather, what they felt their groups were responding to, and the particular stresses they were facing in their lives.

Financial Stresses (Income Generation)

When asked why they joined their groups and what major issues they were facing at home, the first response in all of the groups was unanimously "financial stress," specifically food insecurity, inadequate housing, and the strains of school fees. Financial stress – and the hope that the groups would help them to generate incomes and access resources – was always cited among their primary motivations for organizing. As one gogo in Molweni explained:

> I live in a one-room house that has a metal roof and the roof is now old. When it is raining, we get rained on. The building is also falling apart. The other thing is that there are lots of us and the house is small for all of us. I have people sleeping on the floor. In the morning, I worry whether the children will eat before school, and whether we will have money to pay their fees ... At least now there is some chance, I mean if we sew things and sell them in the pension points, that we will ease some of these worries. (August 2008)

The underlying causes of these financial stresses most often included loss of income earners in their families, high unemployment levels, and difficulties accessing (or maintaining) grants. Indeed, so many difficulties around grants were reported that a closer look at these issues is warranted. The grandmothers claimed that pensions and child support grants were being stopped unexpectedly and that they lacked identity documents (birth and death certificates) for themselves or for the children in their care. They also reported barriers to accessing foster care grants, specifically being turned away for not having the death certificates for both parents of their grandchildren. In the majority of cases, their children had never been married and they had never known their grandchildren's fathers.

In discussing these financial strains, intense power struggles were revealed within many of the gogos' families. As one grandmother from Lower Molweni described:

> I was taking care of this child before both his parents passed away. While I was sick, one of my children stole this baby's birth certificate

without my consent and went and applied for the grant for the baby, claiming that the baby was hers. She did not say anything to me; I only found out that the baby was already receiving a grant when I went and tried to apply for the grant myself. (August 2008)

Among the financial tensions discussed were adult children stealing the gogos' pensions or the child grants intended for children in their care, parents "abandoning" their children with the gogos and collecting child grants for themselves, and teenage grandchildren bullying the gogos into giving them grants (and pensions) to buy cellphones, expensive clothes, alcohol, and drugs. In many cases the influx of resources through grants, although vital to counter-balancing poverty in the grandmothers' families, seemed to expose, exacerbate, and/or create deep intergenerational tensions.

Violence, Abuse, and Insecurity (Protection and Witnessing)

As trust developed in each community, discussions shifted to focus on the tremendous violence and insecurity the grandmothers were enduring in their daily lives, and the view that, by gathering and sharing their experiences, they became witnesses to each other's violation, pain, and grief. This was certainly revealed by Sihle's story at the opening of chapter 4. The words of a gogo from KwaNyuswa also reflect this widely felt sentiment:

This is a safe place for us, unlike our homes and communities. Here we pray and speak and mourn openly. It is important that we can tell others about the abuse and violence we have in our lives, so others will know the truth. This is what women do, this is what we have always had to do to protect ourselves. (August 2008)

The gogos in all four communities reported extremely high levels of violence and insecurity, both within their homes and in their broader communities, supporting similar findings elsewhere in South Africa of how violence and abuse shape the everyday lives of many older caregivers.[7] In a particularly difficult focus group in KwaNyuswa, for instance, one of the gogos described her loss of eight children, three of whom were murdered. Her grief was palpable, and yet, by telling her story and weeping, and by having the others comfort her with touch and prayer, she was able to carry on. The following is an excerpt from this conversation in August 2008:

R: I have eight children that passed away so I'm also in bereavement for losing children. The three children that I am left with are sick. I am the sole breadwinner in my family … I am taking care of one orphan and I am still in grief. I have even started taking high blood pressure pills because I am stressed and I worry a lot.

I: How many are you now at home?

R: There are three of us and I lost eight children.

I: You said you have sick people in your family?

R: Yes, there are three people; none of them are well. They are always visiting doctors.

I: What are they sick with?

R: They have TB.

I: The children you lost, do you mind if we ask what they died of?

R: Some were sick, and two were shot, and one was hanged and murdered. [Sobbing. Long pause.] The one that was hanged was very young; I think she was about nine years old when she died. There was no reason, maybe they wanted something from her. [Silence. More sobbing. Mumbles from other participants.]

I: Was she hanged here in this community?

R: Yes. They kidnapped her.

I: Oh, Ma, we are sorry. [Movement. Other participants comforting her.]

Many gogos also described the fear and insecurity they felt as a result of being accused by their families or communities of practicing "witchcraft," as was the case with both Sihle and Mandisa. Such accusations were often attributed to "jealousies" within their families or instances in which there appeared to be "mysterious deaths" taking place. In these cases, the gogos were ostracized by their families and/or neighbours, making them extremely vulnerable to home invasions and other acts of violence. One gogo from Lower Molweni explained this as follows:

After my daughter passed away, then the accusations started. They [the neighbours] started saying I was doing witchcraft. My other son left and won't come back here. I am by myself a lot. The other night I heard them banging on the doors. I ran out the back, terrified that they would murder me. They probably would have. My one neighbour who still talks to me let me in, and I was safe there. But then they said "see, if you weren't doing witchcraft, you would not have been scared to be caught." I am on guard all the time. I cannot even grieve properly. They will use this as their excuse to get rid of me. (August 2008)

As part of the accounts of violence came terrible stories of domestic abuse of all forms (physical, emotional, and financial), with the most common being directed towards the grandmothers and the young children in their care. This gender-based violence (in every reported case of physical abuse in my research, the abuser was male and the abused was female) was commonly described as follows: a teenager or young adult child stole money from the grandmother/household, abused alcohol and/ or drugs, and then became physically and emotionally abusive towards the women or girls in the home. Many grandmothers did not trust their family members not to steal their possessions, and some said they had no privacy or security in their homes: even when they were trying to pray, they were interrupted in disrespectful, often abusive, ways. As this gogo from KwaNyuswa explained:

I have a cardiac problem because I have to deal with my children who are drunkards. They steal my possessions so that they can sell them to satisfy their drinking habits. They steal my pension and drink it away, and then there is nothing left for the family. And one son, he takes my money to buy drugs, and then at night he comes to the house and harasses me. He knocks on the door and would kick it down if I did not open it. I worry for myself and the other girls because he is so abusive when he is like that. (July 2008)

Likewise, this excerpt from a focus group in Inchanga depicts the depth of the insecurity in many of the gogos' lives:

R: I have something to add. I have not mentioned that one of my sons is very abusive towards me, especially when he is drunk. If I try talking sense to him, he would even spit on me and destroy my furniture and other household belongings, such as the windows and the burglar guards. He is really abusive; last week I even went to the police. He left home for four years and when he came back, he came back with nothing except a sick child. I had to bury his child for him with my money.

I: Is he sick?

R: No, he is not sick.

I: Did the police help you?

R: I was hoping that the police would help me evict him from my home, but they said I should not chase him away, I should just pray for him because if I chase him away he would have nowhere to go. If he and his girlfriend have groceries, they cook alone. But when they do not have food, he comes here and takes the children's food. Then it becomes my problem because these children also have to eat. If I say anything, he loses his temper. That can be very scary. (July 2008)

Many of the gogos reported that their support groups functioned as "safe places" to pray, weep, grieve, and speak about what was happening at home, noting the importance of having other women witness the violence in their lives. It was also evident that violence had deep roots in their families and communities, reflecting the discussion of intergenerational and inter-spatial cycles of violence in the previous chapter: they spoke frequently about alcoholism and spousal abuse when their husbands were alive, as well as about the impacts of numerous murders, home invasions, armed conflicts, and house burnings on their families and communities. As Noku suggested in the vignette at the start of the previous chapter, gathering with other women to bear witness to each other's lives had long been one of their responses to this profound stress.[8] Thus, even before the devastating effects of AIDS in these communities are taken into consideration, some of the gogos' complex reasons for mobilizing become apparent – their groups were clearly responding to the longstanding and endemic stresses of poverty and violence.

HIV/AIDS (Support and Resistance)

As discussed earlier – and as revealed dramatically in this chapter's opening scene – the gogos in my research did not describe their groups as responding specifically or solely to the impacts of HIV/AIDS on their families, despite their connections to the HACT (an AIDS organization) and Noku's presence during many of our conversations. Yet it was clear that most of their families were deeply affected by the epidemic and that part of what motivated the gogos to join these groups was their need for support in dealing with the (at times indirect) impacts: they expressed, for instance, their need for spaces in which to grieve the deaths of their children without fear of discrimination. When asked directly, most of the gogos discussed the profound toll the epidemic was taking on them, as family members with HIV became sick slowly and intermittently, suffering on and off over long periods of time. The combination of the ways AIDS progresses and the silence that surrounds it was devastating to many. This gogo's experience is illustrative:

> When we take care of our kids, we get drained emotionally and physically. We get so drained emotionally that we end up getting sick. The reason is that when they have this thing, they don't die soon. It is painful. They get sick for a while, then better, then sick again. You even sometimes wish to lock the door and not let anyone in because you are so drained emotionally and physically ... You see your child, but you see that it is not his body. You see nothing, only bones. When I saw my child like this I begged him, "my son I can see that you have this disease, be free and just tell the truth and be at ease." But he was hurt and didn't want to talk about it. He was in pain. They really don't die easily. (Gogo, KwaNyuswa, August 2008)

The tragedies associated with AIDS came on top of, and served to exacerbate, existing insecurities, tensions, and financial burdens. Gogos described the distinct financial impacts of HIV/AIDS on their families – impacts that have been reported elsewhere.[9] They explained that the epidemic was depleting their family resources, leading to increased medical, food, transport, childcare, and funeral expenses, and resulting in a loss of income earners. This woman's story reflects a widespread finding in my research:

My daughter had this thing and it was terrible. First she would not talk about it and she would not get tested, and she would not tell me what it was. She got sick and we were taking her to the doctors and traditional healers, spending so much on transport here and there, and on different cures. Nothing worked. Then she finally disclosed to me what was happening ... We went to the clinic and they started the treatment with her, and they also had to treat her for TB and diarrhea. She was very sick but she did get a little better. I cared for her, selling off everything to pay for transport back and forth to the hospital to get her treatment and to pay for her food. I had hopes that she would live. Even her sister, who was fourteen, told me that she was working to pay for her transport and treatment, but I am scared to think what she was doing ... then it got worse again ... She turned into a skeleton. We were cleaning up diarrhea all the time, right up until she died. I borrowed money to bury her. This was one year ago but we still haven't recovered. (Gogo, Molweni, September 2008)

As conversations evolved, many gogos described the complex emotional consequences of HIV/AIDS for them, including their feelings of fear, anxiety, helplessness, and betrayal. Much of this stemmed from difficult intergenerational communication: while the grandmothers encouraged their children to be tested for HIV, many of their children did not disclose their status to them. These gogos felt betrayed by this, sensing that their children did not care enough about them to try to protect them. As one gogo from Inchanga explained:

We thank God because we did not contract this disease when we were caring for our children. They did not tell us that they were sick with this disease, so we did not protect ourselves by using gloves when bathing them and caring for them. This happened to me. Even though I gave my daughter everything, I cared for her up until her death, she never trusted me enough. She did not care about me enough to tell me to use gloves. (July 2008)

Another grandmother similarly described the emotional toll this secrecy took when she told about taking in her HIV-positive newborn granddaughter so that the mother (her son's ex-girlfriend) could attend school elsewhere. The mother did not disclose the baby's status. The grandmother cared for her sick granddaughter but was never allowed to accompany her to the clinic. It was only when the baby was near death that she found out about the condition – but it was too late to start pediatric ARVs. The grandmother was heartbroken. She felt she could have provided proper care and tried to access appropriate medical treatment if only she had known, and that perhaps the baby would have had a chance to live. She recognized that it was the continued stigma around HIV that had killed her granddaughter, but she could not shake off her feelings of anger and betrayal towards the child's mother.

In telling these stories, many gogos expressed high levels of fear and felt that no one was safe once HIV entered the family. They never uttered the words "HIV" or "AIDS" but instead referred either to "this thing" or to "this disease," as is evident from the opening scene of this chapter. Some of the gogos described the virus as a kind of supernatural force or mystical being, something "unnatural" and out of their control, which would enter a family and slowly destroy one member after another, while creating conditions of extreme stress for all who witnessed it. As conversations about HIV/AIDS became more open, the grandmothers steadily began to disclose some of their worst traumas – the immeasurable pain of caring for loved ones who were suffering. They revealed the horrors of watching children wither into skeletons, of cleaning maggots out of genitals, of digging graves for their grandchildren – the list went on.

One woman's story, from a focus group in Inchanga in July 2008, described the kind of terrible experiences faced by many caregivers. She was unaware at the time that her daughter was HIV-positive, although her daughter had long been sick and was in and out of hospital for weeks. On her last visit to the hospital, she was vomiting blood and could barely walk, yet she was released and sent home. Her mother was told to make her as comfortable as possible:

RI: On that night she called me to her bedroom. When I got there she said there was something coming out from her stomach. When I asked what it was she said she did not know, maybe it was an animal. When I looked I got the shock of my life: a baby was coming out. I took the baby out. So she tried sleeping again. She was still in pain. She called me again and told me that something was coming out again. It was another baby.

R2: It was twins?

RI: Yes, the first one was a baby boy, but the second one was a deformed fetus that had rotted in her stomach. So in the middle of the night I went and buried this fetus.

[Sobbing. Pause]

RI: When I got back she said she was hungry so I went and made her porridge. The reason I am crying is because of the grief I went through.

[Pause. Others singing for her.]

RI: In the morning, schools were re-opening and I had to give one of the children at home money to go to school. But there was no money because I had spent all the money taking care of my sick daughter. I went to loan sharks to get money so that I could give it to the child who was at school. I left them and told the children to give her the porridge once it was fine. Unfortunately she did not eat that porridge. When I got back I saw all the neighbours in my house from afar and I knew that she was gone ... She left me with the child and the child has grown and is about six years old now ... I was shattered, totally devastated. I don't even remember what I did. My neighbours were good to me in those days. They buried her. I am better now, but I will never really heal.

At the height of these discussions, we asked the gogos whether and how their groups were responding to the epidemic. The following response, from a gogo in KwaNyuswa, reinforces what was revealed at the opening of this chapter and highlights the complexity of the answers we received in every group:

As women, we have long come together to pray and to support each other, and to witness the stresses we each face. Now we are witness-ing this disease too, even if many still do not want to admit it. So it is not that our group is meeting because of this disease. We are dealing with illness and death in our families, but this is from TB, murders, meningitis, car accidents, and some are probably from this thing too. Our group gives us a place to grieve and get support ... Another thing is, it is harder to handle deaths now, especially if the person was young, because everyone talks and says it was this thing. It can be very stressful and you feel all alone, no one wants to come near you because you have been touched by this. But in the group we don't ask questions, and we feel open to talk the truth, and we don't turn people away who are caring for their kids who have this. (August 2008)

Like many of the gogos, she did not distinguish between death associated with AIDS and death from other causes but conflated the epidemic's impacts with the existing strains of caregiving and the grief of losing family members; she did not disentangle the trauma associated with the epidemic from other traumas in her life, although she did note the increased stigma for caregivers as a result of the epidemic.[10] In contrast to the dominant Canadian discourses of unprecedented and exceptional stresses, she articulated the widely held view among gogos that AIDS was one part of their multifaceted and longstanding struggle. She also alluded to the history of women gathering to witness each other's lives – and thus to the possibility that this form of mobilization pre-dated the epidemic.

Older women, then, were bearing witness to suffering and death far beyond what they considered to be "natural." The deaths they experienced were caused not only by HIV/AIDS but also by violence, crime, road accidents, and other illnesses such as TB. Over time, these had become linked in their minds – their far-too-common experience was that of burying the younger generations. Their groups, while not responding to AIDS exclusively, were sources of support and spaces in which they could attempt to resist the fear, discrimination, isolation, and stigma associated with HIV.

Spiritual Survival

Violence, illness, and poverty, intertwined with family tensions and stigma, were clearly causing extreme emotional trauma. Many gogos suggested that they barely had time to grieve because so many people depended on them, and that they did not have the privacy to pray in their own homes. It is hardly surprising, then, that many described one of their group's central functions as providing them with time and space to grieve, mourn, and pray for guidance and acceptance:

> If you ask us, we will tell you right away that our group is about trying to generate incomes. But many of us would agree that we really need this group for our spiritual survival. It helps us keep our faith. (Gogo, Inchanga, July 2008)

According to Noku, most of the gogos were Christians who drew heavily on their faith to resist, and organize around, the dehumanizing conditions they faced. Yet, many gogos described the spiritual impacts of their recent traumas:

> Having my children pass away one after the other, it affects me spiritually. I am devastated. I am just devastated. It shatters my spirit, you know, it shatters me spiritually. But all I can do is accept it. I pray to God. I accept His wishes. (Gogo, Molweni, August 2008)

Some gogos suggested that, with the combined pressures on them, they were experiencing a transformation in their own spirituality and faith. Experiences of loss had led most to a stronger faith, but some were beginning to question how God could allow so many children to die in such ways. The following excerpt from a focus group in Lower Molweni in August 2008 illustrates a finding that, while not necessarily a dominant trend, emerged at several points in my research:

> I: How do you cope with all of this? Where do you draw your support from?
> RI: We cry; what else can we do?
> R2: We pray, and if you cannot, you cry.
> R3: You just ask God to be with you during your hardships. Other than that there is nothing you can do.
> RI: If God does not answer your prayers by providing you with help, you cry.
> I: Does your prayer comfort you? Does it help you accept what has happened?

R1: We have to accept. We have to accept what God has chosen. We just pray for God to be with us.

R4: I have to say something. I used to accept this, that everything was in God's plan, but now, now that I've lost everyone and seen innocent children dying, I am wondering how this could be? Could this be His choosing?

R2: Yes, that is true.

R4: I pray, but it does not comfort me as much anymore.

In all four groups, gogos asserted that their associations were at least in part about spiritual survival. As this gogo, who was part of the above conversation, expressed:

Our group helps us keep our faith, though. We help each other spiritually. We remind each other it is important to pray. It is how we survive spiritually. (Gogo, Lower Molweni, August 2008)

The possibility that the gogos' faith – so central to their lives – might have been undergoing a transformation speaks to the magnitude of the stress they were experiencing, while the fact that they still came together regularly in song and prayer suggests that many were continuing to draw on their faith in resisting the dehumanization they faced. Their groups provided not only support, but also, crucially, time, space, and acceptance.

Intergenerational Survival

On top of, and related to, these profound stresses, gogos worried about their age and, with such losses among the middle generations in their families, about who would look after the children when they passed away. These concerns highlight issues of aging and sustainability, raised in the previous two chapters with respect to succession among the Canadian grandmothers and the HACT nurses. In the case of the Valley gogos, most were suffering from chronic illnesses (such as hypertension, arthritis, and diabetes), making it difficult for them to care for others, as well as making them acutely aware of their own physical limitations. Their fears also extended to concern over who would look after them when they could no longer provide care for others:

Here we are looking after the kids. And they are making us sick with
blood pressure and diabetes because of their behaviours. But there
is no one else. What will happen to the kids, the little ones, when we
die, or when we no longer can do it? And who will look after us in
the end? (Gogo, Inchanga, September 2008)

Many felt that their adult children and grandchildren – those who were
still living and healthy – did not have the kind of commitment and sense
of responsibility towards extended family that their generation of women
had. These gogos alluded to the changing mobility of young girls, declining marriage rates, and a shifting sense of family responsibility among
young adults:[11]

I don't think my children or grandchildren will be here when I
need them, which is very sad. The girls are now in the city running
around, just like the boys. Some of them are here, some of them are
helping us, but a lot are healthy enough but don't want to be stuck
here where there are no jobs. It's different now. We always expected
that we would look after the children, and then the children would
look after us. But now families don't stay together this way anymore.
And the girls are not getting married too. That's the other thing
is that we don't know the fathers of the children and the men
don't feel they should send money even. (Gogo, Lower Molweni,
September 2008)

In the context of this perceived family breakdown, alongside the middle-
generation loss and the grandmothers' declining health, several of the
gogos said that their groups functioned as a kind of security net. As one
gogo from Molweni poignantly explained:

As old women, our group can look out for each other ... because we
are old and sick, and we might not be around forever. Our children
are dead or they have gone away, and we don't see the mothers
taking the same responsibility as we take. They are in the city or
running around. They don't support us. We are on our own to raise
the children with nothing. What will happen next? At least like this,
we can watch out for each other's children and make sure someone

raises them. In our group, we support each other and take care of each other when our own kids don't. (July 2008)

Their groups were, therefore, not only about physical, economic, emotional, and spiritual survival but also about intergenerational survival. As many gogos were reporting the reconfiguration of their families, their groups were functioning, in part, to build and re-build communities that could act as extended caregiving networks.

In considering these findings – the extreme stresses in the gogos' lives and the ways in which these underpinned their mobilizations – it is worth reiterating that trends did not differ significantly or systematically from one community to the next, between what was revealed in focus groups versus interviews, among older versus younger gogos, or among gogos receiving versus not receiving old-age pensions. Noku also believed that these reflected circumstances across the Valley settlements and had not changed significantly over the course of my research. This analysis therefore reveals the strength of these findings and the ways in which the reported stresses and traumas were likely embedded in larger societal processes (such as ensconced violence, poverty, gender inequality, and so on).

MOBILIZING GRANDMOTHERHOOD PART 4: GOGOS' PERCEPTIONS

In chapter 3 I discussed the central mobilizing discourses of the Canadian Campaign, including the idea of building solidarity on the basis of a shared grandmother experience or identity and the notion of AIDS as an unprecedented and exceptional stress in many African women's lives. In chapter 4 I noted that, by 2010, neither the director nor the nurses at the HACT viewed their Grandmother Project as being about burdens faced by gogos exclusively as a result of AIDS; nor did they believe the gogos viewed themselves as connected to a transnational solidarity movement. Against this backdrop and moving towards a deeper analysis of the productive "friction" within this network, I now explore how the gogos themselves framed their roles as grandmothers, understood their groups, and perceived their connections to efforts outside their own communities.

Contingency of "Gogo"

In 2008, I asked the gogos how they saw their roles as grandmothers and why they continued to care for children they felt were abusive and not committed to their families. Their responses pointed to the intricate pressures, expectations, hopes, and emotions surrounding their relationships with their families. Many expressed a combination of deep love for their families and a sense of duty. One gogo in KwaNyuswa expressed a widely held view: "We stay here because we love our families, we love the children, and it is our job to raise them" (August 2008). Some also drew on the African philosophy of *ubuntu* – an ethos of wellbeing that comes from communalism or the bonding sense of shared destinies, resilience, and mutual assistance – suggesting that their own wellbeing, and their happiness in the afterlife, depended on the wellbeing of those around them, particularly their kin.[12] Many further suggested that it was their duty to God to care for their families.[13]

In addition, as these conversations evolved, it became clear that most gogos had been raised by their own grandmothers, as the HACT nurses had suggested, and that they felt "bound" to their families because "this is what grandmothers have always done." As noted previously, grandmothers throughout the region have historically been involved in childrearing through reciprocal relationships: younger adults would provide financial support, often through remittances from distant jobs, and in return gogos would care for the family's young.[14] Many of the gogos in my research referred to the reciprocal nature of their work, explaining that raising children had, in the past, meant that there would be someone to care for them when they could no longer carry on and that they would be afforded some financial support. Thus, in contrast to certain Canadian assumptions, these gogos described their roles in their families as motivated by more than love, altruism, and caring: most were also motivated by family expectations, prospects of reciprocity, and longstanding practices.

Furthermore, while none of the gogos spoke of a radical transformation in their roles as a result of AIDS, most did allude to the more subtle changes underway. Many lamented that, with so many young adults dying or not taking responsibility for their families, they now felt they must provide both care and financial support, with no guarantees that they would ever be cared for themselves. With such an abundance of material, emotional, and intergenerational strains, some also alluded to changes in the way they perceived their roles and duties. While they still considered themselves "bound" to their families, some yearned for certain things they would not have considered in the past: privacy, a place to pray in peace, their own rooms, their own houses, orphanages, and old-age homes. In each community, the gogos revealed their limits: despite pressures to uphold certain gender and generational norms, some explicitly remarked that they could not continue to give of themselves indefinitely:

> I am left with these six boys who are not helpful; the only thing
> that they know is alcohol and dagga [marijuana] ... If it were up to
> me, I would make a boarding house or school where these children
> could be kept. They would only visit their grannies during holidays.
> I know this is not our way but they are really troublesome. We
> do have our limits. Some grannies are not able to deal with such
> situations. (Gogo, KwaNyuswa, August 2008)

They expressed a change in their vision of grandmotherhood: it was not that they were being denied their retirement or that AIDS was radically altering their roles as caregivers but that the reciprocity of their caregiving relationships was being undermined. Being a grandmother now entailed caring for others indefinitely, while accepting that in the end they could be left with no one. This gogo's words express a widely held sentiment:

> We raise our children with high hopes that they will take care of us
> once they have jobs ... You have hopes that this would be the child
> who will help you out from the poverty that your family has; that
> their children will respect you and help you; that they will look after
> you when you get too old. Instead, they give you children to look
> after, they drink, they run around, they abuse you, they get sick,
> and from there they die. That is what it is to be a grandmother now.
> (KwaNyuswa, August 2008)

Exploring further these gogos' views of grandmotherhood, in 2010 I asked some groups to explain what "gogo" meant to them and where these meanings came from. Their answers not only reinforced certain differences in perceptions between Canadian and South African actors but also revealed the ways in which meanings and experiences of grandmother-hood are contingent on particular social histories.[15] This excerpt from one such conversation is illustrative:

> When we hear "gogo," I guess it means a position of respect, as elders. We usually think of gogo as loving, caring, the one to raise the children; also we think of her as stern, the one who has to make the rules so that teens do not become unruly. She is the one who would have approved the children's marriages. She would have been in charge of the home, especially because the grandfathers were never there, or they died. And now, gogo is also the one with the pension, the one who the younger ones have to treat well if they want money or airtime. "Gogo" means the breadwinner. So she does have some power. (Gogo, KwaNyuswa, April 2010)

It became evident that "gogo," which commonly refers to women of "grandmothering" age (in this context, women who are in their forties and older), holds both symbolic and material power. As Noku explained, older women historically held a certain power on their homesteads: as a result of South Africa's labour migration system, older women were often left in charge of daily decision-making (including control over division of labour and dispersal of incoming remittances and resources), while husbands and sons worked away for long periods of time. Gogos were also the nurturers and disciplinarians of young children, so that "gogo" became imbued with softness and love, on the one hand, and sternness, control, and power on the other. But with employment rates declining, younger women migrating to cities, young adults increasingly requiring care (often associated with the high HIV/AIDS levels), and old-age pensions becoming more valuable and easier to access, the meanings and expectations of "gogo" altered slightly. As Noku explained, with so many young mothers ill or looking for work, older women became even more vital as the nurturers and caregivers of children. They were also caregivers for enormous numbers of sick teens and young adults. And, with many families dependent on old-age pensions as one of the only income sources, "gogo" also became increasingly associated with resources: the family breadwinners. Noku's words, in May 2010, explained this well:

"Gogo" means softness, the one who loves and cares for the children. She is a hero in the epidemic. She cares for her family. But for many she is also someone who you want on your side because she is the only one with some money coming in. She can do nothing wrong. She is untouchable. She is divine. She is powerful. We don't often see that she is also grieving, hurting, in need of support. She is seen as someone who will always be there holding everything together.

Just as "grandmother" in Canada conjured meanings of altruism, love, restful retirement, and a changing, less pressured, role in family life, in the Valley "gogo" also evoked meanings associated with love, nurturing, continued (or renewed) caregiving responsibility, economic power, sternness, and perhaps even infallibility.

In contrast to the dominant Canadian perceptions of grandmotherhood cited in chapter 3, these gogos felt bound to their families not only by love and responsibility but also by longstanding practices based in reciprocity. They had expected to be caring for young children at this time in their lives, and did not perceive their roles as grandmothers as radically altered (by AIDS or anything else). They had no notion that they were being denied a "restful retirement." They did, however, describe more subtle reconfigurations of their roles as gogos connected with their sense of family change, intergenerational strains, and, to some extent, societal transition more broadly (rising unemployment, increased population mobility, declining marriage rates, and the loss of middle-generation family members). These strains were clearly exacerbated by the epidemic but, from the gogos' perspectives, were not seen as a direct result of AIDS.

Perspectives on Their Mobilizations

By now, it should be evident that the gogos perceived their groups as being about survival (in a broad sense) – about responding to the combined daily stresses of poverty, insecurity, violence, death, illness, caregiving, and HIV/AIDS.[16] Described by many as their "lifeline," the groups were providing the gogos with spaces in which to generate incomes, speak openly, witness, gain support, mourn, pray, and grieve; in coming together in this way, many felt that they were resisting isolation, discrimination, stigma, insecurity, and dehumanization. As this gogo in Lower Molweni expressed it:

> This group is my lifeline; it is where I come to pray for strength, and where I receive seeds for my garden and sometimes food. It helps to know we are not alone, to get advice from each other. We have prayed together for a long, long time, but now we are also getting help from Noku. (July 2008)

These women did not, however, describe themselves as coming together (or as sharing some particular bond) as "grandmothers," despite the emotive meanings associated with "gogo" and despite being recently named "gogos' groups" and becoming part of the HACT Grandmother Project. In fact, in 2008, they rarely referred to their groups as "gogos' groups" but instead identified as groups of "widows," "elderly people," "Christians," "chronics" (people with chronic illnesses), "caregivers," "rural women," and "people who are struggling financially." The discourse of grandmotherhood had been introduced by the HACT nurses only the previous year and it was clear that the groups were still in the process of rebranding themselves accordingly. The words of this longstanding member of the Molweni group are illustrative:

> What do we have in common? What is our group about? We are widows. We are religious women, Christians. As elderly people, we are faced with a lot of the same things at home – the children we care for and the problems we have. We know each other's struggles. It is, as Noku says, we are grandmothers. We are starting now to think of ourselves as a group of gogos now. (July 2008)

Furthermore, as I have indicated previously, none of the groups identified as organizing primarily around AIDS, despite their recent affiliations with the HACT. Most of the gogos' families were affected by AIDS and their groups were evidently providing support in the context of caregiving, yet, for a number of complex reasons, they did not specifically frame these groups as AIDS responses: the stigma of the disease, their conflation of AIDS-related deaths with other premature deaths, their sense of organizing around a much broader set of conditions, and, in some cases, the fact that their mobilizations pre-dated the epidemic.

Indeed, it is worth reiterating here that most of the groups were not established as a direct result of the Grandmothers Campaign, the international discourse, or the new resources being made available. Many were, instead, re-inscribing older associations (support groups for the elderly or for people with chronic illnesses) or ways of organizing (prayer circles). In none of the four communities did the gogos see their groups as new (or as responding to something new, exceptional, or unprecedented), but many did note important changes that had taken place as a result of their connections to Noku and to the HACT:

> We have met like this for a long time. But now we get advice from Sister Noku. We get so much help from her, she teaches us, and brings us materials, and she is helping us get training to sew and sell our things. She has transformed our group and our lives. This is why so many other groups want to be part of her project too. (Gogo, KwaNyuswa, September 2008)

Through the course of the focus groups, and especially during my follow-up work in 2010, it also became clear that these groups understood that (re)naming or (re)framing their groups as "gogos' groups responding to AIDS" would help them maintain their connections to the HACT's growing Grandmother Project, thereby allowing members to benefit from the support it offered.[17] A gogo from Inchanga expressed this well:

> It is not exactly about being grandmothers or about this epidemic that we started to come together like this. It was more about dealing with our insecurity and our losses and our financial stress. But when we call ourselves "gogos' groups" like this, we stay attached to Sister Noku. Sister Noku understands who we are and what we are doing. She knows it is about training and empowerment. She has helped us so much. (April 2010)

The gogos in my research viewed themselves and their groups as responding to their daily struggles – not as "grandmothers" or as "AIDS groups" per se but as longstanding associations of women caring for their families under harsh conditions of exclusion, poverty, and insecurity. However, the HACT's Grandmother Project, and the discourse of "gogo" more broadly, clearly resonated with them in part because of the composition of their groups – the majority were, in fact, grandmothers caring for vulnerable children – and in part because of the power vested in this position, discourse, and identity. The HACT's Grandmother Project also, importantly, promised to provide new, much-needed support. Thus, these women were eager to (re)frame their groups as "gogos' groups" and to formalize their linkages to Noku and the HACT. The notion of grandmotherhood, so central to the Canadian Campaign, took on different meanings in this South African context, and yet it came to be similarly deployed as a mobilizing discourse in the Valley of 1000 Hills. These contrasting perspectives speak to Tsing's notion of the "friction" that drives mobilizations across distance and difference, where words can take on different meanings across these divides, even as actors within a transnational network might have overlapping goals and a desire to engage.[18]

Framing of Solidarity and Global Connections

I have, in previous chapters, explored the varied ways Canadian grandmothers framed and practiced "grandmother to grandmother solidarity."[19] But how did the Valley gogos view their connections to the Canadian Campaign? Did they understand where the various discourses of grandmotherhood and AIDS originated? Did they perceive, experience, or practice solidarity as connected to the grandmothers' movement and, if so, in what ways?

When asked about their connections to other groups or networks, none of the gogos in my research perceived their groups to be linked to anything or anyone beyond the Valley. Despite Noku's reports on the Canadian Campaign and their visits from Canadian grandmothers, all four groups insisted that they were not part of any larger network or movement; they certainly did not perceive themselves to be linked to anything or anyone outside of South Africa.[20] All of the groups expressed a similar sentiment: "Our group is just us. We are not connected to other groups here or anywhere else. We did get some training from a church, but that is all" (Gogo,

Inchanga, July 2008). Or, as this gogo from KwaNyuswa reinforced, "It is just us. As far as I know, we are not connected to any other group or movement or anything like that" (September 2008).

When asked specifically about how they perceived the Canadian grandmothers who visited, including Rosemary, they repeatedly told me how grateful they were to these "charitable women" and reminded me of the gifts they had brought. They did not describe a sense of "solidarity" with the Canadians (as per the dominant discourse in Canada), but they were clearly appreciative of their interest in their lives:

> We were visited by these Canadian women, who brought us 10-kilo bags of rice, and by sister [Rosemary] too. We are very grateful to them. We wish they could bring cabbages and mealie meal too. We danced for them with our traditional clothing, and we sang. They enjoyed themselves very much. (Gogo, Lower Molweni, August 2008)

One of the gogos from Inchanga similarly explained it like this:

> It is charitable that they take an interest in us. Sister [Rosemary] has brought clothing and notebooks for the children and we thank her for that. The other women who came, they listened to our stories and brought us rice. They are welcome here. (April 2010)

None of the groups perceived their mobilizations to be about social justice or to be part of a solidarity movement. Part of this, as one gogo explained, had to do with the fact that this was "not like the struggle for freedom [we] came through because there is no one to overthrow anymore" (Gogo, Molweni, August 2008). Their perceptions likely also had to do with their deeply rooted expectations of older women's roles as care providers in their families and communities.

In 2010, I asked the two gogos who accompanied Noku to Swaziland, and thus were exposed to the transnational mobilization firsthand, whether they felt their groups were tied into this network and whether the ideas of social justice and solidarity resonated with how they understood their associations. They responded with very similar answers, captured well in this passage:

Well, it is like, there are these groups who were invited to this conference [in Swaziland], who came together to learn from each other, and the Hillcrest Centre was one of them, that's why we were lucky to be able to go too. I don't think our little group is really part of this, except that we get support from Sister Noku. I don't believe that the women in our group are fighting for their justice or concerned with having an international movement. It is really more that we are supporting each other to survive, we are trying to generate some incomes, we are praying together. (Gogo, Inchanga, May 2010)

This passage highlights how the gogos framed their mobilizations in the Valley predominantly as a matter of survival and as separate from any broader solidarity effort.[21] Yet, as discussed previously, the collective struggles of the gogos against the oppression of violence, stigma, and isolation were enhanced, deepened, enabled, and extended as a result of Noku's presence. Given the support Noku reported as emanating directly from her Canadian alliances, I would argue that the gogos' associations were also indirectly strengthened as a result of the wider movement. Meanwhile, the grambassadors, Rosemary, and the other Canadians who, in various ways, developed relationships with the women in the Valley described these connections as profoundly meaningful and as fuelling their ongoing efforts to build their movement.[22]

There were notable differences in how various associations were named, understood, and practiced among the different actors associated the grandmothers' movement in the Valley and in Canada. It was clear, however, that without the gogos ever drawing on the discourse of "solidarity," and without their perceiving a connection to a wider movement, the practices of women joining together to challenge oppression facing the gogos was having profound effects in South Africa and Canada.

SUMMARY AND CONCLUSIONS

Against the backdrop of the Canadian Campaign and the perspectives of the HACT staff, this chapter provides an in-depth look at the Valley gogos' lives and perspectives. The majority of the gogos were grandmothers (and great-grandmothers), who were, for the most part, caring for extended families, including many vulnerable children, adolescents, and young adults, while relying on the limited resources they could access from government grants. They were raising their grandchildren and great-grandchildren amidst rising unemployment levels, deepening poverty, entrenched domestic violence, and a massive AIDS epidemic. These struggles were reflected in how they framed the objectives of their groups and their motivations for organizing: as a matter of physical, emotional, economic, spiritual, and intergenerational survival.

Their lives and perspectives complicate certain dominant Canadian discourses. Noting the longstanding practice of grandmothers caring for children and the fact that many of the groups pre-dated the start of the HIV/AIDS epidemic in KwaZulu-Natal, for instance, many gogos described their circumstances and mobilizations more in terms of continuity with the past than a radical change caused by AIDS or any other single stressor. Yet, amidst the extreme trauma they so vividly described, some pointed to more subtle changes taking place: spiritual shifts, increased mobility of family members (especially for girls and young women), changing parenting dynamics (with declining marriage rates), loss of middle-generation family members, and an undermining of longstanding caregiving arrangements based on reciprocity. Reconfiguration was also occurring in their groups, as they (re)named themselves as "gogos" and gained vital support, resources, and ideas from the HACT nurses. While the Canadian Campaign was part of this change (through its impact on the HACT nurses), the gogos did not perceive themselves as connected to this solidarity network. Thus this chapter revealed important points of productive "friction" within this transnational network.

A number of possibilities also emerged, or were reinforced, throughout this discussion. The gogos' mobilizations clearly speak to the power of women coming together – of women physically gathering in localized groups – even with limited resources or institutional support. Through their gathering, the gogos were resisting the stigma, discrimination, isolation, and dehumanization they faced, generating some sense of social security for themselves and their grandchildren, witnessing, and thereby validating, each other's experiences of endemic violence, and working towards being able to generate incomes to meet their basic needs. Their efforts were augmented by their connections to the HACT nurses and the associated influx of support, counselling, training, education, and resources. Indeed, their organizations were reconfigured so that new and renewed forms of support were extended to thousands of people in the Valley of 1000 Hills as a result of the HACT's newly mobilized Grandmother Project and thus as an indirect result of the Canadian Campaign. This, then, also speaks to the possibility for transnational solidarity to provide aid and support – albeit indirectly and unknowingly – with relatively few resources, and for these resources, ideas, and discourses to contribute, in complex ways, to positive change in distant parts of the world. I explore these possibilities further in the final chapters of the book.

6 | GLOBAL CONNECTIONS

I sat with Noku, Sibongile, and Ntombifuthi (the leader of the Inchanga gogos) in their hotel room as they packed their belongings for their early morning departure. Unlike the previous nights, when grandmothers could be heard socializing in every corner of the hotel grounds, tonight the hotel was silent. The African Grandmothers' Gathering had come to an end and its delegates, exhausted, had retired to their rooms. This was our chance to quietly debrief together after the powerful events of the previous days.

"Was there anything that surprised you about the gathering?" I asked. "Anything you didn't expect?"

Noku translated my question and the three women discussed it at some length in isiZulu. When they paused, Noku responded: "They were saying that they were surprised about this morning, like that they did not expect there to be a rally as part of this conference."

I flashed back for a moment to the solidarity march: to the thousands of Swazi grandmothers who had been bussed in from the rural areas to participate, to the SWAPOL volunteers handing out signs reading "stop violence against bogogo,"[1] "build hope for bogogo," and "include bogogo in community development," and to the sounds of singing that filled the streets as the crowd snaked through the city's downtown.

"Like, they were surprised," Noku continued, "that this was part of the program, I think, because they thought we were only going to meet the other groups and didn't expect that we would be at a rally like this. It was very exciting."

"Oh, I see," I said, wondering to what extent the march and its messages resonated with these women, "that's interesting. What about you? Did you find this surprising too?"

"Well, I guess, I was surprised a little bit too to hear the findings that came out," Noku reflected thoughtfully. "Not that there has been so much change, but if I understood, it seems that the grannies here, their basic needs are being met now. It was very good to hear."

I thought for a moment of the Manzini Statement, which I had read numerous times that morning and to which Noku was referring:

> We are gathered here in Manzini, Swaziland – 500 grandmothers
> from fourteen countries, sharing our experience and knowledge,
> and celebrating our progress in beating back the ravages of HIV and
> AIDS ... In 2006 we were battered by grief, devastated by the deaths
> of our beloved sons and daughters, and deeply concerned for the
> futures of our grandchildren. We stand here today battered, but not
> broken. We are resilient, and stand unwavering in our resolve to
> move beyond basic survival, to forge a vibrant future for the orphans
> and grandmothers of Africa.

"Well, we have seen change too," Noku explained, "and now that we have this funding that just started from the Stephen Lewis Foundation, we can buy sewing machines and do training, so maybe this is the change we will see. The grannies' groups we work with are still really struggling, though; they are struggling to survive still. But we are very hopeful this will change now. Maybe this will happen with the new training, and they will be empowered too, like we heard about today. It gives me hope."

Our conversation that evening reinforced two of the three themes that I had, by then, come to recognize would be central to this book. Noku's perception that what she was witnessing in her community did not (or did not yet) reflect the kind of "progress" articulated in the Manzini Statement reminded me of the importance of bringing attention to such instances of "friction," of probing areas of contrasting perspectives, in order to better understand how transnational linking works in practice.[2] It also highlighted the contingency of these women's experiences and demonstrated how the experiences of women from particular communities could function to challenge certain more dominant views, perceptions, and narratives.[3] This chapter pays close attention to these themes (with the third, possibility, pivotal to the final chapter). I move beyond previous discussions of the mobilizations that transpired in each place, explicitly probing the global connections that constituted this transnational alliance.

MOBILIZING GRANDMOTHERHOOD PART 5: ANALYSIS AND RETROSPECTIVE

The first and perhaps most significant "zone of awkward engagement" apparent in my research was the dissonance between how Canadian and South African grandmothers perceived their associations and framed the issues around which they were organizing. Extending my discussions of "mobilizing grandmotherhood," I now examine more closely what grandmotherhood – the central discourse of the Canadian Campaign – meant for different actors in Canada and South Africa, how it was mobilized in each context, and what effects this had.

Contrasting Perspectives and Discourses

From its inception, the Canadian Grandmothers Campaign drew extensively on the powerful discourse of grandmotherhood. This was reflected in Stephen Lewis's Massey Lectures, in which he named elderly African women as "grandmothers" and thereby imbued them with a sense of loving familiarity. The SLF then launched its campaign, connecting this emotive discourse to a situation it described as unprecedented, exceptional, and unjust. It framed AIDS as profoundly and exceptionally altering the lives of grandmothers in southern Africa and suggested that, for the first time in the history of humanity, an entire generation was unnecessarily losing its children and being left, with little or no support, to raise its grandchildren.

These discourses resonated deeply with a large cohort of Canadians – the "early baby boomers," with their abundance of skills, organizing know-how, and longstanding sympathies for feminist struggles, at a time when they were nearing retirement and entering grandmotherhood – and the campaign grew rapidly. Although there was diversity among the Canadian women involved, and a handful of groups had been operating prior to the launch of the SLF's campaign, many Canadian grandmothers soon described their movement as building solidarity around the unjust burden of AIDS on African grandmothers: most explained that they were driven to mobilize by their love for their own grandchildren and their empathy for African women losing their children and raising their grandchildren. Many also felt spiritual connections to the campaign based on seeing themselves reflected in their kin and on their sense of connection to other women who had likewise gone through the passage into grandmother-hood. Words like "meaning," "connection," and "community" were motifs in my discussions, as were many Canadian women's perceptions of their shared roles and identities – as grandmothers – with their "African sisters."

Indeed, resonating strongly with the "second wave" feminist notion of "the sisterhood" – in which all women are assumed to share similar experiences of oppression as a result of patriarchy's pervasiveness – the Canadian mobilization hinged upon a universalizing narrative of "grandmother to grandmother solidarity." This was based on grandmothers' "undying devotion" to their children and grandchildren, the "special love that every grandmother knows," and the "wisdom that comes with age" (as expressed in the Toronto Statement), even while some voices within the campaign were beginning to nuance these ideas. Many Canadian grandmothers also articulated outrage that, as a result of AIDS, African grandmothers were being unjustly denied the rest and retirement that they deserved and would otherwise have enjoyed. Thus, the "grandmother narrative" drew on specific ideas about grandmotherhood based on predominantly white, middle-class, twenty-first–century Canadian (or North American) notions of the nuclear family, old age, and retirement. In this context, becoming a grandmother was often associated with a time when women could retire from their productive and reproductive responsibilities and be cared for by their children, thereby enjoying different and less pressured relationships with their families.[4]

Yet, detailed investigation in South Africa revealed that these Canadian perspectives did not reflect the perspectives of the gogos in the Valley of 1000 Hills. Most of the gogos (although there was diversity among them, too), for instance, did not view their roles as caregivers as resulting solely from the HIV/AIDS epidemic or as being unjust. Many spoke about the history of grandmothers as caregivers in South Africa, noting that grandmothers in their communities had long raised children in rural or remote areas, often with limited resources and support, while young adults worked and/or resided elsewhere.[5] Most of the gogos had been raised by their own grandmothers and expected that they too would one day raise their own grandchildren. They lamented the additional grief, stigma, and compounding stresses brought on by the epidemic, but they did not see their roles as fundamentally transformed or altered by AIDS. Moreover, while many suggested that what kept them going was their love for their grandchildren and their sense of duty to their families and to God, it was also clear that their motivations were more complex than love and altruism: many, in fact, were driven by the prospects of longstanding, reciprocal caregiving arrangements and by societal and familial pressures. Expectations that they would one day raise their grandchildren, together with the lack of a clearly identifiable "oppressor" (which had been apparent in their long struggle for democracy), help explain why these gogos did not frame the impacts of AIDS as unprecedented, exceptional, or unjust.

This heterogeneity in perspective was reinforced in discussions with the Valley gogos about their organizations. The gogos were adamant that their groups were not responding to AIDS impacts in isolation but instead to the combined daily stresses of violence, poverty, illness, stigma, and grief; they described their groups as a matter of physical, financial, emotional, spiritual, and intergenerational survival. They were also clear that their groups were not (at least initially) intended as "gogos' groups" but that they collectively identified in a number of other ways – as people with chronic illnesses, as Christians, as rural women, and as caregivers. In addition, many of the gogos' organizations were not initiated as a result of AIDS or the Grandmothers Campaign but instead reinvigorated and re-inscribed existing associations, which often pre-dated the start of the epidemic in KwaZulu-Natal. Moreover, most of the gogos, even those who had direct contact with Canadian grandmothers, were unaware of the Canadian solidarity movement and the SLF. They did not see their groups as making transnational connections, even as they described the Canadian women with whom they had contact as "kind," "caring," and "charitable" women.

Nevertheless, despite this notable contrast in perspectives, when the opportunity arose these women chose to (re)name their groups as "gogos' groups" for several reasons: they were predominantly grandmothers, they recognized the power imbued in "gogo" in this context (as nurturer, decision-maker, and breadwinner) and, perhaps most significantly, they understood that this (re)naming would allow them to tap into vital support from the HACT nurses and the Grandmother Project. Thus, they mobilized discourses and identities originally deployed by the Canadian Campaign (grandmotherhood) in unexpected ways in order to propel, resource, and reconfigure their associations, even while they were not entirely aware of the campaign itself. Meanwhile, the Canadian grandmothers, including those who visited the Valley, remained unaware of the gogos' contrasting perspectives and the ways in which they were redeploying the campaign's discourses. Thus, in both contexts grandmotherhood was actively deployed in order to shape women's mobilizations and demarcate their own social and political goals.[6] For the most part, Canadian and South African grandmothers had very different perceptions of the issues around which they were organizing, largely as a result of their contrasting life experiences, knowledge, expectations, histories, geographies, and social practices. These differences speak to the contingent nature of this transnational network; they also raise important questions about what roles such "friction" can play in shaping mobilizations and global connections.

"Friction," Power, and Change

It is not simply the existence of a disjuncture in perspective between Canadian and South African grandmothers that is important but also (and perhaps more significantly) the broader implications: understanding how such "friction" can alter arrangements of power.[7] As outlined in chapter 2, grandmotherhood was likely first introduced as a mobilizing discourse in the Valley of 1000 Hills following, and as a direct result of, Noku's and Kholiwe's participation in the Toronto Gathering in 2006. It was in Toronto that the nurses were introduced to the idea that AIDS is an issue affecting "grandmothers"; it was also there that they learned about "grandmothers" requiring support as a result of the "new and exceptional" stresses posed by AIDS. This early international encounter led to profound discursive and programmatic shifts: for the first time, the nurses focused their attention on understanding the impacts of AIDS on "grandmothers" in the Valley and on developing new grandmother-centred support groups. They also began to identify as "grandmothers" themselves and as part of a budding transnational grandmothers' movement.

This reconfiguration, however, did not mean that the campaign's discourses were adopted in any straightforward or uncritical way.[8] The nurses did not simply assume that the particular conditions in their communities matched the international narratives. Instead, prior to beginning to mobilize the gogos, they initiated research. In addition, while they initially set out to work with "grandmothers caring for orphans" – in line with the discourses circulating at the Toronto Gathering – they quickly nuanced how they conceptualized the key issues. Their discourse soon shifted away from assumptions that African grandmothers' lives were being radically altered by the epidemic (and the accompanying "AIDS orphaning") towards a more historically and geographically appropriate narrative, much closer to what I described as the gogos' perceptions of their groups. By mid-2008, the nurses spoke of supporting older women's efforts to respond to the multiple pressures in their lives, including, but not limited to, HIV/AIDS; two years later, they framed the groups even more broadly, as efforts in "women's empowerment" and "community upliftment."[9]

In 2010, Noku reflected critically on these discursive changes and their dissonances with the Canadian Campaign, while also noting the positive impacts the Grandmother Project was having at the HACT and across the Valley. Four key findings emerged. First, thousands of vulnerable women, men, and children were benefitting from the HACT's Grandmother Project and especially from Noku's support and counsel. Second, Noku, who was also deriving tremendous satisfaction from this work, drew much support from her encounters with the Canadian Campaign and certain Canadian grandmothers; these encounters propelled her work, provided her with basic resources (particularly during Rosemary's early visits), and gave her the vital sense of being part of a larger movement. Third, the HACT was starting to receive some funding for its Grandmother Project from local donors and the SLF and its staff felt that the "grandmother" label was important for attracting and maintaining this support. Therefore, despite the fact that the groups extended beyond grandmothers and AIDS response, the HACT continued to call its outreach work the "Grandmother Project" and to frame it as support for gogos affected by AIDS. Fourth, the gogos themselves were keen to join the Grandmother Project, even if this meant (re)naming their groups; their eagerness reflected the fact that most of the groups were comprised of grandmother caregivers (often with orphans in their care) and the knowledge that the power imbued in localized meanings of "gogo" presented an opportunity to gain new support.

This shift – in which Canadian discourses were re-conceptualized and redeployed by key South African actors – is pivotal to understanding how linking across distance and difference took place in this instance; it also challenges assumptions that international donors exert totalizing power over subjects in the Global South.[10] By strategically mobilizing grandmotherhood, the nurses, HACT director, and gogos all exercised their power to direct these global encounters. They shifted the dynamic from one where the SLF exerted its power to generate and deploy the dominant discourse of grandmotherhood around which this transnational mobilization would ensue, to one where South African actors took control of this discourse and redeployed it for their own ends. In other words, contrasting perspectives, or "friction," led to reconfigurations of power and functioned to steer the course of this mobilization.[11] The South African actors mobilized grandmotherhood (conceived of and understood differently in the Valley than in Canada) in order to support and obtain resources for existing forms of community organizing.

What did this mean in the Canadian context? Did this disjuncture diminish Canadian efforts? In considering these questions, it is worth revisiting the SLF's goal of being "project-driven" – of not radically altering community responses in sub-Saharan Africa. The SLF mobilized the powerful "grandmother narrative" in order to engage Canadians and, directly following the Toronto Gathering, the mobilization of this narrative led to unanticipated changes among the HACT nurses and in the Valley of 1000 Hills. While this was clearly beneficial to the Valley gogos, the SLF had not intended to have such a radical influence over South African discourses. On the other hand, the shift in power dynamics that occurred when the South African actors redeployed the "grandmother narrative" was more in line with the campaign's philosophy of supporting its African partners' own initiatives.[12] By 2010, resources from the campaign were improving lives in the Valley, while Canadian discourses were being critically renegotiated by key South African interlocutors. In unexpected ways, this complex dynamic appeared to meet the objectives of all involved: the Grandmothers Campaign was able to help resource and strengthen African women's existing associations, the HACT could draw support from this powerful network while continuing to work in a community-driven manner, and the Valley gogos gained new forms of support without sensing any significant Canadian presence in their communities.

Solidarity, Contingency, and Difference

These findings clearly speak to the contingent nature of these mobilizations and to the need to move beyond identity politics in building transnational solidarity. They support, for instance, the notion that identities – including that of "grandmother" – are not static, fixed, or essential, as Cooper, Bernstein, Hilhorst, and many other scholars have pointed out.[13] Despite the Canadian Campaign's recourse to such seemingly innate "grandmother" attributes as love, caring, and responsibility for future generations, the Valley gogos' roles and motivations were based as much on longstanding practices and prospects for reciprocity as on these qualities. The history of grandmothers as caregivers in South Africa stands in direct contrast to the twenty-first century Canadian notions of the nuclear family, old age, and retirement. Thus, context is central to understanding older women's roles and what grandmotherhood means (or has meant) in different times and places, supporting Oyewumi's critique of the appropriateness of Western gender (and age) categories in African contexts, as well as Scheper-Hughes's assertion of the socially constructed nature of motherhood.[14]

The importance of context in understanding how grandmotherhood was mobilized also supports emerging ideas about transnationalism not as supra-local or placeless but rather as constituted through grounded encounters and organizations produced in specific times and places.[15] In Canada, timing, demographic trends, and the presence of an iconic figure were all pivotal in the early and most rapid phase of mobilization. In the Valley of 1000 Hills, understanding the gogos' present-day mobilizations required some historical analysis of their life stresses and collective responses. Recognizing the Canadian and South African processes as situated in their respective contexts sheds light on how the HACT's Grandmother Project reflected aspects of both continuity and reconfiguration, where discourses, ideas, emotions, and resources mobilized at a particular time in Canada functioned to alter and support existing associations in the Valley.

Finally, despite obvious differences in perspective and ways of identifying, and despite the fact that "grandmother to grandmother solidarity" was layered with contrasts in meaning and experience, this transnational alliance had observable, positive effects on women's lives in South Africa (and in Canada as well). This speaks to the idea that solidarity does not necessarily require that actors identify in similar ways or that they share uniform social positions, life experiences, or views of injustice. Understanding it in this way is in line with the conceptual shift associated with the transition from "second wave" to "third wave" feminism. In this transition, scholars and activists sought to move beyond solidarity as necessarily based on sameness or identity politics towards understanding how social difference and contrasting perspectives can function to shape various forms of organizing across borders.[16] I revisit these ideas in the final chapter of the book.

In summary, the ways in which grandmotherhood was perceived and mobilized differently in Canada and in South Africa led to certain rearrangements of power: the SLF's power to deploy the "grandmother narrative" was redeployed by South African actors according to their own meanings and needs, thereby shaping the transnational relationships that were formed. In both contexts, the meanings and experiences attributed to "grandmother" were contingent on social history, political economy, and demographic change. This "friction," alongside the beneficial impacts of the alliance on women's lives, suggests that transnational solidarity, while initially based on universalizing assumptions about grandmotherhood, was in fact propelled by social difference and did not depend on sameness or uniformity of perspective.

MULTIPLE APPROACHES TO SOLIDARITY-BUILDING

A second "zone of awkward engagement" emerged around the issue of whether Canadian grandmothers (or grandmothers' groups) should forge direct, unmediated relationships with African projects. The SLF did not encourage Canadian grandmothers to forge direct relationships with the projects it funds in sub-Saharan Africa. In fact, from the campaign's inception, it strongly discouraged Canadians from travelling to Africa to visit or volunteer with these groups. According to several SLF staff, such relationships undermined the SLF's central message that African groups do not need Canadians to "go over and help"; they risked burdening the groups, which might feel compelled to expend time and resources on managing volunteers; they could undermine autonomy and create conditionality, with project leaders making decisions in order to safeguard these relationships; and they raised questions about how inputs of resources are monitored and whether they can be sustained once individual volunteers are no longer available.[17] A number of Canadian grandmothers, however, held different views from those of the SLF and chose different approaches to engaging in this movement.

This area of "friction" was embodied in Rosemary's role at the HACT, as her approach clearly contrasted with the SLF's practices and ideology. Recognizing Rosemary as an important link between the Canadian movement and the Valley gogos, I examine her engagement further, prefacing this discussion with two points. First, while it might appear counter-intuitive to focus such attention on one grandmother, it is worth reiterating that Rosemary was the most direct, sustained, and intimate connection between the Canadian grandmothers and the Valley gogos between 2006 and 2010; it is also noteworthy that she was perceived at the HACT as the "face of Canadian granny solidarity" (according to Noku, 2010). Thus, her involvement in the Valley had both material and symbolic significance for understanding how the Canadian mobilization was perceived and how it played out in this part of South Africa. Second, this discussion inevitably takes on a more personal tone, requiring me to probe certain individuals' perceptions and actions rather than highlighting broader themes and perspectives. Yet, as Tsing notes, such individual interlocutors and their potentially contentious interactions are crucially important to understanding the complexities and possibilities of transnational linkages and to unpacking how power can operate across distance and difference.[18]

From Rosemary's perspective, then, she had built an ethical, caring, committed, and sustained relationship with Noku, the HACT, and the gogos, developing trust over the course of several years. For her, the experience of assisting Noku for a month or longer each year to build up the HACT's Grandmother Project was "life-changing," "heart-breaking," and "enlightening." She understood the contention between the SLF's approach and her own and thus, as her relationship with the HACT solidified (during her first visit in 2007), she distanced herself from the Canadian Campaign. As of 2007, she no longer fundraised for the SLF. However, she maintained close ties with grandmothers' groups, speaking regularly in Canadian venues and keeping a blog that was accessible to these groups. She explained that she felt comfortable straddling these positions, in part because of the gratitude she received in South Africa.

From the HACT's perspective, Rosemary was a cherished volunteer – what she did was described by several HACT staff as "sustained, on-the-ground solidarity." She helped build its Grandmother Project in ways that could not have been foreseen at the time of the Toronto Gathering. During her annual visits, she provided a rental car and access to cash to pay for gas, tea, food, materials, and events; at times, it was this support that made Noku's work with the gogos possible, especially prior to 2009, when there was very limited funding in place for the gogos.[19] Her presence was also a source of personal support to Noku and she worked with the HACT team to bring publicity to the Grandmother Project. Thus, her volunteering made a material difference in many people's lives, while bringing new meaning and experience to her own. Jennifer regularly referred to Rosemary as "a gem" and as "one of us."

Despite her distance from the SLF, she continued to be viewed by many at the HACT as closely connected to the Canadian Campaign for a number of reasons: her initial contact had been at the Toronto Gathering, she was a Canadian grandmother, and she regularly reinforced the discourse of "grandmotherhood" mobilized in Canada, drawing on its assumed universality in building connections with her "Zulu sisters." She was, from Noku's perspective, the face of the Canadian grandmothers and an embodiment of their solidarity. This perception makes it even more important to consider what her actions produced, consolidated, and re-signified both for the gogos and for Canadian solidarity efforts.

In further exploring this question, it is important to consider the complexities around how she raised and dispensed funds. Rosemary explained that most of the money she raised in Canada went directly towards supporting her work with the Valley gogos. The following excerpt from our June 2010 interview explains her approach in her own words:

I: How do you see yourself vis-à-vis the campaign? If I were to describe your relationship to the campaign, how would I describe it? Are you in fact part of a group here in Canada?
R: I guess I am a group of one ... I talk all over the place, in churches, schools. And I do promote SLF and Grandmothers to Grandmothers.
I: Are you raising money for the SLF?
R: Nope. Except that I do sell Little Travelers [beaded crafts from the HACT] to other groups at cost so that they can sell them for whatever they like and the money they raise goes to the SLF.
I: So you're not actually fundraising directly for the SLF at this point?
R: No. But I did, at the start, make some donations there.

I: Are you fundraising for Hillcrest?

R: ... For the [Canadian] grandmothers' groups, I speak without charging them anything and I sell them Little Travelers at cost. But anything that's not an SLF grandmother group, then I charge an honorarium, which I either give to Hillcrest, or I use it to offset me being at Hillcrest. Because being there, you know, it's on my own nickel, and when I'm there I buy food everyday, and I buy absolutely everything.[20]

I: Are you making donations to Hillcrest or do you simply have a pot of money to buy stuff like food for the grandmothers' groups?

R: Good question. Last year I did a talk, which was strictly a fundraiser for the hospice [HACT respite unit] ... The rest of the time ...

I: And that money got donated to Hillcrest, earmarked for the hospice?[21]

R: Ya. But the rest of the time the money goes into a bank account and then every day at Hillcrest I take my bank card, or you know, once a week, I'll just take my bank card and pull money out and use it for everything. Notebooks and pencils, or fabric, or food, and I feel very comfortable just being able to pull money out all the time, so whatever's needed, I just keep doing it.

Thus, for the most part, Rosemary fundraised in Canada to purchase materials directly for the gogos. In the Valley, this small pot of money was invaluable in supporting the growth and development of the Grandmother Project.

Yet, as one SLF staff member pointed out, this money was not being funnelled through an organization like the SLF, which has monitoring mechanisms in place to make sure funds are dispersed equitably, nor was most of it being donated directly to the HACT, so that the HACT could prioritize how and where to spend it. Instead, it remained under Rosemary's control, often requiring that she be physically present for it to be dispensed in the Valley. This kind of approach raised concerns among some SLF staff about how much influence someone in Rosemary's position might (inadvertently) end up having over the groups' activities and priorities and about what kind of power dynamic was being established in general, especially since these practices might be perceived as connected to the Canadian Campaign. Such concerns were never raised at the HACT but several SLF staff members and Canadian grandmothers in my research asked the following provocative questions: How much influence did Rosemary have, as a physical presence and dispenser of resources, in shaping the HACT's Grandmother Project? Could this form of involvement inadvertently undermine the autonomy of the HACT? Was this relationship creating an unsustainable dependency on one person? Was it reinforcing practices of conditionality, in which access to resources was tied to Rosemary's physical presence in the Valley? While it is possible that not all of the actors involved (especially in South Africa) were fully aware of these questions, they reveal important heterogeneities in vision and approach within the Canadian movement. In this case, Rosemary's practices stood in contrast to the Canadian Campaign's guiding philosophies; at the same time, her actions had undeniably positive impacts on the lives of many in South Africa, a goal ultimately shared by all Canadians engaged in this movement.

This example demonstrates some of the contradictions and intricate power dynamics embodied in this transnational network, further revealing how power can operate, often subtly, among various actors, and how organizations and networks are not homogeneous bodies but made up of individuals with contrasting knowledge, priorities, approaches, and positions. Rosemary's encounters with the HACT functioned to benefit the lives of many gogos, while simultaneously challenging some of the Canadian Campaign's goals. This disjuncture between certain ideals and practices involved in working in solidarity suggests that each contingent encounter must be examined and evaluated according to what it produces in practice. In this instance, Rosemary's contribution to improving lives and building a movement was significant, even as her approach raised provocative questions that need to be considered.[22]

AGING AND SUSTAINABILITY

The final area of complexity I wish to highlight is the issue of how to sustain mobilizations among aging populations.[23] As noted in previous chapters, challenges surrounding the sustainability of these mobilizations were mentioned repeatedly both in Canada and in South Africa, further revealing the contingency of this transnational network.

Part of this concern had to do with leadership: the importance of individual champions to these mobilizations and the fact that these champions were themselves aging. In Canada, Stephen Lewis was pivotal in drawing supporters into the campaign. Well into his seventies at the time of my research, he continued to work tirelessly as an AIDS advocate and as a public speaker. Many Canadian grandmothers worried about what would happen when he could no longer be the public face of the movement: some felt that a critical mass of leadership had developed across the country and would carry the campaign forward, but many wondered whether the campaign could be sustained without him.

Among most of the gogos in the Valley of 1000 Hills, Lewis was an unknown entity. For them, however, and for their recent mobilizations, it would be difficult to overstate the importance of Noku's leadership, enthusiasm, and skill.[24] Yet, in 2010, Noku was in her late sixties and quickly approaching mandatory retirement at the age of seventy. While efforts were in place to train younger assistants for the HACT Grandmother Project, and while Noku admitted that she was unlikely to stop working with the gogos once she retired, there remained pertinent questions about what would happen to the gogos' groups when they were no longer infused with her dedication, energy, and passion. Noku remarked, however, that, unlike the situation in Canada, many of these groups had existed prior to the Grandmother Project and thus there was some chance they would outlive her, perhaps eventually reconfiguring again, shifting, or changing form.

Concerns over sustainability were not limited to the issue of leadership: the general membership of these groups and networks was aging as well. In Canada, some efforts were in place to fortify the Canadian Campaign by bringing younger people on board, in part in reaction to the fact that some Canadian groups were becoming inactive after key members fell ill or died. This was reflected in a shift in the campaign's focus (in 2009 and 2010) from mobilizing around grandmotherhood to mobilizing around intergenerational solidarity, with prioritized activities increasingly including school outreach and intergenerational events.

In South Africa, meanwhile, the question of sustainability was more complex still, as the HIV/AIDS epidemic was itself transforming population demographics. This raised concerns over whether there would be an upcoming cohort of older women to take over as the next generation of caregivers and community organizers. With mortality rates among women in their twenties through forties increasing each year, an important question in the South African context was what will happen when today's grandmothers die. In addition, the gogos perceived a shift in priorities among young women in their families, suggesting that, even among those who were alive and well, there was not the same level of commitment to caregiving as in previous generations.[25] Like the Canadian grandmothers, the gogos were acutely aware of the challenges posed by their aging: many worried about what would happen in their families when they died, and some felt that their groups provided a safety net for the children in their care.

Understanding these grandmothers' mobilizations and linkages in terms of the future requires grappling with the additional complexity of aging. My research revealed certain challenges associated with sustainability both in Canada and in South Africa, while also reinforcing the important ways these complexities are emplaced in particular contexts.

SUMMARY AND CONCLUSIONS

This discussion has revealed how "friction" within a transnational network can lead to new and unpredicted arrangements of power, as was evident in the way the Canadian-branded discourse of grandmotherhood was actively redeployed in the Valley of 1000 Hills. Power was not an all-encompassing or unidirectional force exerted by the SLF on the HACT or the gogos, and neither was knowledge imposed in any straightforward way. Rather, within this network, power circulated and discourses were critically negotiated within complex and contingent relationships. This power was enacted not only as control over resources but also as discursive influence and emotional labour.

The "zones of awkward engagement" examined in this chapter depicted global connections as playing out in unexpected ways, with the potential to benefit some actors while simultaneously undermining the efforts of others, as was the case with Rosemary's volunteer work. This suggests that such encounters should be assessed according to what they produce in practice rather than according to the assumptions or ideals of any one group of actors.[26] The connections that make up this network also appeared to be forged as a series of contingent encounters, conditioned by particular histories, geographies, and individual personalities, indicating that this transnational alliance needs to be understood according to the context(s) in which it arose and operated, not as a uniform body but as comprised of different actors with contrasting perspectives, social locations, and approaches.

The challenge of sustaining mobilizations among aging women was also raised as a concern by grandmothers in both Canada and South Africa. This is particularly worrying in South Africa, where the gogos are pillars of support for their families and communities, and where it is as yet unknown whether, in the context of HIV/AIDS, there will be a next cohort of grandmothers to take over as caregivers and community organizers.

KwaNyuswa, South Africa
September 2008

On a crisp Tuesday morning, Noku, Mbhali, and I drove slowly up the unpaved driveway to the one-room building – the local pastor's rondavel – where the KwaNyuswa group met. We were arriving later than usual, expecting to find the gogos well into their opening prayers. But, when we arrived, the gogos were not praying; they were milling about in anticipation of our arrival.

"We have something to show you," I picked out from the flood of isiZulu greetings. Then we were off, making our way along the meandering footpaths, up the brown, grass-covered hills. As we travelled further from the pastor's house, the footpaths grew narrower and steeper, and the condition of the cement houses and cabbage gardens deteriorated. Up we climbed, arriving at our destination fifteen minutes later: a large stack of bricks perched on the hillside, next to a small house made of mud and stone.

Out of breath, one gogo started to sing. Her melody spread as each woman, in turn, joined in. Louder and louder, they repeated in rounds, "We thank you, Jesus, Amen," harmonizing in an uplifting soundscape of togetherness.

When they stopped, Lungile, one of the gogos, spoke quietly in isiZulu: "This is my house you see here. It is falling down. When it rains, the rain comes in. There is a hole in the roof there and one in the wall ... And there is no security here." Lungile continued, "It is just me and my two daughters, who are both sick, so it is scary sometimes to sleep here at night." As she spoke, she exuded dignity and pain. "How can I look after my daughters here?"

Two gogos began singing again, quietly. Lungile waited patiently for them to finish. "We wanted you to see these bricks," she said. "We started a few months ago, each of us taking some money from our pensions and putting them together in a savings. We plan to use this to re-build our houses."

"Mama Lungile will be the first," another gogo offered, "because she is the most in need. But we will continue to do this until we can all have proper houses. This is the first load of bricks we could buy with our new scheme. We wanted you to see."

Applause followed and the singing started again. Noku threw her arms around Lungile and energetically joined in the group's prayer. As we started back down the path in a musical procession, Noku spoke softly. "I am shocked and delighted," she told me. "I had no idea they were doing this. These groups are spreading now, and they are also taking ownership ... They are going to transform their communities."

This scene and the stack of bricks perched on Lungile's property were etched in my mind that morning: amidst undeniable trauma and devastation, this was one of the greatest moments I witnessed in my research. It revealed the power of hope and the politics of possibility.[1]

Ottawa, Canada
May 2011

A lump formed in my throat as I read Kelly's email. For five years, Kelly and Jane had co-chaired one of Ottawa's oldest grandmothers' groups – a group of women I admired deeply and with whom I had become quite close. A vibrant leader and, for most of the time I knew her, a picture of health, Jane had returned from a camping trip in July 2010, at the age of sixty-three, with some unusual aches and pains. She was diagnosed shortly thereafter with an aggressive form of cancer and the deterioration was rapid. Less than one year later, she died.

As I re-read Kelly's email, I fluctuated between sadness and disbelief. I pictured Jane in action, working tirelessly alongside the other members of her group to fundraise and advocate for African grandmothers. I remembered the time her group invited me to speak at one of their first meetings, a potluck dinner in 2006, and how Jane, who had just been selected to attend the upcoming Toronto Gathering, took copious notes and challenged me with her questions. I pictured sitting in her home a year later, admiring the ease with which she billeted, and connected with, an SLF-led delegation of African grandmothers. I thought of her lifting boxes at garage sales and sound equipment at benefit concerts, of her calm, efficient way of facilitating meetings, and of the strength, caring, dedication, and persistence she brought to the campaign, even through some extremely difficult periods in her own life.

I stared out my window, thinking now of the many times – the too many times – I had received similar news from South Africa: news of losing friends, associates, and colleagues. I felt paralyzed, once more, with grief. It was all so unreal, so unexpected. I had not anticipated mourning in this context. These Canadian grandmothers were, after all, young by Canadian standards, well educated, health-conscious, and living in well-resourced communities with access to top-quality medical care.

Yet, underlying my sadness I felt a small sense of hope – hope tinged with a growing conviction that I had not sufficiently acknowledged one of the most unexpected and inspiring outcomes of the Canadian Campaign: the way it built new forms of community in Canada. The depth of the connections generated by the campaign was unveiled to me in this tragic moment. I had witnessed this group rally around Jane throughout her illness, supporting her and her family, providing meals, and driving her to medical appointments; and now I learned that it was Kelly who had shared her final moments with her in her home when she passed away. These women had not known each other when they started their group five years earlier, and neither had joined the campaign in search of personal support. They had joined in order to make a difference in the lives of African grandmothers. In so doing, they had also made an enormous difference – one that should not be overlooked – in their own lives and communities.

What I witnessed during Jane's illness mirrored what I had observed throughout my years of research: the ways in which this alliance generated, in unexpected and often unintended ways, new spaces of social and material support in South Africa and Canada. While documenting the campaign's effects in Canada was never my primary objective, I cannot readily dismiss the profound changes. Like the scene at Lungile's home in 2008, what I witnessed in Canada was yet another reminder of the possibility for older women to generate change by organizing and joining forces. This final chapter focuses on this third, and perhaps most salient, theme: possibility.

POSSIBILITY FOR CHANGE

My focus on "friction" and contingency stems from a belief that it is from within the "messiness" of lives lived in specific times and places that openings – or the possibility – for change can occur. As Gibson-Graham explains, any norm can be destabilized and social change can ensue as a result of people's daily actions. This "politics of possibility"[2] underpinned one of the book's central questions, which, in drawing this story to a close, I revisit one final time: what was being produced, consolidated, or re-signified through grandmothers' mobilizations – in the Valley of 1000 Hills, in Canada, and through their interlinking – and what were the consequences for the various women's lives and social practices?

Reconfiguring Lives, Communities, and Places

The mobilizations documented in my research undoubtedly had profound effects on the lives of the women involved. They generated new forms of community, positioned older women as development experts and social justice actors, and provided deep personal and interpersonal meaning and fulfillment during times of life transition and stress.

In the Valley, the Canadian Campaign positioned the HACT nurses as international interlocutors, experts, and producers of knowledge, while also naming older women as "gogos" and thereby connecting them to a powerful network of support, resources, and ideas. The associated influx of resources, validation, and knowledge created new and renewed forms of support for thousands of people. Indeed, while some gogos' groups were new and others were reconfigured forms of older associations, all benefitted from their connections to the HACT nurses (and, given the nurses' Canadian affiliations, from the Canadian Campaign). It cannot be overemphasized that the support provided by these groups (and by Noku) was a lifeline for hundreds of vulnerable families. In some instances, I also witnessed "spin-off" effects: the initiative described at the start of this chapter, where group members in KwaNyuswa were pooling their pensions to re-build houses for members most in need, is just one example. These outcomes clearly reveal the possibility for solidarity and aid to generate life-changing support and widespread change, with relatively few resources, by drawing on the emotional labour and organizing know-how of older women.[3]

In Canada, the campaign grew from a handful of disparate groups into an extensive and sophisticated network. It generated invaluable new forms of community and support for many aging women. It also mobilized thousands of Canadian women (predominantly grandmothers at the pivotal "retirement" point in their lives) as social justice actors, and it did so, in part, by generating alternative and meaningful ways for them to engage in international issues. Furthermore, the movement has had an important (though difficult to measure) impact in Canada more widely: in its early years, it garnered extensive media attention and thereby significantly raised public awareness about the gendered and generational implications of the HIV/AIDS epidemic in southern Africa. More recently, Canadian grandmothers have advocated for policy changes (e.g., to amend Canada's Access to Medicines Regime). While these changes have yet to be achieved, the public and media presence of these grandmothers has again served to educate Canadians – this time about how their own government has participated in the production of global health inequalities.

Much of the life-changing reconfiguration that took place, in both South Africa and Canada, was a result of localized mobilizations – a facet of the support and energy derived as women gathered together in their own ways and of their own accord. These small groups formed (or were renewed) in an effort to build solidarity across distance and difference (in the case of Canada) or as an indirect effect of key translocal and transnational inputs (in the case of the Valley). The ability of this transnational network to alter lives, places, and relations lies in both the power of localized associations and the influence of particular encounters between African and Canadian grandmothers.

Re-conceptualizing Spaces of Old Age

In addition to this reconfiguration, these grandmothers' mobilizations also destabilized a number of broader narratives, assumptions, and representations. Most obviously, they challenged existing narratives of older women as disengaged, apolitical, passive, victimized, frail, and/or a drain on their families and communities.[4]

The contributions of these grandmothers were numerous and impressive: the grandmothers were, among other activities, raising children, building houses, and challenging policies. As well, through their mobilizations, they were extending their associational spaces beyond the more conventional (and still vital) kitchen table meetings, church groups, and beading circles to include large international meetings, political demonstrations, and government proceedings. I observed older women acting as keynote speakers, organizing international marches, lobbying politicians, and standing together against the stigma of AIDS.

The fact that this transnational mobilization produced thousands of African and Canadian grandmothers as development experts and social justice actors, and as integral to global AIDS response, strengthens calls for an immediate re-conceptualization of what are sometimes considered "spaces of old age" or assumptions that aging is necessarily associated with marginalization or disengagement.[5] This re-conception requires shifting the existing lens from its focus on the *challenges* associated with aging to recognizing the the many *contributions* older women are making to their communities and societies.

Re-framing Global Connections

This transnational alliance also challenged certain assumptions about global connections and global AIDS response, contributing to a growing body of scholarship that refutes narratives of development and globalization as all-consuming, imposed, homogenizing, placeless, or predictable forces.[6] The SLF, for instance, sought to challenge certain norms around international engagement in the Global South. Its approach to supporting African organizations contrasted with assumptions that international donors are a homogeneous group that necessarily acts out of economic self-interest and is likely to co-opt organizations by placing economic or ideological conditions on their funding.[7] Without discounting the many ways the SLF exerted power (from influence over discourses and representations to control over resources), it is important to note that, between 2006 and 2010, its philosophies and practices actively resisted victimizing, patronizing, and colonial discourses. Indeed, the SLF regularly positioned African and Canadian grandmothers as experts in global AIDS response, thereby shifting ideas about who should be deemed development experts and global actors. The SLF also attempted to remain responsive and project-driven, and to place minimal conditions on, or obstacles around, its funding. This supports Gibson-Graham's assertion that donor-recipient relationships must be analyzed as contingent upon specific personal, institutional, historical, and economic contexts, and according to what they produce in practice.[8]

The complex way power operated within these transnational relationships further destabilized narratives of globalization and development as totalizing forces.[9] While the SLF exerted both material and discursive power in the Valley, this power was not all-encompassing: this was made clear when South African actors actively remobilized powerful Canadian discourses to channel context-appropriate support to those most in need in their communities. This finding also contests the idea that discourses, meanings, and knowledge "flow" within global systems and that these "converge" towards some universal aspiration or understanding.[10] Rather, in this network, meanings and discourses were negotiated and deployed in complex, sophisticated, and contingent ways by all actors and in all encounters.

Shifting Ideas about Solidarity

Finally, the way in which this transnational alliance formed and operated – with its heterogeneous perspective and approach – challenged lingering assumptions that solidarity requires those involved to share a uniform position, way of identifying, social location, or perception of injustice.[11] Resonating with the "second wave" feminist idea of "the sisterhood," the Canadian Campaign initially relied on the emotive idea of a universal experience of grandmotherhood or the bond of a shared identity as grandmothers. However, the gogos revealed very different experiences, meanings, and motivations guiding their mobilizations, suggesting that "gogo," while equally powerful as a discourse, must be understood within a particular social history and political-economic context.[12]

In seeking to better understand this alliance, then, it is important to move beyond identity politics to look at how the discourses that were mobilized reflected social and historical differences. "Friction," social difference, and contrasting perspectives, alongside common goals of improving lives, propelled this movement. This clearly supports a broader shift in thinking about solidarity that has taken place among many "third wave" feminist scholars; indeed, it is line with feminist scholars who probe the social differences and intersectional workings of power that inform how and why people organize.[13]

FINAL REFLECTIONS

Alongside moments of deep trauma, sorrow, struggle, and grief, this story is one of remarkable hope – about the power of older women to alter their own lives through their collective actions and about the ability of transnational solidarity to effect positive social change. Across two continents and immense social difference, this global alliance was driven, in part, by strong leadership, institutional support, emotional energy, and material resources. Yet, equally, and indeed most significantly, it was also propelled by the ways in which key people – many of them older women – from opposite sides of the world strategically mobilized "grandmotherhood" as a discursive category.

This book explored this discursive mobilization in detail. In doing so it revealed that, despite universalizing Canadian narratives of "grandmother to grandmother solidarity," the immense emotional power of "grandmotherhood" as a rallying discourse did not lie in shared social positions or unified understandings of what it means to be a grandmother, nor did it rest on identical perspectives on how AIDS has affected family life and older women in southern African communities. Rather, multiple and contrasting meanings were attributed to grandmotherhood, contingent on time and place, and conditioned by major social, political-economic, demographic, and historical shifts; these played out in localized ways in Canada and South Africa. In Canada, for instance, the growth of the Grandmothers Campaign and the strong resonance of the associated "grandmother narrative" clearly reflected, among other factors, changes that had taken place in the latter half of the twentieth century in gender roles, family life, and women's rights (as a result, largely, of North American feminist movements) and in demography (with the aging population). In South Africa, the power of "gogo" highlighted both continuity and change in gender and generational roles, with increases in pension access, female migrancy, and middle generation attrition (resulting from democratic transition, violence, urbanization, and the AIDS epidemic) all influencing contemporary meanings associated with "gogo."

Driven by such contingency and by the areas of "friction" noted throughout, these grandmothers' associations nevertheless generated profound changes – altering the lives, spaces, and relations of the women involved in both Canada and South Africa. An important conclusion that emerges, then, is that within this kind of transnational alliance, it is unnecessary (and perhaps impossible) to attain some unified perspective (or a single approach) in order to generate significant material and discursive change. In other words, in this instance, exploring the differing ways grandmotherhood was understood, lived, and mobilized in each place revealed that the multiple actors in this network did not need to share matching logics, perspectives, motivations, or discourses in order to achieve their collective goals: their solidarity did not depend on unified understandings or fixed ways of identifying.[14]

This remarkable story of strength, struggle, and contribution calls into question stereotypes about older women's passivity, disengagement, frailty, and marginality. It disrupts simplistic ideas about global AIDS response, and development and globalization more broadly, as forces that are supposedly imposed mechanistically by large international actors on communities in the Global South. It also contests lingering assumptions that solidarity requires uniform perspectives and social positions. The story of the Canadian Grandmothers Campaign and its linkages in the Valley of 1000 Hills has important implications, then, which extend well beyond Canada and South Africa, working to nuance and expand existing conceptualizations of old age, global connections, and solidarity. It reveals the possibility for older women's everyday actions and encounters to change lives, reconfigure norms, and, in so doing, create hopeful futures for generations to come.

NOTES

....

PREAMBLE

1 Note that I use pseudonyms to identify all of the participants in my research, including my colleagues and research assistants. The only exceptions are certain high-profile people, such as Stephen Lewis and his daughter, Ilana Landsberg-Lewis, whose identities are important for understanding why and how the mobilization I document in the book unfolded the way it did. I discuss this further in chapter 1.

2 In doing this, I draw on a number of scholarly methodological ideas, which have informed my approach to both research and writing. For excellent works on engaged, feminist, participatory, anti-oppressive, and indigenous methodologies, and on the democratization of knowledge production more broadly, see Brown and Strega, *Research as Resistance*; Cooke and Kothari, *Participation: The New Tyranny?*; Hickey and Mohan, *Participation: From Tyranny to Transformation?*; Kobayashi, "Negotiating the Personal and the Political"; Maguire, "Feminist Participatory Research"; Ruddick, "Activist Geographies"; and Tuhiwai Smith, *Decolonizing Methodologies*. For insights into the emotional dimensions of community-engaged research, feminist ethics, and ethics of care, see Carmalt and Faubion, "Normative Approaches"; McEwan and Goodman, "Place Geography"; and Meth, "Violent Research." For scholarly conversations relating to the need for critical reflexivity around researchers' shifting roles and positions, see Ruth Butler, "From Where I Write"; Mohammad, "'Insiders' and/or 'Outsiders'"; and Rose, "Situating Knowledges." For those around the production of knowledge as situated within social, economic, political, and personal contexts, see Haraway, "Situated Knowledges." Finally, for further insights into grounded approaches to analysis and the idea of basing theoretical production on women's particular lives and experiences, see Abu-Lughod, *Writing Women's Worlds*; Crang, "Filed Work"; and Scott, "Experience."

3 This is not to discount the value of formal guidelines for ethical research practice. This research underwent ethics reviews through Carleton University in 2006, 2008, 2009, and 2010.

4 In Canada, my work was not initiated by the SLF or the Grandmothers Campaign but by me. Because the SLF is a powerful donor organization in southern Africa, as well as a powerful organizing body for the Grandmothers to Grandmothers

Campaign in Canada, I felt it was important to keep my research at arm's length; as such, I never sought to partner with the SLF in the way that I did with the HACT. However, in line with my guiding philosophies, I solicited regular feedback from the SLF and shared findings through presentations, reports, and articles.

5 This research was funded by the Social Sciences and Humanities Research Council of Canada, the Pierre Elliott Trudeau Foundation, HEARD, and Carleton University.

CHAPTER ONE

1 See www.hillaids.org.za.

2 I am drawing, in this instance, on the four official racial categories defined by the apartheid regime: "African" (or "black"), "Indian," "coloured," and "white." While I recognize that it is deeply problematic to reiterate such language, that the meanings of such racial terms have been fluid and contested, and that the very concept of race is socially constructed and not ontologically stable, these categories are still widely used in South Africa today, including among the women in my research. They remain salient for understanding (and redressing) historical inequalities and the ways in which these inequalities linger in material and symbolic ways in contemporary South Africa, despite the fact that, after 1994, the post-apartheid constitution adopted a language of non-racialism (Hunter, *Love in the Time of AIDS*).

3 Demographic, health, and economic statistics for the area produced by eThekwini (Durban) Municipality tend to be skewed, as they group affluent and impoverished communities into common wards, creating average household incomes, literacy levels, and so on for each ward. On this basis, between sixty-one and sixty-eight percent of households in the Valley are estimated to live on less than R400 (C$70) per month, and unemployment levels are estimated at approximately 45.5 percent (KwaZulu-Natal Department of Economic Development, "KwaZulu-Natal Economic Overview"). The South African census data, however, clearly depict stark inequalities, and particularly the racialization of these inequalities, or what Hunter (*Love in the Time of AIDS*) calls the "racial structuring of households". Here it emerges that, nationally, unemployment, broadly defined, is at 4.6 percent among "whites" and 42.5 percent among "Africans" (Statistics South Africa, *Census 2001*, 57–9). The best estimates for HIV prevalence in the Valley are aggregated by province from antenatal clinic data, which indicate that approximately 39.6 percent of women attending these clinics in KwaZulu-Natal are HIV-positive (Department of Health, "National Antenatal Sentinel").

4 Analyses of caregiving for children and the roles of grandmothers in the context of AIDS in South and sub-Saharan Africa have proliferated in the past decade. For examples specific to South Africa, see Bohman et al., "We Clean Our Houses"; Campbell et al., "Supporting People with AIDS"; Casale, "I Am Living a Peaceful Life"; Freeman and Nkomo, "Guardianship of Orphans"; Hosegood and Timaeus, "Impact of Adult Mortality"; Ogunmefun, Gilbert, and Schatz, "Older Female Care-

givers"; Ogunmefun and Schatz, "Caregivers' Sacrifices"; and Schatz and Ogunmefun, "Caring and Contributing." For comparative examples that extend beyond South Africa, see Kuo and Operario, "Caring for AIDS-Orphaned Children," and Monasch and Boerma, "Orphanhood and Childcare Patterns."

5 See www.stephenlewisfoundation.org. Also, I would like to interject a note on identifiers. Although all of my participants consented to be identified by name, after extensive consultations I have chosen to maintain the privacy, as much as possible, of those involved. I use pseudonyms when telling the stories of particular grandmothers (e.g., "Ntombi," whose story is told at the opening of this chapter, is a pseudonym) and when referring to staff members from the Hillcrest AIDS Centre and the Stephen Lewis Foundation. Where Hillcrest Centre and SLF staff are concerned, I recognize that the identities of these actors are available in the public domain; nevertheless, it was felt that the use of pseudonyms remains appropriate and does confer some level of privacy. I also use pseudonyms to refer to my RA's, including "S'fiso," whom I discuss in the preamble. In assigning pseudonyms, I use only first names, in line with twenty-first–century North American norms of familiarity and to avoid implying some arbitrary distance or formality between researcher and researched in a context where personal relationships were central to carrying out this work. The only two actors in my research to whom I refer by their real names (and most often only by their surnames) are Stephen Lewis and Ilana Landsberg-Lewis; my rationale here is that understanding the positions of these well-known and powerful international interlocutors is important to the analysis I undertake.

6 For the complete Toronto Statement, see http://www.grandmotherscampaign.org/wp-content/uploads/2012/03/Toronto_statement.pdf

7 I discuss the mobilizations of "grandmothers," both in the Valley of 1000 Hills and in Canada, throughout the book, despite the fact that it is not only "grandmothers" who are involved in these efforts. This is not meant to subsume all those involved within the category of "grandmother," nor is it intended to discount the important roles of "non-grandmothers." I draw on this language to avoid cumbersome modifiers, recognizing that it is the language used most frequently by the SLF and the HACT and that most participants in my research were in fact grandmothers, defined in biological terms as women whose offspring had offspring. Among those who were not biological grandmothers, many identified with a social grandmothering position, based on their own sense of being an elder within their community and their feelings of responsibility for future generations of children.

8 I use "Grandmothers Campaign," "Canadian Campaign," and "campaign" in the book as interchangeable short-forms for "Grandmothers to Grandmothers Campaign."

9 Joint United Nations Programme on HIV/AIDS (UNAIDS), *Global Report*.

10 HelpAge International, *Older Women*.

11 A number of international declarations have committed governments to addressing the needs of older people in high-prevalence communities: the UN Declara-

tion of Commitment on HIV/AIDS (2001), the Madrid International Plan of Action on Ageing (2002), and the Valetta Declaration (2005). Yet it was not until 2006 – following the Grandmothers' Gathering in Toronto – that the "plight of Africa's grandmothers" and their "heroic struggles" became more widely evident to international audiences.

12 As noted earlier, it is evident that older women are playing important caregiving roles in the context of HIV/AIDS (e.g., Bicego, Rutstein, and Johnson, "Dimensions of the Emerging Orphan Crisis"; Bohman et al., "We Clean Our Houses"; Campbell et al., "Supporting People with AIDS"; Casale, "I Am living a Peaceful Life"; Freeman and Nkomo, "Guardianship of Orphans"; HelpAge International, *Older Women*; Hosegood and Timaeus, "The Impact of Adult Mortality"; Kuo and Operario, "Caring for AIDS-Orphaned Children"; Monasch and Boerma, "Orphanhood and Childcare Patterns"; and Schatz and Ogunmefun, "Caring and Contributing"). Collectively, this literature indicates that caring for vulnerable children in the region is placing profound financial, physical, and psychological strains on caregivers – the majority of whom are aging women – but that these women are also tremendously strong and their family caregiving arrangements are fluid. Less research emphasis has, however, been placed on understanding grandmother caregivers' collective responses, sources of support, complex lived experiences, and diverse family situations. Moreover, excellent ethnographic studies now provide nuanced analyses of sexualities, gendered vulnerabilities, perceptions of AIDS, and experiences of migrancy, inequality, unemployment, stigma, and changing household dynamics, among other issues (e.g., Campbell, "Migrancy, Masculine Identities, and AIDS"; Elder, *Hostels, Sexuality, and the Apartheid Legacy;* Fassin, "The Embodiment of Inequality"; Hunter, *Love in the Time of AIDS*; Leclerc-Madlala, Simbayi, and Cloete, "Sociocultural Aspects"; Robins, "'Brothers Are Doing It for Themselves'"; Robins, "From 'Rights' to 'Ritual'"; Robins, "Long Live Zackie"; Schoepf, "Structure, Agency, and Risk"; Susser, *AIDS, Sex, and Culture*; Thornton, *Unimagined Community*; and Young and Ansell, "Fluid Households"). Yet, among these other AIDS ethnographies, this book is unique in its focus on the gogos.

13 For a recent analysis and critique of global financial commitments to AIDS response, see amfAR and AVAC, *Action Agenda to End AIDS.*

14 United Nations, *World Population Ageing 2007.*

15 See, for example, Bandy and Smith, *Coalitions Across Borders*; Dufour, Masson, and Caouette, *Solidarities Beyond Borders*; Guidry, Kennedy, and Zald, *Globalization and Social Movements*; and Tripp, "Evolution of Transnational Feminisms."

16 I have explored "vulnerabilities" to HIV/AIDS in Chazan and Whiteside, "The Making of Vulnerabilities."

17 Recent efforts to reveal older women's contributions to working for social change include, among others, Hepworth, *Old Age and Agency*; Kutz-Flamenbaum, "Code Pink"; Narushima, "A Gaggle of Raging Grannies"; Roy, *The Raging Grannies*; Dana Sawchuk, "Peace Profile"; and Dana Sawchuk, "The Raging Grannies." While the term "older" in research and policy circles often refers to those over the age of sixty

or sixty-five, in this book I do not use such age categories; rather, the women I write about self-identified as "older," "elders," "grandmothers," or "gogos." In taking this approach, I recognize that age and life-course categories are context-specific and that women can be considered elders and can become grandmothers long before the age of sixty. See African feminist scholar Oyewumi, *The Invention of Women*, for an important critique of Western age and gender categories.

18 Frank, "AIDS Ethnography," 143.

19 See, for example, Mahmood, *Politics of Piety*, for a critical overview of this work.

20 See, for example, Abu-Lughod, *Veiled Sentiments*, and Wikan, *Behind the Veil*.

21 This scholarship avoided framing women as powerless in the face of structural oppressions, and it often moved beyond the structure-agency binary to unveil women's capacity to act even in the most restrictive conditions. In line with this theoretical thrust, and of interest in the context of this research, is the analogy put forward by Ogundipe-Leslie, *Recreating Ourselves*, and later discussed by Gqola, "Ufanele Uqavile," of African women as metaphorically carrying six mountains on their backs: "The six mountains on our backs ... represent the meanings emanating from our location in Africa with the accompanying history of interlocking oppressions in the burdens we carry. However, because these are on our backs ... we are able to move with them. This analogy is mindful of the nexi of power relations at play in Blackwomen's lives whilst acknowledging the agency with which we engage them" (12). The conceptualization of agency that I draw upon in this book extends from this idea that, even within structural constraint, people always continue to act; understanding agency, as I consider it (and as I discuss throughout this chapter), means not simply looking for evidence of women's actions but rather recognizing the possibility for their repeated daily actions to change norms.

22 Mahmood, *Politics of Piety*.

23 Boddy, *Wombs and Alien Spirits*.

24 It is worth clarifying what I mean by "the feminist political project." I recognize that there is no universal experience of gender subordination or male dominance (or, as Abu-Lughod writes in her preface to *Writing Women's Worlds*, that patriarchy is neither simply nor singularly expressed). However, I also concur with South African feminist scholar and activist Amina Mama that using the term "feminist" implies some motivation to redress gender injustices and transform gender relations. In a similar argument to that of Mahmood (*Politics of Piety*), Mama (in Salo, "Interview with Amina Mama," 61) warns of the mistake of assuming that all women's "mobilizations" are informed by feminist politics. She cites instances in which women were mobilized or took to the streets to support agendas that were not in any way about resisting oppression or transforming oppressive power relations.

25 I would like to add two additional points of context here. First, I am drawing on critiques offered by Mohanty, "Under Western Eyes," among others, who, in the 1990s, drew attention to how scholars and development practitioners in the Global North tended to homogenize "Third World women" in a strategy that not only disregarded and misrepresented the diversity among women across the Global

South but also justified understanding them as a singular category of people to whom modernizing interventions could be directed. For similarly influential critiques around the oversights of Western/Northern feminism in Africa, see Amadiume, *Male Daughters, Female Husbands*, and Oyewumi, *The Invention of Women*. Second, I would like to draw attention to important critiques of many feminists from the Global North, particularly prior to the late 1980s, that deal with their dominance in setting international feminist agendas, their overarching tendency to assume that there existed (or could exist) a universal feminist project, and their widespread assumption that feminist politics began in the North and spread to the Global South, when in fact there was often parallel, region-specific, feminist activity taking place (Tripp, "The Evolution of Transnational Feminisms"). Practices shifted in the 1990s to acknowledge multiple feminisms and the plurality of women's struggles for emancipation. See Desirée Lewis, "Introduction," for example, for a discussion of the diversity of feminist perspectives subsumed under "African feminisms."

26 Abu-Lughod, "The Romance of Resistance," 43.
27 Ibid., 53.
28 Mahmood, *Politics of Piety*, 9.
29 Ibid., 16.
30 For example, Judith Butler, "Contingent Foundations"; *Gender Trouble*; and *(Un)doing Gender*.
31 Judith Butler, *Gender Trouble*, xxiv.
32 For other critical ethnographies of social mobilization, see Hilhorst, *The Real World of NGOs*; Rutherford, "Desired Publics"; Tsing, *Friction*; and Watts, "Antinomies of Community."
33 Cooper, "The Politics of Difference."
34 Bernstein, "Celebration and Suppression."
35 Judith Butler, *Gender Trouble* and *(Un)Doing Gender*.
36 Mahmood, *Politics of Piety*.
37 Scheper-Hughes, *Death without Weeping*, 341.
38 Desirée Lewis, "Introduction," 6.
39 Backhouse and Flaherty, *Challenging Times*.
40 I choose my words carefully in this discussion. Like Kim Sawchuk, "Feminism in Waves," I would argue that the very metaphor of feminist "waves" – and the embedded assumptions that struggles for gender equality in the Global North have taken place in distinct and bounded periods of activity, with peaks of activity followed by decades of near-inactivity, and with certain people, ideologies, concepts, objectives, and ways of organizing neatly categorized within each period – is likely overly simplistic. While I see this metaphor as useful in terms of representing major shifts that have taken place in feminist thinking (and thus I draw on this language as a shorthand for these shifts), I remain critical of the stability and boundedness of these categories. In other words, I recognize that gender struggles were likely ongoing, if perhaps less prominent, even during the apparent ebb

times, and that the concepts and ideologies attached to each "wave" were probably present, albeit less clearly articulated, in the discourses of previous generations of feminists. In addition, the "waves," as they are most often invoked, tend to portray a North-centric version of feminist history. In response to this, Tripp, "The Evolution of Transnational Feminisms," offers an excellent framework for re-imagining the "waves" from a transnational perspective, suggesting that scholars in the "West" often define "the global movement with respect to the first and second waves of feminism in the West as though these phases occurred universally and as though Western movements were the precursors to similar movements in other parts of the world." She also explains that, "[l]ooking through the prism of the history of transnational feminism, instead one sees national and local trajectories always featured significantly, creating regional waves of feminism with their own dynamics and pace that did not necessarily correspond to feminist trends" (692). Her framework and critique are especially salient given my examination of women's transnational mobilizations.

41 For example, Collins, *Black Feminist Thought*; Crenshaw, "Mapping the Margins"; McClintock, *Imperial Leather*; Mohanty, "Under Western Eyes"; Mohanty, "'Under Western Eyes' Revisited"; and Oyewumi, *The Invention of Women*.

42 While much feminist scholarship now elicits the ways in which gender, class, race, sexuality, and geography intersect to condition women's mobilizations, age has not been widely incorporated as an intersecting axis of difference in this work. An important exception here is the intervention by Oyewumi, *The Invention of Women*, who argued that Western categories around gender are often inappropriate to African contexts, in part because they ignore other key positions, such as seniority. This book helps to address such limitations by specifically attending to the dynamics of older women's mobilizations, recognizing age and life course as crucial dimensions of intersectional analysis.

43 For example, Judith Butler, *Gender Trouble*.

44 As articulated by Salo, "Interview"; Tripp, "The Evolution of Transnational Feminisms"; and many others.

45 I draw from Mohanty, *Feminism without Borders*, to consider explicitly how difference and diversity are central values that must be respected in building (and in analyzing) alliances. Like Featherstone (in *Solidarity*), I define solidarity as relations or collectivities forged through struggles that seek to challenge forms of oppression, leaving open that these relations are often forged across considerable social difference and can be approached and understood differently among the different actors involved. This shift to understanding how differences in position and perspective shape solidarities has emerged as an important theme among scholars theorizing solidarity, alliances, and coalition movements both within feminist scholarship and elsewhere. See, for example, Bilge, "Developing Intersectional Solidarities"; Brown and Yaffe, "Practices of Solidarity"; Davis, *Alliances*; Pratt, "Collaborating across Our Differences"; Steans, "Negotiating the Politics of Difference"; and Sundberg, "Reconfiguring North-South Solidarity." See also the

important series of papers compiled by Gouws, *(Un)thinking Citizenship,* for varied perspectives on South African feminist debates around identity politics and social difference in the context of the post-apartheid struggle for citizenship and gender rights.

46 It is worth making explicit here that "solidarity" as a discourse was deployed in Canada as central to the mobilization of the Grandmothers Campaign; for the most part, then, when I discuss "solidarity" throughout the book, I am referring to the transnational relations forged in connection with the Canadian Campaign and movement. In line with Mahmood, *Politics of Piety,* I would caution that "solidarity," like "resistance," can carry with it assumptions of a certain set of motivations or progressive politics. In order to avoid falsely ascribing such pre-determined motivations to women for whom these may not be meaningful, I try to refrain from assuming (or at least I seek to call into question) that the gogos perceived "solidarities" either within their localized groups or with the Canadian Campaign. Instead I probe what motivated their mobilizations and how they viewed their various relations in an attempt to understand their associations on their own terms. I also focus on what their mobilizations and linkages produced, consolidated, or re-signified – regardless of how they named them. Furthermore, I draw on Brown and Yaffe (in "Practices of Solidarity") to inform my thinking about "grandmother to grandmother solidarity" in three additional ways. First, like them, I contend that how solidarity is framed cannot be understood in isolation from how it is practiced and thus I focus on grounded acts of collective struggle, how these take place, and what effect they have. Second, while international solidarity is frequently presented as "asymmetrical flow[s] of assistance traveling from one place to another" (35), they consider these relations in terms of complex, entangled, and reciprocal flows; I likewise remain open to the possibility that the "solidarity" I document, while initially mobilized in Canada by Canadian actors as efforts to assist African grandmothers, might operate in more intricate and multi-directional ways. Third, like them, I examine whether the complex solidarities at play within the grandmothers' movement might generate new political possibilities and re-configure relationships between distant places (in this case Canada and South Africa), with social change happening in unexpected ways in more than one place simultaneously.

47 For example, Gibson-Graham, *A Postcapitalist Politics,* and Tsing, *Friction.*

48 These assumptions derive predominantly from postcolonial scholarship, which has illuminated the continuities between colonialism and contemporary practices and discourses associated with development and globalization (e.g., Cowen and Shenton, *Doctrines of Development*; Escobar, *Encountering Development*; and Ferguson, *Global Shadows*). These scholars point to the persistence of conditions placed on former colonies' access to development assistance and to the ways in which First World donors continue to represent Third World recipients as inferior, threatening, incapable, and underdeveloped. Many suggest that deep-rooted beliefs in trusteeship – a philosophy that it was the duty of colonial powers to instil

civilization and to protect the infantile "natives" in their colonies – continue to justify external control over foreign aid. They also argue that such conditionality has been reinforced by post–Cold War discourses of "economic globalization" as inevitable and unstoppable, and by a pervasive narrative of "the global" as some homogenizing and placeless force that implies not only interconnecting flows but also the existence of certain universal aspirations and desires (Gibson-Graham, *A Postcapitalist Politics;* Tsing, *Friction).* These critiques resonate with much of the thinking about "global AIDS response." Indeed, several initiatives have involved placing ideological conditions on funding to AIDS-related programming (see, for example, de Waal, *AIDS and Power,* for an account of conditions placed on PEPFAR funding). In addition, in many instances the "global" of "global AIDS response" falls within the same discursive assumptions associated with globalization – viewed as an abstract, homogeneous, and externally led mass of resources and ideas rather than as a series of particular encounters among diverse initiatives and people.

49 Gibson-Graham, *A Postcapitalist Politics.*
50 Mahmood, *Politics of Piety.*
51 Gibson-Graham, *A Postcapitalist Politics,* xx.
52 Tsing, *Friction.*
53 Gibson-Graham, *A Postcapitalist Politics.*
54 Judith Butler, *(Un)doing Gender.*
55 My focus on "possibility" and on "agency" is also not interchangeable with a focus on the popular concept of "empowerment." While I do consider the possibility that daily actions can consolidate or challenge norms, I believe the assumptions embedded in the language of "empowerment" are tangibly different and quite troubling. These assumptions include the idea that by changing individual attitudes, confidence, skill sets, and so on poor and historically disadvantaged women would somehow improve their own lots in life. The gogos are not lacking in confidence, work ethic, capacity, skills, or any other personal attributes. I do not think that, with the addition of small-scale, individualistic "women's empowerment" programs in the Valley, they would rise from their positions at the bottom of the global hierarchy, overcoming the historical and contemporary workings of white supremacy, patriarchy, and capitalism. I investigate their agency, asking whether and how it might be possible for their actions to destabilize certain routinized practices and social norms, yet I do not intend to portray some simplistic success story, and thus I avoid using the language of "empowerment," except in instances where I am quoting my informants.
56 Tsing, *Friction.*
57 For example, Cooper, "The Politics of Difference"; Gouws, *(Un)thinking Citizenship;* Desirée Lewis, "Introduction"; Mohanty, *Feminism without Borders;* and Oyewumi, *The Invention of Women.*
58 It is worth clarifying what I mean by "feminist ethnography of global connections." First, I view this as a "feminist" ethnography for several reasons. I align with feminist goals of bringing visibility to women who have often gone unrecognized – in

this case, older women as key participants in global AIDS response. Feminist scholarship also informs the book's central concepts of agency, mobilization, solidarity, difference, global connections, and so on. In addition, the research draws from feminist (critical, indigenous, and anti-oppressive) methodologies that pay attention to how power operates within all research relationships, situating knowledge within the socio-political contexts in which it is produced and basing research on an ethics of care rather than on the researcher's detachment from her research subjects (see, for example, Brown and Strega, *Research as Resistance*; Kirby, Greaves, and Reid, *Experience Research Social Change*; Kobayashi, "Negotiating the Personal and the Political"; Meth, "Violent Research"; Moss, *Feminist Geography in Practice*; and Tuhiwai Smith, *Decolonizing Methodologies*). Second, while what constitutes the changing nature of "ethnography" in an increasingly interconnected world has been the subject of much debate, I align with Tsing's analysis in *Friction*: I seek to move beyond abstract or universal notions of global interconnection by providing, in contrast, an *ethnographic* account of the "sticky engagements," actual encounters, and everyday lives, contingent on particular histories and geographies, that produce this instance of transnational alliance. See also Appadurai, "Grassroots Globalization," for a similar methodological discussion of what constitutes "ethnographies of global circulations," and Hart, "Geography and Development," for insights into "critical ethnographies."

59 Abu-Lughod, *Writing Women's Worlds*.

CHAPTER TWO

1 This is in line with engaged, feminist, participatory, anti-oppressive, and indigenous approaches to research, and with efforts to democratize knowledge production more broadly, as discussed in the book's preamble. See also Brown and Strega, *Research as Resistance*; Cooke and Kothari, *Participation: The New Tyranny?*; Hickey and Mohan, *Participation: From Tyranny to Transformation?*; Kobayashi, "Negotiating the Personal and the Political"; Maguire, "Feminist Participatory Research"; Ruddick, "Activist Geographies"; and Tuhiwai Smith, *Decolonizing Methodologies*.

2 See http://www.grandmotherscampaign.org/wp-content/uploads/2012/03/Toronto_statement.pdf, as cited in chapter 1.

3 I will refer to members of the Grandmothers Campaign interchangeably as "Campaign members" or "grandmothers." This is not to discount the invaluable contributions of the grandothers but merely to simplify language. Some of the participants in my research were not grandmothers, and thus when I cite them, I will cite them as "grandother" (with the month and year of the interview).

4 See www.grandmotherscampaign.org.

5 Of most relevance to this book are Pat, coordinator from 2006 to 2009, and Jill, coordinator from 2009 to 2011.

6 In 2011, the SLF initiated a split between the Grandmothers Campaign and NAC; NAC has since formed a vibrant, independent advocacy organization, called the

Grandmothers Advocacy Network (GRAN) (see http://www.grandmothers advocacy.org).

7   See http://hillaids.org.za/gogo_support_groups.

8   According to the HACT's 2008–2009 Annual Report, the SLF was its largest donor, accounting for approximately one-third (R1,068,887 or approximately C$140,000) of its total income in 2009. According to Jennifer, this funding was allocated to the home-based care project, which did not include funding for the gogos. Even in the absence of secured funding, however, the gogos' groups were benefitting from their connection to the HACT nurses in a number of ways. The nurses were accessing donated materials to start income-generation projects, setting up training sessions for the gogos, regularly bringing them food and tea, and providing vital counselling, education, and support. According to Jennifer, funding from the SLF increased in 2010: this included both additional funding allocated to the home-based and respite care project and an added R140,000 (or C$20,000) for the gogos.

9   Tsing, *Friction*.

10 Gibson-Graham, *A Postcapitalist Politics*.

11 One of the grambassadors later returned independently to volunteer at the HACT in the respite unit. She had minimal direct contact with the gogos' groups, however, so I have not included her here as a key encounter in the way I have with Rosemary and her relationship with the gogos.

CHAPTER THREE

1   Stephen Lewis, *Race Against Time*, 50.

2   Marais, *Buckling*.

3   See, for example, HelpAge International and International HIV/AIDS Alliance, *Forgotten Families*; Joint United Nations Programme on HIV/AIDS (UNAIDS), *Report on Global HIV/AIDS Epidemic*; Kakwani and Subbarao, *Ageing and Poverty*; World Health Organization, *Impact of AIDS*.

4   See www.stephenlewisfoundation.org/news_speeches for archived speeches.

5   Formerly leader of the Ontario New Democratic Party, Canadian ambassador to the UN, and deputy executive director of UNICEF, named Canadian of the Year by *Maclean's* magazine in 2003, listed by *Time* magazine as one of the one hundred most influential people in the world in 2005, Stephen Lewis has long been a household name in Canada. He comes from an accomplished family: his father was a social democratic political leader in Canada, his spouse, Michele Landsberg, is a prominent feminist activist and former columnist for a major Canadian newspaper, and his son and daughter-in-law, Avi Lewis and Naomi Klein, are renowned film-makers, broadcasters, writers, and anti-globalization activists.

6   Not only was the gathering prominent in the Canadian media but it was also picked up by *The New York Times*, the South African Broadcasting Corporation, and many other international networks. See http://www.stephenlewisfoundation.org/news-resources/news-articles.

7 This was evident, for instance, in the writings of the GAA and HAI. From 2006 onward, the language employed by these and other groups increasingly reflected notions of older women caregivers as "grandmothers" and "heroes." See www.globalaging.org and www.helpage.org.

8 When I refer to different "narratives" of grandmotherhood, I am drawing on the idea that ways of understanding different words, situations, and experiences are socially constructed within specific political, economic, and historical contexts, and that different interlocutors have different abilities to influence these narratives (Cooper, "The Politics of Difference"). This is not intended to imply that these are fabricated "stories"; there is little doubt that AIDS has had profound and widespread impacts on families and communities in sub-Saharan Africa, and it is clear that caregiving is largely falling to older women (Chazan, "Seven 'Deadly' Assumptions"). What is important here is the way this message was delivered at this time, the way it was then understood and deployed by different actors, and the influence it ultimately had.

9 As indicated previously, I will refer to campaign members as "grandmothers" collectively; when citing them, however, I will distinguish between "grandmother" and "grandother" (the latter meaning a campaign member who is not a grandmother). By contrast, I will differentiate South African grandmothers when I cite them by referring to them as "gogo."

10 While a detailed analysis of the diversity among the Canadian campaign members would be worthwhile, it is beyond the scope of this book.

11 There were some men in the campaign, though all my research participants were women.

12 See www.stephenlewisfoundation.org.

13 It is difficult to measure the impact of the campaign on Canadian society or to fully understand the changes that occurred in terms of awareness-raising. Nevertheless, it is worth emphasizing the social importance of Lewis's (and the campaign's) widespread public and media presence in Canada, especially in the year preceding and the year of the campaign's launch (2005 and 2006 respectively). See, for example, Don Butler, "Africa's Gogo Caregivers"; Don Butler, "Small Groups of Thoughtful People"; Cobb, "Grannies Unite"; Cobb, "Granny Power"; Goar, "Africa's Heroic Grandmothers"; Goar, "Virus Exposes Our Ugly Secrets"; Jimenez, "The Burdens Grandmothers Bear."

14 I would like to interject a note here about how this statement was written. While the content of this piece was written to reflect the broader findings of the gathering, certain key interlocutors shaped how these issues were framed as a powerful piece of prose that functioned to motivate and mobilize Canadians. I was peripherally part of this process, as I helped document grandmothers' workshops and compile key notes to be incorporated into the statement. At the time of the gathering, several SLF staff explained that our notes were going to be passed along to Landsberg-Lewis, Lewis, and one of Lewis's close associates, who would work with

selected African delegates to compose the statement, which would then be read by one African and one Canadian grandmother at the culmination of the gathering. In 2011, Landsberg-Lewis clarified that she was not present during the writing of the statement, although she did consult for parts of it via teleconference. The important point here is to recognize both the collaboration that occurred and the role of these important leaders in the framing and generation of this central text.

15 I was again part of this process, as I helped document workshops and compile key notes for the writing of the statement. The statement was written by Landsberg-Lewis, one of her advisors, and a group of SWAPOL staff. See http://www.grandmotherscampaign.org/wp-content/uploads/2012/03/Manzini_statement.pdf for the complete Manzini Statement.

16 To the dismay of many, the bill failed to be passed into law. Subsequently, with the split off of GRAN from the SLF in 2011, many grandmothers not only continued to advocate for changes to CAMR but also began to engage in several other sophisticated campaigns in solidarity with their African counterparts, independently of the SLF but still as central to the wider grandmothers' movement. See www.grandmothersadvocacy.org.

17 Stephen Lewis, *Race Against Time,* 50.

18 Backhouse and Flaherty, *Challenging Times.*

19 As noted in chapter 1, I am cautious about drawing too heavily on the popular "wave" metaphor to categorize periods of feminist struggle (in Canada and elsewhere in the Global North) and their associated ideologies, issues, and tactics. Like Kim Sawchuk (in "Feminism in Waves"), I remain critical of the stability and boundedness (and, at times, embedded ageist assumptions) of these categories, and, like Tripp (in "The Evolution of Transnational Feminisms"), I recognize that the "waves" trope often portrays a North-centric version of feminist history. Nevertheless, it is useful to contextualize what has been associated with these periods, and particularly with feminism's "second wave," in order to situate the ways in which many Canadian grandmothers identified with Canadian feminist movements of the 1960s and 1970s. The "first wave" (1880 to 1920), for instance, generally refers to struggles for women's suffrage undertaken predominantly by white, middle-class, Christian women. The "second wave" (1960s to 1970s) tends to be characterized by the fight (again, often assumed to be dominated by white, middle-class women) for reproductive rights, equal pay, and an end to violence against women, as well as by the universalizing notion of the "sisterhood." Finally, the "third wave" (1980s to present) tends to be associated with increasing transnationalism, more diversity in voices and leadership, more sophisticated coalition-building, and the analytic of intersectionality, influenced by postcolonial and poststructural thought. For further reading on the feminist "waves" in Canada (and North America), see Harnois, "Re-representing Feminisms"; Hogeland, "Against Generational Thinking"; and Purvis, "Grrrls and Women Together." For relevant historical overviews of feminism in Canada, see Bromley, *Feminisms Matter;* Carstairs and Janovicek, *Feminist*

History in Canada; Keough and Campbell, *Gender History*; Newman and White, *Women, Politics, and Public Policy*; Pierson and Cohen, *Canadian Women's Issues*; Pierson et al., *Canadian Women's Issues*; and Prentice et al., *Canadian Women*.

20 Turcotte and Schellenberg, *A Portrait of Seniors in Canada*.

21 It is also worth noting that, at the time of the campaign's launch, there were already well-known precedents in Canada and the United States for social and political organization among this same demographic group, one example being the Raging Grannies. See www.raginggrannies.org.

22 Biccum, "Development and the 'New' Imperialism"; Jones, "When 'Development' Devastates."

23 Judith Butler, *Precarious Life*.

24 Gergin, "Silencing Dissent."

25 Much has been written on the longer-standing influence of neoliberal economic policies (starting in the 1980s) on struggles for women's equality and on feminist and social justice movements in Canada. The findings of this research should be contextualized within this broader historical trend (that is, associated with neoliberalism), and alongside the further (and much more radical) disabling of the welfare state, defunding of civil society, erosion of democratic processes, and shift to social conservatism of the "Harper era" (2006 to present) in Canada. For analyses of these trends in the Canadian context, see Bashevkin, *Women, Power, Politics*; Brodie and Bakker, *Canada's Social Policy Regime*; Caplan, "More Voices"; Dobrowolsky, "The Women's Movement in Flux"; and Knight and Rodgers, "The Government Is Operationalizing Neo-liberalism."

26 Tsing, *Friction*.

27 Mahmood, *Politics of Piety*.

CHAPTER FOUR

1 This violence, which took place in the transition to democracy, is most often described as political violence between members of the Inkatha Freedom Party (IFP), the Zulu National Cultural Movement and political party, founded by Chief Mangosuthu Buthelezi in 1975, and the non-racial democratic organizations of the liberation struggle, including the Congress of South African Trade Unions (COSATU), the United Democratic Front (UDF), and, after its unbanning in 1990, the African National Congress (ANC) (Freund, "The Violence in Natal"). However, as Marks points out ("The Origins of Ethnic Violence," 124), "such explanations may be imposing an official sounding order on the overwhelming confusion and horror of violence where in fact there is no such coherence: only a shifting assortment, a 'kaleidoscope' of explanations."

2 Much has been written elsewhere offering more detailed analyses of the history of South Africa and KwaZulu-Natal. See Hamilton, *Terrific Majesty*, for a critical examination of early colonial encounters. See Christopher, *The Atlas of Apartheid*; Lester, Nel, and Binns, *South Africa*; and Rogerson and McCarthy, *Geography in a*

Changing South Africa, for analyses of apartheid and the transition to democracy. See Etherington, *Peace, Politics and Violence*; Jeffery, *The Natal Story*; and Stephen Taylor, *Shaka's Children*, for additional insights into the transitional violence. See Hunter, "Cultural Politics and Masculinities," and Morrell, *Political Economy and Identities*, for excellent analyses pertaining specifically to KwaZulu-Natal. See Campbell, *Letting Them Die*; Hunter, "Cultural Politics and Masculinities"; Hunter, *Love in the Time of AIDS*; Illiffe, The *African Aids Epidemic*; Marks, "An Epidemic Waiting to Happen?"; Nattrass, *Moral Combat*; Rohleder et al., *HIV/AIDS in South Africa*; and Whiteside and Sunter, *AIDS*, for important analyses and/or historical overviews of the AIDS epidemic. Other excellent and accessible sources include Marais, *Buckling,* and Sparks, *Beyond the Miracle.*

3 Stephen Taylor, *Shaka's Children.*

4 See Hamilton, *Terrific Majesty*, for an important discussion of the rise of "Zulu-ness" during this era.

5 By 1871, Natal had a white population of approximately 17,000 and an estimated black population of 300,000, according to Lester, Nel, and Binns, *South Africa*, 87.

6 Lester, Nel, and Binns, *South Africa.*

7 See Rangan and Gilmartin, "Gender and Traditional Authority." This is not to stereotype all women as "left behind" or to discount evidence that some women did migrate during this time (often in order to work as domestic workers in white areas). Bozzoli alludes to some of this early female migration in *Women of Phokeng*. Yet, the dominant narrative does resonate in the lives and families of most of the gogos in my research.

8 Ngubane, *Body and Mind in Zulu Medicine.*

9 Vilikazi, *Zulu Transformations.*

10 Sparks, *Tomorrow Is Another Country.*

11 Madhavan, "Fosterage Patterns."

12 Stephen Taylor, *Shaka's Children*, 283.

13 Kaarsholm, "Culture as Cure."

14 Vilikazi, *Zulu Transformations*, 11.

15 Ibid.

16 It is also possible that such spaces existed for women in different forms pre-colonization, but I have been unable to locate any such evidence or analysis with regard to what is now KwaZulu-Natal. For an important account and gender analysis of the encounter between Catholic missionaries and the Masai in Tanzania, see Hodgson, *The Church of Women.*

17 Elder, *Hostels, Sexuality, and the Apartheid Legacy.*

18 Schatz and Ogunmefun, "Caring and Contributing."

19 Bond and Desai, "Explaining Uneven and Combined Development."

20 See Naude, "Post-apartheid South Africa."

21 There exists a vibrant South African literature on the economic globalization that took place in the transition to democracy, including analyses of the implications for unemployment levels, inequalities, and social movements. For further reading,

22 Marais, *Buckling*.

23 Hunter, *Love in the Time of AIDS*.

24 See Hosegood, Benzler, and Solarsh, "Population Mobility." As noted previously, there is evidence of female migration beginning long before the transition period (e.g., Bozzoli, *Women of Phokeng*); while women were somewhat excluded from formal labour migration during the colonial and apartheid periods, mobility as a livelihood strategy for women had long been practiced by many, even during periods of legal segregation (see Elder, *Hostels, Sexuality, and the Apartheid Legacy*; Posel and Casale, "What Has Been Happening"). Thus, the existence of mobile and multi-location households was already common at the time of the transition. With the legal changes, the opening up of borders, and the decline in formal employment, mobility became much more fluid and feminized in this period; feminized urban poverty and oscillating urban-rural migration became entrenched (see Posel, "A Review of Current Literature"). For further reading on gender and migration in KwaZulu-Natal, see also Camlin et al., "Gender, Migration and HIV," and Lurie et al., "Circular Migration."

25 Hunter, *Love in the Time of AIDS*.

26 Jeffery, *The Natal Story*.

27 Bonnin, "Claiming Spaces."

28 See Centre for the Study of Violence and Reconciliation, *Tackling Armed Violence*. Violence has indeed been shown to cycle through time (from one generation to the next) and space (from such public forms as police violence to such private spheres as domestic and sexual abuse). Pearce, "Introduction," notes that perpetrators of violence are more likely to have been victims of violence themselves, while experiences of collective political violence increase the likelihood of violence occurring in intimate spaces. She refers to the accumulated impacts of intergenerational and inter-spatial violence as "chronic violence."

29 Fassin, "The Embodiment of Inequality."

30 Department of Health, "National Antenatal Sentinel." See also Welz et al., "Continued Very High Prevalence," for an analysis of a longitudinal study of HIV infection in rural KwaZulu-Natal.

31 According to the Joint United Nations Programme on HIV-AIDS, *Global Report*, thirty-seven percent of those in need – 1,000,000 people – were accessing treatment in South Africa at that time.

32 See Nattrass, "Moral Combat."

33 Marais, *Buckling*.

34 See www.hillaids.org.za.

35 While the HACT aimed to fill the growing gap between the medical and care needs in the Valley and the services being provided through the state health care system, Jennifer critiqued the country's neoliberal economic policies, which she under-

stood to be driving this gap. Elsewhere, similar critiques have been waged around the growth of "civil society" groups in post-apartheid South Africa and how these have often been treated as support and service-delivery mechanisms, offloading and privatizing state responsibilities, e.g., Habib and Kotze, "Civil Society." See also Akintola, "Gendered Home-Based Care," and Marais, *Buckling*, 64, for analyses of how the expansion of "home-based care" as an accepted response to the growing care needs in South Africa has compounded the burdens faced by (poor) women.

36 For example, German Agri Action, Oxfam Australia, and the SLF.

37 There is a large and growing body of literature on the roles of faith-based organizations (FBOS) in HIV/AIDS response in the southern African region. Some recent examples include Akintola, "What Motivates People"; Burchardt, "Faith-Based Humanitarianism"; Currie and Heymann, "Faith-Based Orphan Care"; and Keikelame et al., "Perceptions of HIV/AIDS Leaders."

38 For a discussion of this, see Habib and Kotze, "Civil Society."

39 In South Africa, "pension points" (also called "pay-points") are designated community centres (either established buildings or mobile centres) where people gather, often in long queues, to collect monthly social grants.

40 A "rondavel" is a round building with a thatched roof, common to rural KwaZulu-Natal.

41 "I" refers to "interviewer" and "R" denotes "respondent." In subsequent cases where I cite focus groups with more than one respondent, different respondents are referred to as "R1," "R2," "R3," and so on.

42 This was the word Kholiwe used. While it was evident that she was referring to a Christian priest, it was unclear to which sect of Christianity she was referring.

43 While Noku never described this as a struggle for "justice," she did see it as being about improving the lives of women who had been marginalized and excluded for far too long.

CHAPTER FIVE

1 Referring to these participants collectively as "gogos" is for the sake of clarity and is not intended to diminish the participation of the non-grandmother participants.

2 Elsewhere I have shown that the average age of entering grandmotherhood for the first time among "African" South Africans has been estimated at forty years (Chazan, "Seven 'Deadly' Assumptions"), so this finding reflects a wider trend.

3 Such complexities around orphanhood and children's vulnerabilities in the context of HIV/AIDS have been noted elsewhere: for example, Chirwa, "Social Exclusion and Inclusion"; Kuo and Operario, "Caring for AIDS-Orphaned Children"; Meintjies and Giese, "Spinning the Epidemic"; Richter and Desmond, "Targeting AIDS Orphans"; Sherr et al., "A Systematic Review"; and Skinner et al., "Towards a Definition."

4 Details on accessing government grants are available at http://www.westerncape. gov.za/topics/1397. All of these social transfers are means-tested, with the maxi-

mum values changing each year. As of 2010, criteria and maximum monthly values were roughly as follows: old-age pensions of R1,010 were available to men and women over the age of sixty (this was a change from 2008, when pensions were R820, available to men of sixty-five and women over sixty); child support grants of R250 (up from R190 in 2007) were available to the primary caregivers of children under fifteen years; foster care grants of R590 were available for foster parents of children under eighteen years; and disability grants of R820 were available to mentally and physically disabled adults. There may be some discrepancy between official and actual eligibility requirements; this was certainly reported by the gogos in this study. As mentioned earlier, the roll-out of social security grants has been one of the major successes through South Africa's transition to democracy, as noted by Legido-Quigley, "South African Old-Age Pension." These grants are crucial to the survival of the grandmothers' (often large) extended networks; they are distributed well beyond the "intended" recipients. Many in South Africa are also now lobbying for a Basic Income Grant (see Ferguson, "The Formalities of Poverty").

5 See, for example, Legido-Quigley, "South African Old-Age Pension." See also Booysen and Berg, "The Role of Social Grants"; Leclerc-Madlala, "We Will Eat When I Get the Grant"; Meintjes et al., "Children 'In Need of Care.'"

6 These are basic schematics akin to family trees. Gogos defined their households according to responsibility and entitlements, irrespective of kinship relationships or location of dwelling. For most, these were fluid networks of people, often residing in multiple locations, for whom they felt responsible for providing care. The "maps" were the result of the gogos being asked to detail who they included in these networks (see Hosegood, Benzler, and Solarsh, "Population Mobility").

7 See Bohman et al., "We Clean Our Houses." For further reading on experiences of violence and abuse among older women in South Africa, see also Maitse and Majake, *Enquiry into the Gendered Lived Experiences of Older People*; and Ferreira and Lindgren, "Elder Abuse."

8 These findings suggest that the gogos have forged a collectivity in the face of long-standing oppression – an effort some might deem as a kind of localized "solidarity," although the gogos themselves never used such language. While it is useful to highlight this theme, given the book's focus on building solidarities, it is also important to re-iterate that, following Mahmood, *Politics of Piety*, and others, I have sought to examine the gogos' lives and associations on their own terms without pre-prescribing certain motivations or politics.

9 See Marais, *Buckling*, for an excellent synthesis of South African research on these impacts.

10 See Ogunmefun, Gilbert, and Schatz, "Older Female Caregivers," for further discussion about the stigma facing older women caring for those with HIV/AIDS in South Africa.

11 For an important and critical analysis of the changing nature of love relationships (including marital trends, gender identities, and life in urban shack settlements)

in the context of KwaZulu-Natal's HIV/AIDS epidemic and transitioning political economy, see Hunter, *Love in the Time of AIDS*.

12 Resonating strongly with Marais, *Buckling*.

13 See Schatz and Ogunmefun, "Caring and Contributing," for research carried out with gogos elsewhere in KwaZulu-Natal and for a similar discussion of these older women's roles (and perceptions of their roles) within their families in the context of AIDS.

14 See also Madhavan, "Fosterage Patterns."

15 As discussed in chapter 1, this reflects the idea that experiences and expectations surrounding motherhood tend to be socially, economically, historically, and culturally produced as opposed to based on universal or innate emotions or approaches to care. This is in line with Scheper-Hughes, *Death without Weeping*, and Desirée Lewis, "Introduction."

16 I would like to interject a note pertaining to my finding that many of the gogos described their actions as rooted in "survival." As has been widely debated among African feminist scholars, I recognize that, by framing the gogos' mobilizations as driven by "survival," I could risk reproducing assumptions that women in impoverished African contexts aspire only to survival and thus forego a wide range of other aspirations – for respect and dignity, for freedom from violence, for political, economic, and social change, and for personal and intellectual fulfillment. In these debates, I concur with Mama (in Salo, "Interview," 60) and others that the recurrence of "survival" as a theme in African women's lives is likely due to the fact that many "are trapped in the daily business of securing the survival of themselves, their families and their communities" and that this is not indicative of their limited or apolitical aspirations but rather "symptomatic of a global grid of patriarchal power, and all the social, political and economic injustices that it delivers to women, and to Africans." Nevertheless, like Mahmood, *Politics of Piety*, and as discussed in chapter 1, I view it as important to accurately reflect how the gogos described their motivations without pre-prescribing certain politics to their actions. By drawing on a concept of "agency" based on the idea that daily actions can change norms – regardless of whether these actions are guided by emancipatory politics or material survival – I deliberately move away from any pretence that a "politics of survival" necessarily elides a desire for, or a potential to effect, change.

17 The way these groups changed how they conceived of (and named) themselves following the mobilization of the Canadian Grandmothers Campaign and, subsequently, the start of the HACT Grandmother Project resonates with certain themes within critical development scholarship, particularly those pertaining to the undesired (often unintended) consequences of North-driven poverty-alleviation efforts (as noted, for example, by Cowen and Shenton, *Doctrines of Development*; Escobar, *Encountering Development*; and Ferguson, *Global Shadows*). However, as I discuss further in the next chapter, it is too simplistic to read this as an instance in which a donor from the Global North imposes certain ideas or discourses on a group of

passive recipients in the South. Instead, by further examining this "zone of awkward engagement," as I do in chapter 6, the intricate and contingent ways power operates in these relationships becomes clearer (Tsing, *Friction*).

18 Tsing, *Friction*.

19 As discussed previously, "solidarity" was mobilized as central to the campaign's purpose, drawing often on a feminist discourse based in the quintessentially "second wave" notion of "the sisterhood." For many campaign members, their solidarity was based on the perception of a shared experience as grandmothers; it was frequently framed not as "charity" but as a collective sense of responsibility as women with privilege, resources, time, and the power to raise the alarm on the unprecedented situation in sub-Saharan Africa. They practiced their solidarity in a variety of ways, including building direct (albeit most often SLF-mediated) relationships with gogos (listening to them and witnessing their trauma), raising funds to support their community organizations, raising awareness, and advocating for policy changes within Canada.

20 It is noteworthy that there was no significant difference in understanding of the Canadian mobilization between groups visited by the grambassadors and groups that had had contact with only Rosemary.

21 This focus on survival reflected earlier discussions among the gogos' groups. Indeed, in mid-2010, there did not appear to be the kind of significant shift in the gogos' material conditions that was alluded to in the Manzini Statement, though clearly they were benefitting from the emotional and spiritual support of their groups and from the hope of economic security in the future. There was also no noticeable change in the ways they framed their groups: in contrast to the shift in discourse noted in Manzini, which I revisit in the next chapter, the Valley gogos were very much still struggling for, and organizing around, their basic needs.

22 This aligns with the argument that Brown and Yaffe make in "Practices of Solidarity" that there is a need to understand the complex and multi-directional workings of solidarity within transnational alliances. It is also in line with the central theoretical thrust of this book: the importance of investigating women's associations on their own terms without pre-prescribing particular politics or logics and the focus on understanding what grounded encounters and daily acts can produce, consolidate, or re-signify, recognizing women's agency as performative (Mahmood, *Politics of Piety*).

CHAPTER SIX

1 "Bogogo" means "grandmother" in siSwati (the main language spoken in Swaziland).

2 Tsing, *Friction*.

3 Abu-Lughod, *Writing Women's Worlds*.

4 It is worth reiterating here that, when I discuss "narratives" of grandmotherhood as being constructed within different contexts, I do not mean that these are fabri-

cated or false "stories." Rather, I am implying that how people understand different words, situations, and experiences is contextual and that different interlocutors have different abilities to influence these narratives.

5   As has also been documented in, for example, Madhavan, "Fosterage Patterns."

6   In line with Cooper's work, "The Politics of Difference," as cited in chapter 1.

7   Tsing, *Friction*

8   As discussed in chapter 1 and noted in chapter 5, these findings align with efforts within critical scholarship on development and globalization to move beyond assumptions that all North-South (or donor-recipient) relationships take place in some predictable, imposing, or inevitable way (e.g., Gibson-Graham, *A Postcapitalist Politics,* and Tsing, *Friction*). While recognizing the complex power dynamics at play and the historical and structural inequities embedded in the global political economy, these scholars seek to grapple more fully with the agency of actors in the Global South and the contingency of their grounded encounters. In this case, it is evident that the nurses and the gogos did not passively adopt the Canadian grandmother narrative with all of its embedded meanings: they questioned, investigated, and then actively, strategically, and purposefully re-deployed this narrative in ways that reflected their own experiences and met their own needs (resonating with, for example, Cooper, "The Politics of Difference"). This analysis, with its emphasis on the power of the women in the Valley to actively re-mobilize "grandmotherhood" in this way, and with its insistence on the contingency of these encounters and the heterogeneity among the actors in the Valley, also clearly resonates with feminist critiques that scholars and practitioners in the Global North have tended to homogenize "Third World women" as a category of passive people to whom modernizing interventions could be directed (e.g., Amadiume, *Male Daughters, Female Husbands*; Mohanty, "Under Western Eyes"; and Oyewumi, *The Invention of Women*).

9   I would like to reiterate from chapter 1 that I only draw on the language of "empowerment" in this book in instances where I am quoting participants in my research; the assumptions embedded in such language, while reflective of neoliberal economic trends in South Africa and elsewhere, are not in line with how I conceptualize "agency." Like Judith Butler, *(Un)doing Gender*; Judith Butler, *Gender Trouble*; Gibson-Graham, *A Postcapitalist Politics*; Mahmood, *Politics of Piety*; and others, I frame "agency" as the possibility for daily actions, regardless of their motives, to consolidate or challenge norms. The assumptions embedded in the language of "empowerment" are quite different: these include the idea that, by improving the self-confidence and skill sets of people who have been historically disadvantaged, these individuals somehow gain the capacity to transform their own lots in life. While I do investigate older women's agency throughout the book, nowhere in this analysis do I mean to imply that introducing individualistic "women's empowerment" programs in the Valley would necessarily result in the gogos overcoming the multiple historical and contemporary workings of oppression.

10   Gibson-Graham, *A Postcapitalist Politics.*

11 Tsing, *Friction*.

12 I make this suggestion based on discussions with SLF staff about the campaign's philosophies and objectives, particularly its desire to remain project-driven and to support African projects. At meetings with SLF staff in 2009 and 2010, there was little actual awareness around how Canadian discourses initially played out in the Valley or how they were later remobilized.

13 Bernstein, "Celebration and Suppression"; Cooper, "The Politics of Difference"; and Hilhorst, *The Real World of NGOs*.

14 Oyewumi, *The Invention of Women*; Scheper-Hughes, *Death without Weeping*.

15 As has been argued by Bebbington, "NGOs and Uneven Development"; Sylvie, "Development Geography"; and others.

16 See Kim Sawchuk, "Feminism in Waves," and Tripp, "The Evolution of Transnational Feminisms," for important discussions (including critiques) of the "waves" of feminist history. See Bilge, "Developing Intersectional Solidarities"; Brown and Yaffe, "Practices of Solidarity"; Davis, *Alliances*; Mohanty, *Feminism without Borders*; Pratt, "Collaborating across Our Differences"; Steans, "Negotiating the Politics of Difference"; and Sundberg, "Reconfiguring North-South Solidarity," for salient writings on moving beyond identity politics to build solidarities across difference.

17 These concerns are in line with the postcolonial critiques of development noted in chapter 1 (e.g., Amadiume, *Male Daughters, Female Husbands*; Cowen and Shenton, *Doctrines of Development*; Escobar, *Encountering Development*; Mohanty, "Under Western Eyes").

18 Tsing, *Friction*.

19 At other times, even once funding was in place for the gogos, Rosemary's input of resources supported organizing larger events; for instance, in 2011, her funding went towards organizing "Gogolympics" for some 350–400 gogos in the Valley, as she noted in an email correspondence in 2011.

20 In 2011, Rosemary clarified that she did not fundraise to cover her airfare or main living expenses; these were covered personally by her and her husband.

21 The HACT regularly relied on private donations, both large and small, which could be earmarked for specific projects, and thus this was in line with its practices. As well, it is standard practice in any NGO that volunteers cover their own expenses, whether through personal funds or otherwise; thus, the HACT never inquired about (and was never aware of) the details of Rosemary's fundraising.

22 Alongside this discussion and the SLF's concerns, it is also important not to discount the SLF's immense power: its control over resources, its discursive influence, and its role as initiator and shaper of the Canadian mobilization. While its critiques of the kind of direct contact embodied in Rosemary's work merit attention, it is also noteworthy that a significant number of Canadian grandmothers felt that the SLF's "rules" around direct contact were as much about keeping control in Canada as about the effects on African projects.

23 For further reading relating to mobilizations with aging populations, see Martinson and Halpern, "Ethical Implications"; Minkler and Holstein, "From Civil Rights"; and Sanjek, "Sustaining a Social Movement."

24 Kholiwe was also an important leader in the early days of the mobilization in the Valley; as noted previously, however, she did not remain active in the Grandmother Project after her retirement from the HACT in 2008.

25 It is impossible to know from my research whether this perception was simply a facet of aging, where older generations sometimes sense an ideological gap between them and younger generations, or whether it reflected a real shift in family dynamics and practices. The gogos did make reference to certain trends in their families, which have been documented more widely (e.g., Hunter, *Love in the Time of AIDS*), and which might suggest the latter: these included increasing female mobility and declining marriage rates.

26 This aligns conceptually with the argument put forth by Brown and Yaffe in "Practices of Solidarity" that how solidarity is conceptualized or framed cannot be understood in isolation of how it is practiced and what such practices produce.

CHAPTER SEVEN

1 As introduced in chapter 1 and noted throughout, in drawing on what Gibson-Graham (in *A Postcapitalist Politics*) calls a "politics of possibility," I contend that there is always a possibility that any dominant discourse or norm can be destabilized through the complex actions people take in their everyday lives. This is not, however, meant to deny the interlocking forms of privilege and oppression that create vastly unequal circumstances (and thus vastly different choices and opportunities for action) for different people around the globe (Collins, *Black Feminist Thought*).

2 Gibson-Graham, *A Postcapitalist Politics*.

3 I would like to reiterate here that I do not intend to diminish the interlocking forms of oppression and the historical, structural, and systemic injustices borne by the gogos. As I noted in chapter 1, I neither wish to portray the gogos as heroic and resilient to the point of requiring no external support nor to represent them as fragile, weak, or victims. Rather, recognizing the need for systemic political-economic change and meaningful historical redress, and acknowledging the power of the routinized practices that have maintained the global hierarchy that works against so many African women, I recognize it as vital to unpack specifically how and why these women's repeated actions and encounters have generated material and symbolic changes.

4 Such narratives have been noted, and in some cases challenged, elsewhere. See, for example, Estes, "Sex and Gender"; Hepworth, *Old Age and Agency*; Kutz-Flamenbaum, "Code Pink"; Narushima, "Gaggle of Raging Grannies"; Pain, Mowl, and Talbot, "Difference and the Negotiation of 'Old Age'"; Ray, "Researching to Transgress"; and Dana Sawchuk, "The Raging Grannies."

5 Pain, "Age, Generation and Lifecourse."

6 For example, Gibson-Graham, *A Postcapitalist Politics*, and Tsing, *Friction*.

7 Gibson-Graham, *A Postcapitalist Politics*.

8 Ibid.

9 In line with, for example, Ferguson and Gupta, "Spatializing States"; Gibson-Graham, *A Postcapitalist Politics*; Katz, *Growing Up Global*; and Tsing, *Friction*.

10 As in Tsing, *Friction*.

11 In line with Mohanty, *Feminism without Borders*, and Pratt, "Collaborating Across Our Differences," among others.

12 Supporting the analyses of Oyewumi, *Invention of Women*; Scheper-Hughes, *Death without Weeping*; and others.

13 For example, Cooper, "The Politics of Difference"; Gouws, *(Un)thinking Citizenship*; Desirée Lewis, "Introduction"; Mohanty, *Feminism without Borders*; and Oyewumi, *The Invention of Women*.

14 I would like to re-iterate here, from chapter 5, that while the gogos framed their mobilizations in the Valley as a matter of survival and did not perceive themselves as connected to Canadian solidarity efforts, there was a collective struggle against various forms of oppression taking place within their groups, which could be deemed a kind of localized solidarity but was never described as such. Their associations were enhanced and extended as a result of Noku's support and, given that Noku felt enormous validation from the Canadian movement, it could be argued that the "solidarities" within the gogos' groups were indirectly deepened by their connection to the wider movement. Meanwhile, the Canadian grandmothers who developed relationships with the gogos described these connections as profoundly important for fuelling their ongoing solidarity, which was practiced in a number of ways, from building direct relationships, to fundraising, to advocating for policy changes in Canada. In line with Brown and Yaffe, "Practices of Solidarity," among others, these findings reveal clear differences in how "solidarity" (whether named as such or not) was both understood and practiced among the different actors associated with the grandmothers' movement: no unified perspective or practice of solidarity was required in order for the women's acts and connections to produce meaningful change. Complex and entangled relations were revealed, with changes occurring in multiple places simultaneously; these relations and outcomes challenge assumptions of North-South solidarity as a unidirectional flow of aid.

BIBLIOGRAPHY

Abu-Lughod, Lila. "The Romance of Resistance: Tracing Transformations of Power through Bedouin Women." *American Ethnologist* 17, no. 1 (1990): 41–55.

– *Veiled Sentiments: Honor and Poetry in a Bedouin Society*. Berkeley: University of California Press, 1986.

– *Writing Women's Worlds: Bedouin Stories*, Fifteenth Anniversary Edition. Berkeley: University of California Press, 2008.

Akintola, Olagoke. "Gendered Home-Based Care in South Africa: More Trouble for the Troubled." *African Journal of AIDS Research* 5, no. 3 (2006): 237–47.

– "What Motivates People to Volunteer? The Case of Volunteer AIDS Caregivers in Faith-Based Organizations in KwaZulu-Natal, South Africa." *Health Policy and Planning* 26, no. 1 (2011): 53–62.

Amadiume, Ifi. *Male Daughters, Female Husbands: Gender and Sex in an African Society*. London: Zed Books, 1987.

amfAR and AVAC. *An Action Agenda to End AIDS: Critical Action from 2012–2016 to Begin to End the HIV/AIDS Pandemic*. Washington, DC: amfAR / AVAC, 2012. http://www.amfar.org/uploadedFiles/_amfarorg/Articles/On_The_Hill/2012/GlobalActionAgenda.PDF.

Appadurai, Arjun. "Grassroots Globalization and the Research Imagination." *Public Culture* 12, no. 1 (2000): 1–19.

Backhouse, Constance, and David H. Flaherty, eds. *Challenging Times: The Women's Movement in Canada and the United States*. Montreal: McGill-Queen's University Press, 1992.

Ballard, Richard, Adam Habib, and Imraan Valodia, eds. *Voices of Protest: Social Movements in Post-Apartheid South Africa*. Pietermaritzburg: University of KwaZulu-Natal Press, 2006.

Ballard, Richard, Adam Habib, Imraan Valodia, and Elke Zuern. "Globalization, Marginalization and Contemporary Social Movements in South Africa." *African Affairs* 104, no. 417 (2005): 615–34.

Bandy, Joe, and Jackie Smith, eds. *Coalitions across Borders: Transnational Protest and the Neoliberal Order*. Lanham, MD: Rowman and Littlefield, 2005.

Banerjee, Abhijit, Sebastian Galiani, Jim Levinsohn, Zoë McLaren, and Ingrid Woolard. "Why Has Unemployment Risen in the New South Africa?" *Economics of Transition* 16, no. 4 (2008): 715–40.

Bashevkin, Sylvia. *Regress Trumps Progress: Canadian Women, Feminism and the Harper Government*. Berlin: Friedrich-Ebert-Stiftung, July 2012. http://library.fes.de/pdf-files/id/09205.pdf.

– *Women, Power, Politics: The Hidden Story of Canada's Unfinished Democracy*. Don Mills: Oxford University Press, 2009.

Bebbington, Anthony. "NGOs and Uneven Development: Geographies of Development Intervention." *Progress in Human Geography* 28, no. 6 (2004): 725–45.

Bernstein, Mary. "Celebration and Suppression: The Strategic Uses of Identity by the Lesbian and Gay Movement." *American Journal of Sociology* 103, no. 3 (1997): 531–65.

Biccum, April R. "Development and the 'New' Imperialism: A Reinvention of Colonial Discourse in DFID Promotional Literature." *Third World Quarterly* 26, no. 6 (2005): 1005–20.

Bicego, George, Shea Rutstein, and Kiersten Johnson. "Dimensions of the Emerging Orphan Crisis in Sub-Saharan Africa." *Social Science and Medicine* 56, no. 6 (2003): 1235–47.

Bilge, Sirma. "Developing Intersectional Solidarities: A Plea for Queer Intersectionality." In *Beyond the Queer Alphabet: Conversations on Gender, Sexuality, and Intersectionality*, edited by Malinda Smith and Fatima Jaffer, 19–23. Teaching Equity Matters E-Book Series: Canadian Federation for the Humanities and Social Sciences, 2012.

Boddy, Janice. *Wombs and Alien Spirits: Women, Men, and the Zar Cult in Northern Sudan*. Madison: University of Wisconsin Press, 1989.

Bohman, Doris M., Sharon Vasuthevan, Neltije C. van Wyk, and Sirkka-Liisa Ekman. "'We Clean Our Houses, Prepare for Weddings and Go to Funerals': Daily Lives of Elderly Africans in Majaneng, South Africa." *Journal of Cross-Cultural Gerontology* 22, no. 4 (2007): 323–37.

Bond, Patrick, and Ashwin Desai. "Explaining Uneven and Combined Development in South Africa." In *Permanent Revolution: Results and Prospects 100 Years On*, edited by Bill Dunn, 230–45. London: Pluto, 2006.

Bonnin, Debby. "Claiming Spaces, Changing Places: Political Violence and Women's Protests in KwaZulu-Natal." *Journal of Southern African Studies* 26, no. 2 (2000): 301–16.

Booysen, Frikkie, and Servaas van der Berg. "The Role of Social Grants in Mitigating the Socio-Economic Impact of HIV/AIDS in Two Free-State Communities." *South African Journal of Economics* 73, no. 1 (2005): 545–63.

Bozzoli, Belinda. *Women of Phokeng: Consciousness, Life Strategy, and Migrancy in South Africa, 1900–1983*. London: James Currey, 1991.

Brodie, Janie, and Isabella Bakker. *Canada's Social Policy Regime and Women: An Assessment of the Last Decade*. Ottawa: Status of Women Canada, 2007.

Bromley, Victoria L. *Feminisms Matter: Debates, Theories, Activism*. Toronto: University of Toronto Press, 2012.

Brown, Gavin, and Helen Yaffe. "Practices of Solidarity: Opposing Apartheid in the Centre of London." *Antipode* 46, no. 1 (2014): 34–52.

Brown, Lesley, and Susan Strega, eds. *Research as Resistance: Critical, Indigenous, and Anti-oppressive Approaches*. Toronto: Canadian Scholars' Press, 2005.

Burchardt, Marian. "Faith-Based Humanitarianism: Organizational Change and Everyday Meanings in South Africa." *Sociology of Religion* 74, no. 1 (2013): 30–55.

Butler, Don. "Africa's Gogo Caregivers." *Montreal Gazette*, 16 August 2006.

– "Small Groups of Thoughtful People." *The Ottawa Citizen*, 14 December 2006.

Butler, Judith. "Contingent Foundations: Feminism and the Questions of 'Postmodernism.'" In *Feminists Theorize the Political*, edited by Judith Butler and Joan W. Scott, 3–21. New York: Routledge, 1992.

– *Gender Trouble: Feminism and the Subversion of Identity*. New York: Routledge, 1999.

– *Precarious Life: The Powers of Mourning and Violence*. London: Verso, 2004.

– *(Un)doing Gender*. New York: Routledge, 2004.

Butler, Ruth. "From Where I Write: The Place of Positionality in Qualitative Writing." In Limb and Dwyer, *Qualitative Methodologies*, 264–78.

Camlin, Carol S., Victoria Hosegood, Marie-Louise Newell, Nuala McGrath, Till Bärnighausen, and Rachel C. Snow. "Gender, Migration and HIV in Rural KwaZulu-Natal, South Africa." *PLOS ONE* 5, no. 7 (2010): 1, doi: 10.1371/journal.pone.0011539.

Campbell, Catherine. *Letting Them Die: Why HIV/AIDS Programs Fail*. Bloomington: Indiana University Press, 2003.

– "Migrancy, Masculine Identities, and AIDS: The Psychosocial Context of HIV Transmission on the South African Gold Mines." In *HIV and AIDS in Africa: Beyond Epidemiology*, edited by Ezekiel Kalipeni, Susan Craddock, Joseph R. Oppong and Jayati Ghosh, 133–43. Oxford: Blackwell, 2004.

Campbell, Catherine, Yugi Nair, Sbongile Maimane, and Zweni Sibiya. "Supporting People with AIDS and Their Carers in Rural South Africa: Possibilities and Challenges." *Health and Place* 14, no. 3 (2008): 507–18.

Canadian International Development Agency. "*Canada's International Policy Statement: A Role of Pride and Influence in the World. Development.*" Gatineau: Canadian International Development Agency, 2005.

Caplan, Gerald. "More Voices You Won't Hear in the Election Campaign." *Globe and Mail*, 22 April 2011.

Carmalt, Jean Connolly, and Todd Faubion. "Normative Approaches to Critical Health Geography." *Progress in Human Geography* 34, no. 3 (2010): 292–308.

Carstairs, Catherine, and Nancy Janovicek, eds. *Feminist History in Canada: New Essays on Women, Gender, Work, and Nation*. Vancouver: UBC Press, 2013.

Casale, Marisa. "'I am Living a Peaceful Life with My Grandchildren. Nothing Else.' Stories of Adversity and 'Resilience' of Older Women Caring for Children in the Context of HIV/AIDS and Other Stressors." *Ageing and Society* 31, no. 8 (2011): 1265–88.

Centre for the Study of Violence and Reconciliation. *Tackling Armed Violence: Key Findings and Recommendations of the Study on the Violent Nature of Crime in South Africa.* Johannesburg: Centre for the Study of Violence and Reconciliation, 2010.

Chazan, May. "Seven 'Deadly' Assumptions: Unpacking the Implications of HIV/AIDS among Grandmothers in South Africa and Beyond." *Ageing and Society* 28, no. 7 (2008): 935–58.

Chazan, May, and Alan Whiteside. "The Making of Vulnerabilities: Understanding the Differentiated Effects of HIV and AIDS among Street Traders in Warwick Junction, Durban, South Africa." *African Journal of AIDS Research* 6, no. 2 (2007): 162–75.

Chirwa, Wiseman Chijere. "Social Exclusion and Inclusion: Challenges to Orphan Care in Malawi." *Nordic Journal of African Studies* 11, no. 1 (2002): 93–113.

Christopher, A.J. *The Atlas of Apartheid.* London: Routledge, 1994.

Cobb, C. "Grannies Unite, Get in Tune with Each Other." *Montreal Gazette,* 14 August 2006.

– "Granny Power Delivers Message: 300 African and Canadian Grannies Bond in AIDS Fight." *National Post* (Toronto), 14 August 2006.

Collins, Patricia Hill. *Black Feminist Thought: Knowledge, Consciousness, and the Politics of Empowerment.* Boston: Unwin Hyman, 1990.

Cooke, Bill, and Uma Kothari. *Participation: The New Tyranny?* London: Zed Books, 2001.

Cooper, Barbara M. "The Politics of Difference and Women's Associations in Niger: Of 'Prostitutes,' the Public, and Politics." *Signs* 20, no. 4 (1995): 851–82.

Cowen, Michael, and Robert W. Shenton. *Doctrines of Development.* London: Routledge, 1996.

Crang, Mike. "Filed Work: Making Sense of Group Interviews." In Limb and Dwyer, *Qualitative Methodologies,* 215–33.

Crenshaw, Kimberle. "Mapping the Margins: Intersectionality, Identity Politics, and Violence against Women of Colour." *Stanford Law Review* 43, no. 6 (1993): 1241–99.

Currie, Madeleine A., and S. Jody Heymann. "Faith-Based Orphan Care: Addressing Child-Oriented Goals and Child Rights in HIV/AIDS-Affected Communities." *Vulnerable Children and Youth Studies* 6, no. 1 (2011): 51–67.

Davis, Lynne, ed. *Alliances: Re/Envisioning Indigenous-non-Indigenous Relationships.* Toronto: University of Toronto Press, 2010.

Department of Health. "National Antenatal Sentinel HIV and Syphilis Prevalence Survey in South Africa, 2009." Pretoria: National Department of Health, 2010.

Desai, Ashwin. *We Are the Poors: Community Struggles in Post-Apartheid South Africa.* New York: Monthly Review, 2002.

de Waal, Alex. *AIDS and Power: Why There Is No Political Crisis – Yet.* London: Zed Books, 2006.

Dobrowolsky, Alexandra. "The Women's Movement in Flux: Feminism, Framing, Passion, and Politics." In *Group Politics and Social Movements in Canada,* edited by Miriam Smith, 159–80. Toronto: Broadview Press, 2008.

Dufour, Pascale, Dominique Masson, and Dominique Caouette. *Solidarities beyond Borders: Transnationalizing Women's Movements.* Vancouver: UBC Press, 2010.

Elder, Glen S. *Hostels, Sexuality, and the Apartheid Legacy: Malevolent Geographies.* Athens: Ohio University Press, 2003.

Escobar, Arturo. *Encountering Development: The Making and Unmaking of the Third World.* Princeton: Princeton University Press, 1995.

Estes, Caroll L. "Sex and Gender in the Political Economy of Aging." In *Social Policy and Aging: A Critical Perspective,* edited by Carroll L. Estes, 119–25. Thousand Oaks, CA: Sage, 2001.

Etherington, Norman, ed. *Peace, Politics and Violence in the New South Africa.* London: Hans Zell, 1992.

Fassin, Didier. "The Embodiment of Inequality: AIDS as a Social Condition and the Historical Experience in South Africa." *EMBO Reports* 4, no. S1 (2003): 4–9. doi:10.1038/sj.embor.embr856.

– *When Bodies Remember.* Los Angeles: University of California Press, 2007.

Featherstone, David. *Solidarity: Hidden Histories and Geographies of Internationalism.* London: Zed Books, 2012.

Ferguson, James. "Formalities of Poverty: Thinking about Social Assistance in Neoliberal South Africa." *African Studies Review* 50, no. 2 (2007): 71–86.

– *Global Shadows: Africa in the Neoliberal World Order.* Durham: Duke University Press, 2006.

Ferguson, James, and Akhil Gupta. "Spatializing States: Toward an Ethnography of Neoliberal Governmentality." *American Ethnologist* 29, no. 4 (2002): 981–1002.

Ferreira, Monica, and Pat Lindgren. "Elder Abuse and Neglect in South Africa: A Case of Marginalization, Disrespect, Exploitation and Violence." *Journal of Elder Abuse and Neglect* 20, no. 2 (2008): 91–107.

Foucault, Michel. "Two Lectures." In *Power/Knowledge: Selected Interviews and Other Writings 1972–1977 by Michel Foucault,* edited by Colin Gordon, 78–108. New York: Pantheon Books, 1990.

Frank, Emily. "AIDS Ethnography: How to Begin." *Transforming Anthropology* 13, no. 2 (2005): 143–47.

Freeman, Melvyn, and Nkululeko Nkomo. "Guardianship of Orphans and Vulnerable Children: A Survey of Current and Prospective South African Caregivers." *AIDS Care* 18, no. 4 (2006): 302–10.

Freund, Bill. "The Violence in Natal 1985–1990." In *Political Economy and Identities in KwaZulu-Natal: Historical and Social Perspectives,* edited by Robert Morrell, 179–95. Durban: Indicator, 1996.

Gergin, Maria. "Silencing Dissent: The Conservative Record." *Canadian Centre for Policy Alternatives,* 6 April 2011. https://www.policyalternatives.ca/publications/commentary/silencing-dissent-conservative-record.

Gibson-Graham, J.K. "Beyond Global vs. Local: Economic Politics Outside the Binary Frame." In *Geographies of Power: Placing Scale*, edited by Andrew Herod and Melissa W. Wright, 25–60. Oxford: Blackwell, 2002.

– *A Postcapitalist Politics.* Minneapolis: University of Minnesota Press, 2006.

Goar, Carol. "Africa's Heroic Grandmothers." *Toronto Star*, 4 August 2006.

– "Virus Exposes Our Ugly Secrets." *Toronto Star*, 18 August 2006.

Gouws, Amanda, ed. *(Un)thinking Citizenship: Feminist Debates in Contemporary South Africa*. Aldershot, UK: Ashgate, 2005.

Gqola, Pumla Dineo. "Ufanele Uqavile: Blackwomen, Feminisms and Postcoloniality in Africa." *Agenda: Empowering Women for Gender Equity* 50 (2001): 11–22.

Guidry, John A., Michael D. Kennedy, and Mayer N. Zald, eds. *Globalization and Social Movements: Culture, Power and the Transnational Public Sphere*. Ann Arbor: University of Michigan Press, 2000.

Habib, Adam, and Hermien Kotze. "Civil Society, Governance and Development in an Era of Globalization." In *Governance in the New South Africa*, edited by Omano Edigheji and Guy C.Z. Mhone, 246–70. Cape Town: University of Cape Town Press, 2003.

Hamilton, Carolyn. *Terrific Majesty: The Powers of Shaka Zulu and the Limits of Historical Invention*. Cambridge: Harvard University Press, 1998.

Haraway, Donna. "Situated Knowledges." *Feminist Studies* 14, no. 3 (1998): 575–99.

Harnois, Catherine. "Re-representing Feminisms: Past, Present, and Future." *NWSA Journal* 20, no. 1 (2008): 120–45.

Hart, Gillian. *Disabling Globalization: Places of Power in Post-Apartheid South Africa*. Pietermaritzburg: University of Natal Press, 2002.

– "Geography and Development: Critical Ethnographies." *Progress in Human Geography* 28, no. 1 (2004): 91–100.

HelpAge International. *Older Women Lead the Response to HIV/AIDS*. London: HelpAge International, 2006.

HelpAge International and International HIV/AIDS Alliance. *Forgotten Families: Older People as Carers of Orphans and Vulnerable Children*. Brighton: International HIV/AIDS Alliance, 2003. http://www.helpage.org/silo/files/forgotten-families-older-people-as-carers-of-orphans-and-vulnerable-children.pdf.

Hepworth, Mike. *Old Age and Agency*. Hauppauge, NY: Nova Science, 2004.

Hickey, Samuel, and Giles Mohan, eds. *Participation: From Tyranny to Transformation?* London: Zed Books, 2004.

Hilhorst, Dorothea. *The Real World of NGOs: Discourses, Diversity and Development*. London: Zed Books, 2003.

Hodgson, Dorothy L. *The Church of Women: Gendered Encounters between Maasai and Missionaries*. Bloomington: Indiana University Press, 2005.

Hogeland, Lisa Maria. "Against Generational Thinking, or, Some Things That "Third Wave" Feminism Isn't." *Women's Studies in Communication* 24 (2001): 107–21.

Hosegood, Victoria, Justus Benzler, and Geoff C. Solarsh. "Population Mobility and Household Dynamics in Rural South Africa: Implications for Demographic and Health Research." *Southern African Journal of Demography* 10, no. 1–2 (2005): 43–68.

Hosegood, Victoria, and Ian M. Timæus. "The Impact of Adult Mortality on the Living Arrangements of Older People in Rural South Africa." *Ageing and Society* 25 (2005): 431–44.

Hunter, Mark. "The Changing Political Economy of Sex in South Africa: The Significance of Unemployment and Inequalities to the Scale of the AIDS Pandemic." *Social Science and Medicine* 64 (2007): 689–700.

– "Cultural Politics and Masculinities: Multiple Partners in Historical Perspective in KwaZulu-Natal." *Culture, Health & Sexuality* 7, no. 4 (2005): 389–403.

– *Love in the Time of AIDS: Inequality, Gender, and Rights in South Africa.* Bloomington: Indiana University Press, 2010.

Illiffe, John. *The African Aids Epidemic: A History.* Oxford: James Currey, 2006.

Jeffery, Anthea. *The Natal Story: Sixteen Years of Conflict.* Johannesburg: South African Institute of Race Relations, 1997.

Jimenez, Marina. "The Burdens Grandmothers Bear: They Raise Children in AIDS-Filled Africa, and Canadian Matriarchs Are Offering Help." *Globe and Mail*, 8 March 2006.

Joint United Nations Programme on HIV/AIDS (UNAIDS). *Global Report: UNAIDS Report on the Global AIDS Epidemic 2010.* Geneva: Join United Nations Programme on HIV/AIDS, 2010.

– *Report on the Global HIV/AIDS Epidemic 2002.* Geneva: Joint United Nations Programme on HIV/AIDS (UNAIDS), 2004.

Jones, Peris S. "When 'Development' Devastates: Donor Discourses and Access to HIV/AIDS Treatment in Africa." *Third World Quarterly* 25, no. 2 (2004): 385–404.

Kaarsholm, Preben. "Culture as Cure: Civil Society and Moral Debates in KwaZulu-Natal After Apartheid." *Current Writing: Text and Reception in Southern Africa* 18, no. 2 (2006): 82–97.

Kakwani, Nanak, and Kalanidhi Subbarao. *Ageing and Poverty in Africa and the Role of Social Pensions.* Washington, DC: World Bank, 2005. https://openknowledge.worldbank.org/handle/10986/8535.

Katz, Cindi. *Growing Up Global: Economic Restructuring and Children's Everyday Lives.* Minneapolis: University of Minnesota Press, 2004.

Keikelame, Mpoe Johannah, Colleen K. Murphy, Karin E. Ringheim, and Sara Woldehanna. "Perceptions of HIV/AIDS Leaders about Faith-Based Organisations' Influence on HIV/AIDS Stigma in South Africa." *African Journal of AIDS Research* 9, no. 1 (2010): 63–70.

Keough, Willeen G., and Lara Campbell. *Gender History: Canadian Perspectives.* Don Mills: Oxford University Press, 2014.

Kirby, Sandra L., Lorraine Greaves, and Colleen Reid. *Experience Research Social Change: Methods beyond the Mainstream.* 2nd ed. Toronto: Broadview Press, 2006.

Knight, Melanie, and Kathleen Rodgers. "'The Government Is Operationalizing Neo-liberalism: Women's Organizations, Status of Women Canada and the

Struggle for Progressive Social Change in Canada." *Nordic Journal of Feminist and Gender Research* 20, no. 4 (2012): 266–82.

Kobayashi, Audrey. "Negotiating the Personal and the Political in Critical Qualitative Research." In Limb and Dwyer, *Qualitative Methodologies*, 55–72.

Kuo, Caroline, and Don Operario. "Caring for AIDS-Orphaned Children: A Systematic Review of Studies on Caregivers." *Vulnerable Children and Youth Studies* 4, no. 1 (2009): 1–12.

Kutz-Flamenbaum, Rachel V. "Code Pink, Raging Grannies, and the Missile Dick Chicks: Feminist Performance Activism in the Contemporary Anti-war Movement." *NWSA Journal* 19, no. 1 (2007): 89–105.

KwaZulu-Natal Department of Economic Development. "KwaZulu-Natal Economic Overview." Accessed 16 July 2009, www.kznded.gov.za.

Leclerc-Madlala, Suzanne. "'We Will Eat When I Get the Grant': Negotiating AIDS, Poverty and Antiretroviral Treatment in South Africa." *African Journal of AIDS Research* 5, no. 3 (2006): 249–56.

Leclerc-Madlala, Suzanne, Leickness C. Simbayi, and Allanise Cloete. "The Sociocultural Aspects of HIV/AIDS in South Africa." In *HIV/AIDS in South Africa 25 Years On: Psychosocial Perspectives,* edited by Paul Rohleder, Leslie Swartz, Seth C. Kalichman, and Leickness C. Simbayi, 13–26. New York: Springer, 2009.

Legido-Quigley, Helena. "The South African Old-Age Pension: Exploring the Role of Poverty Alleviation in Households Affected by HIV/AIDS." Conference paper for the Fourth International Research Conference on Social Security, Antwerp, Belgium, 5–7 May 2003. http://www.eldis.org/go/home&id=13604&type= Document#.U6iHgUCrrgU.

Lester, Alan, Etienne Nel, and Tony Binns. *South Africa, Past, Present and Future: Gold at the End of the Rainbow?* Harlow, UK: Pearson Education, 2000.

Lewis, Desirée. "Introduction: African Feminisms." *Agenda* 50 (2001): 4–10.

Lewis, Stephen. *Race Against Time.* Toronto: House of Anansi, 2005.

Limb, Melanie, and Claire Dwyer, eds. *Qualitative Methodologies for Geographers: Issues and Debates.* London, Arnold, 2001.

Lurie, Mark, Abigail Harrison, David Wilkinson, and Salim Abdool Karim. "Circular Migration and Sexual Networking in Rural KwaZulu-Natal: Implications for the Spread of HIV and Other Sexually Transmitted Diseases." *Health Transition Review* 7, no. S3 (1997): 17–27.

Madhavan, Sangeetha. "Fosterage Patterns in the Age of AIDS: Continuity and Change." *Social Science and Medicine* 58 (2004): 1443–54.

Maguire, Patricia. "Feminist Participatory Research." In *Just Methods: An Interdisciplinary Feminist Reader,* edited by Alison Jaggar, 417–32. Boulder: Paradigm, 2013.

Mahmood, Saba. *Politics of Piety. The Islamist Revival and the Feminist Subject.* Princeton: Princeton University Press, 2004.

Maitse, Teboho, and Chana Majake. *Enquiry into the Gendered Lived Experience of Older Persons Living in Conditions of Poverty.* Braamfontein, South Africa: Commission on Gender Equality, 2005.

Marais, Hein. *Buckling: The Impact of AIDS in South Africa*. Pretoria: Centre for the Study of AIDS, University of Pretoria, 2005.

Marks, Shula. "An Epidemic Waiting to Happen? The Spread of HIV/AIDS in South Africa in Social and Historical Perspective." *African Studies* 61, no. 1 (2002): 13–26.

– "The Origins of Ethnic Violence." In *Peace, Politics and Violence in the New South Africa,* edited by Norman Etherington. London: Hans Zell, 1992.

Martinson, Marty, and Jodi Halpern. "Ethical Implications of the Promotion of Elder Volunteerism: A Critical Perspective." *Journal of Aging Studies* 25, no. 4 (2011): 427–35.

McClintock, Anne. *Imperial Leather: Race, Gender and Sexuality in the Colonial Contest*. New York: Routledge, 1995.

McEwan, Cheryl, and Michael K. Goodman. "Place Geography and the Ethics of Care: Introductory Remarks on the Geographies of Ethics, Responsibility and Care." *Ethics, Policy and Environment* 13, no. 2 (2010): 103–12.

Meintjes, Helen, Debbie Budlender, Sonja Giese, and Leigh Johnson. "Children 'In Need of Care' or In Need of Cash? Social Security in the Time of AIDS." *South African Review of Sociology* 36, no. 2 (2005): 238–68.

Meintjes, Helen, and Sonja Giese. "Spinning the Epidemic: The Making of Mythologies of Orphanhood in the Context of AIDS." *Childhood* 13, no. 3 (2006): 407–30.

Meth, Paula. "Violent Research: The Ethics and Emotions of Doing Research with Women in South Africa." *Ethics, Place and Environment* 6, no. 2 (2003): 143–59.

Minkler, Meredith, and Martha B. Holstein. "From Civil Rights to ... Civic Engagement? Concerns of Two Older Critical Gerontologists About a 'New Social Movement' and What It Portends." *Journal of Aging Studies* 22, no. 2 (2007): 196–204.

Mohammad, Robina. "'Insiders' and/or 'Outsiders': Positionality, Theory and Praxis." In Limb and Dwyer, *Qualitative Methodologies*, 101–20.

Mohanty, Chandra Talpade. *Feminism without Borders: Decolonizing Theory, Practicing Solidarity*. Durham: Duke University Press, 2003.

– "Under Western Eyes: Feminist Scholarship and Colonial Discourse." In *The Post-Colonial Studies Reader,* edited by Bill Ashcroft, Gareth Griffiths, and Helen Tiffin, 259–63. London: Routledge, 1995.

– "'Under Western Eyes' Revisited: Feminist Solidarity through Anticapitalist Struggles." *Signs* 28, no. 2 (2003): 499–535.

Monasch, Roeland, and J. Ties Boerma. "Orphanhood and Childcare Patterns in Sub-Saharan Africa: An Analysis of National Surveys from 40 Countries." *AIDS* 18, no. S2 (2004): 55–65.

Morrell, Robert, ed. *Political Economy and Identities in KwaZulu-Natal: Historical and Social Perspectives*. Durban: Indicator, 1996.

Moss, Pamela, ed. *Feminist Geography in Practice: Research and Methods*. Oxford: Wiley-Blackwell, 2002.

Narushima, Mya. "A Gaggle of Raging Grannies: The Empowerment of Older Canadian Women through Social Activism." *International Journal of Lifelong Education* 23, no. 1 (2004): 23–42. doi:10.1080/0260137032000172042.

Nattrass, Nicoli. *Moral Combat: AIDS Denialism and the Struggle for Antiretrovirals in South Africa.* Scottsville: University of KwaZulu-Natal Press, 2007.

Naude, Wim. "Post-apartheid South Africa in the World Economy: An Assessment of Inequality in an Open Developing Country." *Africa Insight* 34, no. 4 (2004): 46–53.

Newman, Jacquetta, and Linda A. White. *Women, Politics, and Public Policy: The Political Struggles of Canadian Women.* 2nd ed. Don Mills: Oxford University Press, 2012.

Ngubane, Harriet. *Body and Mind in Zulu Medicine: An Ethnography of Health and Disease in Nyuswa-Zulu Thought and Practice.* London: Academic Press, 1977.

Ogundipe-Leslie, Molara. *Recreating Ourselves: African Women and Critical Transformations.* Trenton, NJ: Africa World Press, 1994.

Ogunmefun, Catherine, Leah Gilbert, and Enid Schatz. "Older Female Caregivers and HIV/AIDS-Related Secondary Stigma in Rural South Africa." *Journal of Cross-Cultural Gerontology* 26, no. 1 (2011): 85–102.

Ogunmefun, Catherine, and Enid Schatz. "Caregivers' Sacrifices: The Opportunity and Costs of Adult Morbidity and Mortality on Female Pensioners in Rural South Africa." *Development Southern Africa* 26, no. 1 (2009): 95–109.

Oyewumi, Oyeronke. *The Invention of Women: Making an African Sense of Western Gender Discourses.* Minneapolis: University of Minnesota Press, 1997.

Pain, Rachel. "Age, Generation and Lifecourse." In *Introducing Social Geographies,* edited by Rachel Pain, Michael Barke, Jamie Gough, Duncan Fuller, Robert MacFarlane, and Graham Mowl, 141–63. London: Arnold, 2001.

Pain, Rachel, Graham Mowl, and Carol Talbot. "Difference and the Negotiation of 'Old Age.'" *Environment and Planning D: Society and Space* 18, no. 3 (2000): 377–93.

Pearce, Jenny. "Introduction: Researching Democracy and Social Change with Violence in the Foreground." *IDS Bulletin* 40, no. 3 (2009): 1–9.

Pierson, Ruth Roach, and Marjorie Griffin Cohen. *Canadian Women's Issues: Volume II: Bold Visions.* Toronto: James Lorimer, 1995.

Pierson, Ruth Roach, Marjorie Griffin Cohen, Paula Bourne, and Philinda Masters. *Canadian Women's Issues: Volume I: Strong Voices.* Toronto: James Lorimer, 1993.

Posel, Dori. "A Review of Current Literature and Recent Research on Migration in Southern Africa." Working Paper. University of Natal, Durban, March 2002. www.queensu.ca/samp/migrationresources/Documents/Posel_review.pdf.

Posel, Dori, and Daniela Casale. "What Has Been Happening to Internal Labour Migration in South Africa, 1993–1999." *The South African Journal of Economics* 71, no. 3 (2003): 455–79.

Pratt, Geraldine. "Collaborating across Our Differences." *Gender, Place, and Culture* 9, no. 2 (2002): 195–200.

Prentice, Alison, Paula Bourne, Gail Cuthbert Brandt, Beth Light, Wendy Mitchinson, and Naomi Black, eds. *Canadian Women: A History*. 2nd ed. Toronto: Harcourt Brace Jovanovich, 1996.

Purvis, Jennifer. "Grrrls and Women Together in the Third Wave: Embracing the Challenges of Intergenerational Feminism(s)." *NWSA Journal* 16, no. 3 (2004): 93–123.

Rangan, Haripriya, and Mary Gilmartin. "Gender, Traditional Authority and the Politics of Rural Reform in South Africa." *Development and Change* 33, no. 4 (2002): 633–58.

Ray, Ruth E. "Researching to Transgress: The Need for Critical Feminism in Gerontology." *Journal of Women and Aging* 11, no. 2–3 (1999): 171–84.

Richter, Linda M., and Chris Desmond. "Targeting AIDS Orphans and Child-Headed Households? A Perspective from National Surveys in South Africa, 1995–2005." *AIDS Care* 20, no. 9 (2008): 1019–28.

Robins, Steven. "'Brothers Are Doing It for Themselves': Remaking Masculinities in South Africa." In *The Politics of AIDS: Globalization, the State and Civil Society*, edited by Maj-Lis Foller and Hakah Thorn, 156–76. Basingstoke, UK: Palgrave Macmillan, 2008.

– "'Long Live Zackie, Long Live': AIDS Activism, Science and Citizenship after Apartheid." *Journal of Southern African Studies* 30, no. 3 (2004): 651–72.

– "From 'Rights' to 'Ritual': AIDS Activism in South Africa." *American Anthropologist* 108, no. 2 (2006): 312–23.

Rogerson, Christian, and Jeffrey McCarthy. *Geography in a Changing South Africa: Progress and Prospects*. Cape Town: Oxford University Press, 1992.

Rohleder, Poul, Leslie Swartz, Seth C. Kalichman, and Leickness C. Simbayi, eds. *HIV/AIDS in South Africa 25 Years On: Psychosocial Perspectives*. New York: Springer, 2009.

Rose, Gillian. "Situating Knowledges: Positionality, Reflexivity and Other Tactics." *Progress in Human Geography* 21, no. 3 (1997): 305–20.

Roy, Carole. *The Raging Grannies: Wild Hats, Cheeky Songs, and Witty Actions for a Better World*. Montreal: Black Rose Books, 2004.

Ruddick, Sue. "Activist Geographies: Building Possible Worlds." In *Envisioning Human Geographies*, edited by Paul Cloke, Philip Crang and Mark Goodwin, 229–40. London: Arnold, 2004.

Rutherford, Blair. "Desired Publics, Domestic Government, and Entangled Fears: On the Anthropology of Civil Society, Farm Workers, and White Farmers in Zimbabwe." *Cultural Anthropology* 19, no. 1 (2004): 122–53.

Salo, Elaine. "Interview with Amina Mama: Talking About Feminism in Africa." *Agenda* 50 (2001): 58–63.

Sanjek, Roger. "Sustaining a Social Movement: Gray Panther Ideology and Tactics." *Journal of Aging, Humanities, and the Arts* 4, no. 2 (2010): 133–44.

Sawchuk, Dana. "Peace Profile: The Raging Grannies." *Peace Review: A Journal of Social Justice* 25, no. 1 (2011): 129–35.

- "The Raging Grannies: Defying Stereotypes and Embracing Aging through Activism." *Journal of Women and Aging* 21, no. 3 (2009): 171–85.

Sawchuk, Kim. "Feminism in Waves: Re-imagining a Watery Metaphor." In *Open Boundaries: A Canadian Women's Studies Reader*, 3rd ed., edited by Barbara Crow and Lisa Gotell, 58–63. Toronto: Pearson, 2009.

Schatz, Enid, and Catherine Ogunmefun. "Caring and Contributing: The Role of Older Women in Rural South African Multi-generational Households in the HIV/AIDS Era." *World Development* 35, no. 8 (2007): 1390–403.

Scheper-Hughes, Nancy. *Death without Weeping: The Violence of Everyday Life in Brazil*. Berkeley: University of California Press, 1992.

Schoepf, Brooke Grundfest. "Structure, Agency, and Risk." In *HIV and AIDS in Africa: Beyond Epidemiology*, edited by Ezekiel Kalipeni, Susan Craddock, Joseph R. Oppong, and Jayati Ghosh, 121–31. Oxford: Blackwell, 2004.

Scott, Joan W. "Experience." In *Feminists Theorize the Political*, edited by Judith Butler and Joan W. Scott, 22–40. New York: Routledge, 1992..

Sherr, Lorraine, Rebecca Varrall, Joanne Mueller, Linda Richter, Angela Wakhweya, Michèle Adato, and Chris Desmond. "A Systematic Review on the Meaning of the Concept 'AIDS Orphan': Confusion over Definitions and Implications for Care." *AIDS Care* 20, no. 5 (2008): 527–36.

Skinner, Donald, N. Tsheko, S. Mtero-Munyati, M. Segwabe, P. Chibatamoto, and S. Mfecane. "Towards a Definition of Orphaned and Vulnerable Children." *AIDS Behavior* 10 (2006): 619–26.

Sparks, Allister. *Beyond the Miracle: Inside the New South Africa*. Chicago: University of Chicago Press, 2003.

- *Tomorrow Is Another Country: The Inside Story of South Africa's Road to Change*. New York: Hill and Wang, 1995.

Statistics South Africa. *Census 2001. Primary Tables South Africa: Census '96 and 2001 Compared*. Pretoria: Statistics South Africa, 2004.

Steans, Jill. "Negotiating the Politics of Difference in the Project of Feminist Solidarity." *Review of International Studies* 33 (2007): 729–43.

Sundberg, Juanita. "Reconfiguring North-South Solidarity: Critical Reflections on Experiences of Transnational Resistance." *Antipode* Journal Compilation (2007): 144–66.

Susser, Ida. *AIDS, Sex, and Culture: Global Politics and Survival in Southern Africa*. Oxford: Wiley-Blackwell, 2009.

Sylvie, Rachel. "Development Geography: Politics and 'the State' under Crisis. *Progress in Human Geography* 34, no. 6 (2010): 828–34.

Taylor, Rupert. "Justice Denied: Political Violence in KwaZulu-Natal after 1994." *African Affairs* 101, no. 405 (2002): 473–508.

Taylor, Stephen. *Shaka's Children: A History of the Zulu People*. London: HarperCollins, 1994.

Thornton, Robert J. *Unimagined Community: Sex, Networks, and AIDS in Uganda and South Africa*. Berkeley: University of California Press, 2008.

Tripp, Aili Mari. "The Evolution of Transnational Feminisms: Consensus, Conflict, and New Dynamics." In *Gender and Women's Studies in Canada: Critical Terrain*, edited by Marg Hobbs and Carla Rice, 691–702. Toronto: Women's Press, 2013.

Tsing, Anna. *Friction: An Ethnography of Global Connection*. Princeton: Princeton University Press, 2005.

Tuhiwai Smith, Linda. *Decolonizing Methodologies: Research and Indigenous Peoples*. London: Zed Books, 1999.

Turcotte, Martin, and Grant Schellenberg. *A Portrait of Seniors in Canada, 2006*. Cat. No. 89-519-XWE. Ottawa: Statistics Canada, 2007. http://www.statcan.gc.ca/pub/89-519-x/89-519-x2006001-eng.htm.

United Nations. *World Population Ageing 2007*. United Nations Department of Economic and Social Affairs Population Division, 2007. www.un.org/esa/population/publications/WPA2007/wpp2007.

Vilikazi, Absolom. *Zulu Transformations: A Study of the Dynamics of Social Change*. Pietermaritzburg: University of Natal Press, 1965.

Watts, Michael. "Antinomies of Community: Some Thoughts on Geography, Resources and Empire." *Transactions of the Institute of British Geographers* 29 (2004): 195–216.

Welz, Tanya, Victoria Hosegood, Shabbar Jaffar, Jörg Bätzing-Feigenbaum, Kobus Herbst, and Mary-Louise Newell. "Continued Very High Prevalence of HIV Infection in Rural KwaZulu-Natal, South Africa: A Population-Based Study." *AIDS* 21, no. 11 (2007): 1267–472.

Whiteside, Alan, and Clem Sunter. *AIDS: The Challenge for South Africa*. Cape Town: Human and Rousseau Tafelberg, 2000.

Wikan, Unni. *Behind the Veil in Arabia: Women in Oman*. Chicago: University of Chicago Press, 1991.

World Health Organization. *Impact of AIDS on Older People in Africa: Zimbabwe Case Study*. Geneva: World Health Organization, 1990.

Young, Lorraine, and Nicola Ansell. "Fluid Households, Complex Families: The Impacts of Children's Migration as a Response to HIV/AIDS in Southern Africa." *The Professional Geographer* 55, no. 4 (2003): 464–46. doi:10.1111/0033-0124.5504005.

INDEX

Abu-Lughod, Lila, 23–4, 32
abuse, 134–7. *See also* violence
activism: Canadian grandmothers and, 54, 55–6; and charitable status, 76–7; discourse and, 77; SLF and, 76–7
advocacy: Canadian grandmothers and, 55–6, 66–7; by SLF, 62; sustained, 66
African grandmothers. *See* gogos
African Grandmothers' Gathering. *See* Manzini Gathering
agency: of African grandmothers, 81, 193n48; in development, 205n8; feminism and, 52–3, 81; feminist scholarship and, 22–3, 22–5, 28; in globalization, 205n8; grandmotherhood and, 53; Grandmothers Campaign and, 52; and inhabiting of norms, 24; meaning of, 205n9; and norms, 203n16; of older women, 22–5; postcolonial scholarship and, 22; power and, 24–5; and social change, 25
aging: and age in feminist scholarship, 191n42; of leadership, 171–3; population, 21–2; and social change, 182; spaces of, 180; and sustainability, 171–3
Alex/Tara Children's Clinic (Alexandra Township), 49–50
Amalgamated Banks of South Africa (ABSA), 102

Bernstein, Mary, 26, 166
Bill C-393, 67
Boddy, Janice, 23
Bongiwe, 129f, 130–1
Bonnin, Debby, 96

Brown, Gavin, 192n46, 204n22, 207n26
Butler, Judith, 24–5, 26, 29, 194n5
Buyi, 123–4, 125

Canada's Access to Medicines Regime (CAMR), 39, 67, 179
Canadian Broadcasting Corporation (CBC): *Nature of Things*, 61. *See also* Massey Lectures
Canadian Campaign. *See* Grandmothers to Grandmothers Campaign
Canadian Charter of Rights and Freedoms, 76
Canadian grandmothers. *See* grandmothers, Canadian
Canadian International Development Agency (CIDA), *A Role of Pride and Influence in the World*, 76
Canadian Legal AIDS Network, 67
Christianity: and gendered roles, 92–3; and gogos, 126, 143; HACT and, 100; and HIV/AIDS, 106; introduction of, 92–3; Jennifer and, 106
colonization/colonialism: and development, 192–3n48; and gender roles, 92–3; and globalization, 192–3n48; and segregation/apartheid, 90, 91; and Valley of 1000 Hills, 90, 91
contingency: and change, 178; defined, 32; and development discourses, 28; of differing experiences, 159; of encounters in transnational network, 173–4; and globalization, 28; of grandmotherhood, 182; and mobilization, 74–8, 165–7; and solidarity, 171

Cooper, Barbara M., 26, 166

demography: family reconfiguration, 144–6, 147–8; and grandmotherhood, 32, 167; and Grandmothers Campaign, 57–8, 74–5, 85, 166; and grandmothers' movement, 54; HIV/AIDS and, 172–3; and social change, 182; and sustainability, 172–3

development: agency in, 205n8; colonialism and, 192–3n48; discourses, 28; possibility and, 29–30; and security, 75–6; simplistic understandings of, 28; SLF and, 181; transnational relationships and, 181

difference(s): among gogos, 79–81, 89, 125–6, 161–2; and contingent nature of transnational networks, 163; and discourses, 181–2; and friction, 81–4, 159, 163, 165, 182; in perception of grandmotherhood discourse(s), 160–3; and solidarity, 166–7, 191n45

discourse(s): African actors and remobilization of Canadian, 181; changes over time, 120–1; context and negotiation/deployment, 181; destabilization of dominant, 29, 32; development, 28; differences and, 181–2; friction from critical negotiation of, 173; gogos' groups and, 162; Grandmother Project and, 117; and grandmothers, 52–3; of Grandmothers Campaign, 57, 119, 163–4; S. Lewis and, 52; Manzini Gathering/Statement and, 65–6, 67; mobilization of, 26; nurses and, 117–19; and political activism, 77; reiterative structure of norms and, 25; Rosemary and, 169; social locations and, 26; solidarity as, 192n46

discourse(s) of grandmotherhood: context of, 32, 85, 183; difference(s) in perception of, 160–3; emotivity of, 53; and friction, 85, 183; gogos and, 151; and Grandmothers Campaign, 53, 85, 160; Jennifer and, 120; Kholiwe and,

34–5, 117, 120, 163–4; S. Lewis and, 52, 53, 160; and mobilization(s), 32, 53, 70, 85, 154, 163, 182; Noku and, 34–5, 117–19, 120, 163–4; Rosemary and, 169; at Toronto Gathering, 35–6; and universal/shared identity/experience, 85, 161, 183. *See also* grandmother narrative

Durban Association for the Aged (DAFTA), 41, 103

Elder, Glen S., 94

11 September 2001 attacks, 75–6

Embo Crafts, 105

employment: and childrearing, 95; and household income, 128, 130–1; labour migration for, 42, 90–1, 95, 149, 161; and rural-urban migration, 95, 145; scarcity of, 17, 133, 149

empowerment, 193n48, 205n9

equality/inequality: mobilization and, 85; second wave feminism and, 75; transition to democracy and, 94; in Valley of 1000 Hills, 89, 90

exceptionality, 70–1, 72–3

Eyetsu Community Centre, 102

families: abuse within, 134–7; breakdown of, 145; gogos' love for, 147, 161–2; HIV/AIDS and, 138–9; intergenerational survival, 144–6; middle generation in, 131, 132, 144; power struggles within, 133–4; reconfiguration of, 144–6, 147–8, 156; and sustainability, 172–3

feminism: and agency, 52–3, 81; Canadian grandmothers and, 54, 56, 71–2, 160; first wave, 27, 75, 197n19; Grandmothers Campaign and, 72–3; neoconservatism and, 76; political project, 189n24, 190n25; second wave, 27, 68, 75, 78, 161, 166–7, 181, 197n19; and sisterhood, 68, 161, 181, 197n19, 204n19; solidarity, 27; third wave, 80, 166–7, 182, 197n19; waves of, 190–1n40, 197n19 feminist scholarship: and agency, 22–5, 28; ethnography, 30–3; and grand-motherhood, 26–7; transition from second to third wave of, 26–7; and women as identity group, 27

Foucault, Michel, 24

friction: and change, 178; complexity/diversity of African grandmothers' lives and, 79–81; contrasting perspectives and, 81–4, 159, 163, 165; critical negotiation of discourses and, 173; defined, 32; and discourses reflecting differences, 182; global/transnational connections and, 146, 156, 159, 163; and mobilizations, 163, 165; personal contact and, 37, 38, 81–4; possibility and, 29–30; and power, 29, 163, 173; and reconfigurations of power, 165; and zones of awkward engagement, 78–9. *See also* zones of awkward engagement

funding: contingencies of, 28; global financial crisis and, 21; for gogos' groups, 42–3; for Grandmother Project, 43, 47, 164; of HACT, 9, 99, 164; project-driven, 77–8; SLF and, 18–19, 43–4, 99

fundraising: accountability and, 73; Grandmothers Campaign and, 37; by Rosemary, 83, 169–71; SLF and, 38, 62

Gibson-Graham, J.K., 28, 29, 178, 181, 207n1

global, the, 29, 30–3

Global Action on Aging (GAA), 51

global AIDS response: meaning of, 29; older women and, 50; retraction of resources for, 76; stereotypes regarding, 183

global connections: about, 28–30; defined, 28, 45; forces shaping, 28; friction and, 163; gogos and, 119; gogos' groups and, 153–5; and Grandmother Project, 115; grounded encounters as, 38, 45–7; Jennifer on, 109; Toronto

Gathering as first in series, 36. *See also* transnational connections

globalization: agency in, 205n8; colonialism and, 192–3n48; contingency and, 28; possibility and, 29–30; power within transnational relationships and, 181; simplistic understandings of, 28; stereotypes regarding, 183; transition to democracy and, 95

gogos: abuse and, 134–7; adoption of campaign's discourses, 163–4; agency of, 81, 193n48; ages/aging of, 126, 144–5; Canadian grandmothers and, 73–4, 81–4, 108–9; and care of selves in old age, 144–5, 147, 148, 161; caring for children, 126–7; as Christians, 126, 143; complexity of lives, 79–81; and contingency of "gogo," 147–50; and death, 142; diversity among, 79–81, 89, 125–6, 161–2; empowerment and, 193n48; familial change/reconfiguration and, 145, 147–8, 156; family network fluidity and, 126–7, 156; family power struggles and, 133–4; finances/income sources, 127–8, 129f, 130f, 131f, 141, 147, 149; gendered roles, 90–1; and global connections, 119; "gogo" discourse, 181; and government grants, 127–8, 131; and grandmother narrative, 165, 205n8; and Grandmother Project, 164; and grandmother role, 147–50; as great-grandmothers, 126; as heroes, 19, 61, 80, 81, 117; HIV/AIDS and, 41, 70–1, 85, 122–4, 138–42, 161–2, 163; household maps, 128–31; insecurity and, 126, 134–7; and intergenerational survival, 144–6; labour migration and, 42, 145; love for families, 147, 161–2; Manzini Statement and, 66; meanings of "gogo," 148–50, 196n9; and middle generation, 131, 132, 144; as multigenerational caregivers, 132; numbers of children cared for, 128–30, 131, 132, 149; nurses' commonality with, 116; and orphans, 125, 127, 163–4; perspectives on

sense of community, 73–4; SLF and, 8, 9, 10, 36, 37, 40, 56–7, 62; and social justice, 78; and solidarity, 27, 70, 77–8, 116, 192n46, 204n19; spiritual connections to, 160–1; Toronto Gathering/Statement and, 19, 36–7; and twinning relationships, 37–8, 78
grandothers, 37, 55, 196n9
great-grandmothers, 126

Health Economics and HIV/AIDS Research Division (HEARD), 3, 6, 7, 8, 9, 11, 30–1
HelpAge International (HAI), 20, 51
Hilhorst, Dorothea, 166
Hillcrest AIDS Centre Trust (HACT): about, 7, 17, 97–100; Canadian grandmothers' visits, 46, 63, 108–9; and Christianity, 100; establishment of support groups, 41–2; focus/purpose of, 17, 97, 98–9; founding of, 97; funding for, 9, 99, 164, 170; and gogos' groups, 17–18, 100, 105, 156–7, 178; Grandmother Project (see Grandmother Project); Grandmothers Campaign and, 48, 165; and HIV/AIDS, 97–9, 99–100; home-based care program, 40, 41, 43, 98–9, 106–7; income-generation projects, 99, 100; Jennifer as director of, 98–100, 105–6, 109 (see also Jennifer); Kholiwe's employment at, 34; and KwaNyuswa support group, 104; leaders of, 100; Lewis's visit to, 46–7; location of, 17, 90, 99–100; and Lower Molweni support group, 103, 104; Noku's employment at, 34; nurses (see Kholiwe; Nokuthala (Noku)); nurses at Toronto Gathering, 9, 34; palliative care activities, 98; private donations to, 206n21; respite unit, 98–9, 106–7; Rosemary and, 83–4, 168–71; SLF and, 9, 99, 173; staff/volunteers, 100; stresses and, 97; Toronto Gathering and, 40–1; use of term "grandmothers," 187n7

Hillcrest Methodist Church, 97
HIV/AIDS: anti-retroviral (ARV) therapies, 98, 140; CAMR and, 67; Christianity and, 106; deaths from, 142; elderly people and, 51; emotional consequences, 139–40; financial impacts of, 138–9; flat-lining of funding to, 77; global financial crisis and flat-lining of funding for, 21; global response to, 21–2; and gogos, 41, 69, 70–1, 85, 122–4, 138–42, 161–2, 163; gogos' groups and, 105, 122–4, 125, 138–42, 151–2; and Grandmother Project, 164; and grandmothers, 35, 50, 52–3, 59; Grandmothers Campaign and, 8, 160, 179; grassroots connections/movements and, 64; HACT and, 97–8; incidence/prevalence of, 4, 96; Jennifer and, 106; and justice, 85; Kholiwe and, 34; Manzini Gathering and, 64; in Manzini Statement, 159; Noku and, 34; and older women, 7, 9; and social change, 18, 96; and solidarity, 160; stigma of, 4, 17, 97, 140, 142, 161, 180; and stresses, 7, 117, 120; testing/counselling, 99–100, 139; and transformation of Africa, 70–1; and transition to democracy, 96–7; treatment campaigns, 96–7; and violence, 88

identity: feminism/sisterhood and, 68; gogos' groups and, 162; grandmotherhood and, 35–6, 70, 85, 163, 181; mobilization and, 26; performativity and, 26; and solidarity, 27–8, 166–7, 183; and transnational solidarity, 165–6; and women as group, 27
Imana Soup Company, 103
Inchanga (settlement): about, 17; grandmothers in, 15–17; HACT and, 90; household map for Bongiwe, 129f, 130–1; segregation and, 90
Inchanga gogos' group(s): about, 17, 102, 152, 153–4, 155; Canadian connection to, 20, 154; chairpersons, 102;

formation of, 41, 102; grambassadors'
visit to, 46, 102; insecurity in gogos'
lives, 136-7; location, 102; and Noku,
114-15; Ntombifuthi as leader, 17, 41,
158; partnerships, 102; purpose of, 143;
sewing, 102; and training workshops,
102; violence and, 87-9; on visits by
Canadians, 154
inequality. *See* equality/inequality
insecurity: food, 97, 121; and gogos, 126,
136-7, 138-9; HIV/AIDS and, 96, 138-9;
as reason for group mobilization, 120,
133, 134-7, 150-1, 152; transition period
and, 94. *See also* stresses
International AIDS Conference, Toronto,
18, 53

Jane, 176-7
Jennifer: about, 106-10; on Canadian
grandmothers' movement, 108; and
direct contact between Canadian and
African grandmothers, 108-9; and
discourses of grandmotherhood, 120;
and Grandmother Project, 105-8,
116-17, 118; as HACT director, 98-9,
100, 105-6, 109; and HIV/AIDS work,
106; on Kholiwe, 108; motivation, 119;
on naming of gogos' groups, 118; and
Noku, 106-7, 108; qualities, 109, 110;
and Rosemary, 108-9, 169; and SLF,
43-4, 106, 109; on transitional period
and gogos, 94
Jill, 63, 64, 81-2
justice. *See* social justice

Kelly, 176-7
Kholiwe: about, 114-15; commonality with gogos, 116; discourse on
grandmothers, 34-5, 117, 120, 163-4;
and Grandmothers Campaign, 48,
115; group formation by, 41-2; on
HACT, 97-8; and HIV/AIDS, 34;
interactions with gogos, 116; Jennifer
and, 100, 107, 108; as leader, 207n24;
motivations, 115-16, 119-20; original

conceptualization of groups, 125;
raised by grandmother, 92; retirement,
42; Rosemary and, 83-4; second trip to
Canada, 41, 46; at Toronto Gathering,
9, 34-5, 40-1, 115, 163-4; transition
period and, 94
Klein, Naomi, 195n5
KwaNyuswa (area): community health
workers in, 105; HACT and, 90; mobilization in, 104-5; number of groups
in, 104; segregation and, 90; Women's
Day gathering in, 104-5
KwaNyuswa gogos' group(s): about,
104-5; activities, 104, 105; formation
of, 41, 104; goal, 104; HACT and, 104,
105; home rebuilding, 104, 175-6,
179; location, 104; partnerships, 105;
sewing, 104, 105
KwaZulu Homeland, 91, 95
KwaZulu-Natal province, 15, 17, 95

Landsberg, Michele, 195n5
Landsberg-Lewis, Ilana, 19, 56, 58-9,
77, 196-7n14. *See also* Stephen Lewis
Foundation (SLF)
Lewis, Avi, 195n5
Lewis, Desirée, 26
Lewis, Stephen: about, 195n5; and
advocacy, 71; advocacy by, 171-2; age
and sustainability of leadership, 171-2;
in CBC's *Nature of Things* program,
61; characteristics, 58; critical inquiry
and, 29; and director of HEARD, 11;
and founding of SLF, 19; and grandmother discourse, 52, 53, 160; and
grandmother narrative, 84-5; and
Grandmothers Campaign, 57, 58, 77,
85; and grandmothers' movement, 58;
on grassroots solutions, 71; influence
of, 58, 171-2; Massey Lectures, 49-51,
52-3, 56, 57, 160; meetings with older
women in Africa, 59; political values
of, 77; *Race Against Time*, 52, 53, 57; and
Toronto Statement, 196-7n14; as UN
HIV/AIDS special envoy, 19, 52, 58, 61;

visit to HACT, 44, 46–7; and women affected by AIDS, 50, 52–3. *See also* Stephen Lewis Foundation (SLF)

life expectancy, 21, 75

Lower Molweni (area): HACT and, 90; household map for Mandisa, 131–2

Lower Molweni gogos' group(s): about, 103–4; activities, 103, 104; formation of, 41; grambassadors' visits, 46, 104, 154; HACT and, 103, 104; and HIV/AIDS, 122–5; leadership, 103; as lifeline, 151; location, 104; spiritual survival in, 143–4

Lungile, 175–6

Mahmood, Saba, 23, 24, 26, 28, 81, 192n46

Mama, Amina, 189n24

Mandisa, 131–2, 135

Manzini Gathering: about, 36, 64–7; Canadian grandmothers attending, 64; Grandmothers Campaign and, 36, 37; Jennifer on, 107–8; Noku at, 45, 47; and personal connections between African/Canadian grandmothers, 38; purpose of, 39–40; SLF and, 64; and SLF funding of HACT, 43; solidarity march, 158–9; SWAPOL and, 64

Manzini Statement, 64–6, 159, 204n21

Marais, Hein, 50, 95

Massey Lectures, 49–51, 52–3, 56, 57, 61, 160

Mbhali, 87, 122–3, 124, 125, 175

middle generation, 131, 132, 144

migration: labour, 42, 90–1, 149, 161; rural-urban, 90, 95, 145

mobilization(s): aging and sustainability of, 171–3; alternative forms of engagement and, 71–3; as community outreach, 116–17; daily survival struggles and, 117; and discourses, 26; effects of, 178–9; extension of associational spaces and, 180; factors in transnational alliance, 182; financial stresses and, 133–4; friction/complexity and, 78–84, 163, 165; of gogos'

groups, 116–20, 132–46, 154–5; gogos' perceptions on, 150–3; grandmother narrative and, 84–5; of Grandmothers Campaign, 59–62, 84; grassroots, 71–2; HIV/AIDS and, 138–42; and identities, 26; income generation and, 133–4; intergenerational survival and, 144–6; in KwaNyuswa area, 104–5; localized, 179; Massey Lectures and, 52; SLF and, 35, 38; social justice and, 154–5; spiritual survival and, 142–4; strategic, and power, 164–5, 167; stresses and, 120, 146; sustainability of, 174; Toronto Gathering and, 53; violence/insecurity and, 134–7; and women's equality, 85

mobilization(s) of grandmotherhood: about, 25–8; analysis/retrospective, 160–7; Canadian grandmothers' perspectives, 67–74; context and, 26, 162–3, 183; contingency and, 74–8, 165–7; discourse(s) and, 32, 53, 70, 85, 154, 163, 182; exceptionality and, 70–1; gogos' perceptions of, 146–55; grandmother to grandmother solidarity and, 27–8, 153–5; identities and, 26; interlocutors/catalysts, 51–67; perceptions of gogos', 116–20; and power, 164–5; solidarity and, 68–70; strategic, 164–5; transnational connections and, 153–4

Mohanty, Chandra Talpade, 189–90n25, 191n45

Molweni (community): HACT and, 90; household map for Vuyelwa, 130f, 131; segregation and, 90

Molweni gogos' group(s): about, 102–3; activities, 103; DAFTA and, 103; formation of, 41, 102–3; literacy course, 103; location, 103; membership, 103; partnerships, 103; purpose, 151

Natal, 91, 95

National Advocacy Committee (NAC), 39, 67

neoconservatism, 75–6

neoliberalism, 95, 198n25, 200–1n35

Nokuthala (Noku): about, 110–15; age/retirement, 172; bereavement counselling workshop, 102; church/community life, 113–14; discourse on grandmothers, 34–5, 117–19, 120, 163–4; and gogos, 113–14, 116, 143, 146, 149–50; and gogos' groups, 41, 42–3, 44–5, 100–1, 117–19, 125, 153; and Grandmothers Campaign, 48, 115, 153, 164; and HIV/AIDS, 34; and Inchanga groups, 102; influence on groups, 152, 153, 155, 178; interactions with gogos, 116; Jennifer and, 100, 106–7, 108; and KwaNyuswa groups, 42, 104, 105, 175–6; and Lower Molweni group, 103–4; at Manzini Gathering, 45, 47, 102, 158–9; and Molweni group, 41, 103; motivations, 115–16, 119–20; qualities, 172; raised by grandmother, 92; Rosemary and, 38, 46, 83–4, 119, 164, 168, 169; and sewing training sessions, 102; speaking tours in Canada, 46; and stresses in gogos' lives, 146, 155; at Toronto Gathering, 9, 34–5, 40–1, 115, 163–4; transition period and, 94, 95–6; and violence, 87–9, 95–6, 137; on women's prayer circles, 93

non-grandmothers, 125–6, 187n7

Nonhlanhla, 123–4, 125

norms: agency and, 24, 203n16; destabilization of, 29, 178; entrenchment by grandmothers, 25; as performative/reiterative, 25, 29; shared grandmotherhood and, 79; SLF's challenges of, 180–1

North-South Institute, 5–6

North-South relations: feminism and, 27; as global connections, 28; imposition of North-centric on, 45; negotiation of, 28; older women's, 14. *See also* global connections; transnational connections

Ntombifuthi (Ntombi), 17, 20, 41, 158

nurses, from HACT. *See* Kholiwe; Nokuthala (Noku)

Ogundipe-Leslie, Molara, 189n21

older women: agency, 22–5; as care providers, 154; challenges of, 22; child-rearing by, 90–2; collective actions altering lives of, 31, 182; contributions by, 22, 180; democratic transition and, 95; existing narratives of, 180; and global AIDS response, 50; as household heads, 96; named as grandmothers, 51, 53; and possibility, 183; and prayer, 96; and SLF, 59; and social change, 22; stereotypes regarding, 33, 183; sustainability of caregiving role, 172–3, 174; and victimhood, 22, 25; violence and, 96. *See also* gogos; grandmothers; grandmothers, Canadian

orphans, 20–1, 41, 42, 49–50, 125, 127, 163–4

Oyewumi, Oyeronke, 166, 191n42

Pat, 39, 61, 63, 77–8, 80–1

patriarchy: agency and, 23; in feminist scholarship, 23; postcolonial scholarship and, 23; second wave feminism and, 27, 68, 75, 161; sisterhood and, 27, 68, 161

pensions, 18, 65, 127–8, 133, 149

possibility: complex solidarities and, 192n46; defined, 32; and destabilization of discourses/norms, 207n1; and development, 29–30; and globalization, 29–30; older women and, 183; politics of, 29, 178; for solidarity, 179; transnational solidarity and, 157

postcolonial scholarship: and agency, 22; and development, 192–3n48; and globalization, 192–3n48; and resistance, 23; and third wave of feminism, 197n19; and women as identity group, 27

poverty: apartheid and, 91; direct/twinning relationships and, 37–8; family power struggles and, 133–4; and gogo role, 148; gogos' groups and, 101, 133–4, 137, 150, 162; HACT and, 99; HIV/AIDS and, 96, 117, 125; reciprocal caregiving and, 148; and spiritual survival, 142–3; transition to democracy and, 17, 94–5; urban, 95

power: and agency, 24–5; donors and, 109, 164; friction and, 29, 163, 165, 173; of "gogo," 162, 182–3; gogos' groups and, 156–7; of grandmotherhood, 32; grandmother narrative and, 165; Manzini Statement and shift of, 66; reiterative structure of norms and, 25; resistance and, 24; Rosemary and, 170–1; SLF and, 83, 180; strategic mobilization of grandmotherhood and, 164–5, 167; struggles within families, 133–4; and subjectivities, 24–5; in transnational relationships, 171, 181

prayer: circles, 93, 101, 113–14, 117, 152; vigils, 96

queer theory, 27

Race Against Time (Lewis), 52, 53, 57
reciprocal relationships in caregiving, 147, 148, 156, 162
research practice/methodology: anti-oppressive, 5; and colonialism, 5; community-engaged, 4–5, 7, 9, 11; and ethics of care, 7–8; feminist ethnography, 30–3; feminist scholarship and, 22–8; global AIDS response and, 21–2; Indigenous approaches, 5; and older women's stories, 6–7, 22, 25; personal relationships in, 9–10; sources of, 185n2
resistance: agency and, 22; feminist scholarship and, 23–4; Grandmothers Campaign and, 78; postcolonial scholarship and, 23; respect for, 24
Robin Hood Foundation, 43
A Role of Pride and Influence in the World (CIDA), 76
Rosemary: about, 46, 168–71; on connections with Valley women, 155; as direct/independent volunteer,

38, 40, 46, 83–4; fundraising by, 83, 169–71; gogos' attitudes toward, 154; and Grandmother Project, 46, 168–9, 170–1; and Grandmothers Campaign, 83, 168, 169, 170–1; HACT's attitude toward, 168–9; influence/power of, 170–1; Jennifer and, 108, 109, 169; Noku and, 38, 46, 83–4, 119, 164, 168, 169; resources provided by, 43, 46, 154, 164, 168–9, 170–1; and SLF, 83, 84, 168, 169, 170–1; at Toronto Gathering, 83, 169; and transnational solidarity, 169; as zone of awkward engagement, 173

Sawchuk, Kim, 190–1n40, 197n19
Scheper-Hughes, Nancy, 26, 166
segregation/apartheid: colonization and, 90, 91; decline of, 94
S'fiso, 3–4, 6, 7–8, 10, 11–12
Sibongile, 122–3, 124, 158
Sihle, 87–9, 134, 135
sisterhood, 27, 68, 161, 181, 204n19
social change: agency and, 25; aging and, 182; Canadian grandmothers and, 54, 58; contingency and, 178; demography and, 182; destabilization of norms and, 178; friction and, 178; grandmotherhood and, 53; grandmothers' associations and, 183; HIV/AIDS and, 18, 96; older women and, 22; solidarity and, 31, 182; transition to democracy and, 18
social justice: Canadian grandmothers and, 54, 179; child care by grandmothers and, 69; exceptionality of HIV/AIDS epidemic and, 71; Grandmothers Campaign and, 78, 179; HIV/AIDS epidemic and, 85; and mobilization, 154–5; neoconservatism and, 76; population aging and, 21–2; second wave feminism and, 75
solidarity: contingency and, 171; defined, 191n45; difference and, 166–7, 191n45; differences in perception of, 208n14; as discourse, 192n46; diversity and, 191n45; feminist, 27; and global/

sustainability: aging of leadership and, 171–3; of gogos' caregiving roles, 172–3; of mobilizations, 174

Swaziland Women for Positive Living (SWAPOL), 36, 64, 158

Thembe, 123

Toronto Gathering: about, 18–20; as global connection, 45–6; and grandmother narrative, 165; and Grandmother Project, 45; and grandmothers' movement, 36–7; influence of, 35–6; Kholiwe at, 9, 34–5, 40–1, 115, 163–4; Manzini Gathering compared to, 65–6; media coverage of, 53; and mobilization in Canada, 53; and mobilization of Grandmothers Campaign, 59–61; Noku at, 9, 34–5, 40–1, 115, 163–4; and personal connections between individual African/Canadian grandmothers, 38; Rosemary at, 83, 169; SLF and, 18–19; solidarity at, 119; and visibility of African grandmothers, 53

Toronto Statement, 19–20, 53, 59–61, 65, 66, 161, 196–7n14

transition to democracy: and economic change, 95; and globalization, 95; and HIV/AIDS epidemic, 96–7; and inequalities, 94; Jennifer and, 106; and older women/gogos, 95; positive changes, 94; and societal change, 18; and urban-rural migration, 95; and Valley of 1000 Hills, 94–7; and violence, 17, 94, 95–6

transnational connections: context and, 166, 173–4; differences as contingent nature of, 163; friction and, 146, 156, 159; gogos' groups and, 162; mobilization factors, 182; and possibility, 157; power in, 171, 181; reconfigurations by, 178–9; as series of contingent encounters, 173–4; solidarity within, 204n22; Toronto Statement and, 19; unification of perspective for change, 183. *See also* global connections

Tripp, Ailli Mari, 191n40, 197n19

trusteeship, 192–3n48

Tsing, Anna, 29, 78–9, 153, 168

tuberculosis (TB), 123, 125, 139

ubuntu, 147

Umlazi, 3–4

Valley of 1000 Hills: Christianity in, 92–3; colonization and, 90, 91; contrasts/inequalities in, 89, 90; HACT in, 7, 17; HIV/AIDS in, 97; location of, 89–90; topography, 15, 89–90; Toronto Gathering and, 35–6; transition to democracy and, 94–7; violence in, 87–9

victimhood: of African grandmothers, 19, 52, 53, 61, 79, 80; of Africans, 22; of older women, 22, 25; of women, 23

Vilikazi, Absolom, 92–3

violence: and children, 96; cycling of, 198n28; and deaths, 131; as deep-rooted in families/communities, 137; and gogos, 126, 134–7; against grandmothers, 65; HIV/AIDS and, 88; as intergenerational/inter-spatial, 137; older women and, 96; as reason for group mobilization, 134–7; and spiritual survival, 142–3; transition to democracy and, 17, 94, 95–6; in Valley of 1000 Hills, 87–9

Vuyelwa, 130f, 131

Warwick Junction, 3, 6–7

witchcraft, 132, 135–6

witnessing, 96, 125–6, 134, 137, 141, 142

Yaffe, Helen, 192n46, 204n22, 207n26

zones of awkward engagement, 29–30, 78–9, 84, 167–71, 173–4. *See also* friction

Zululand, 91